At Trump Plaza with Pete Bevacqua and Donald Trump announcing the 2017 Senior PGA and 2022 PGA Championship. We felt that Mr. Trump would make sure that the PGA had "the greatest championships ever." I hope he gets the chance.

CLASSICS OF GOLF
*The world's best reading golf books.*

# UNFRIENDED

The Power Brokers, Political Correctness and Hypocrisy in Golf

## Ted Bishop

### 38th President of the PGA of America

Classics of Golf
120 Research Drive
Stratford, CT 06615

For information on special discounts for bulk purchases, please contact Classics of Golf, 120 Research Drive, Stratford, CT 06615, info@classicsofgolf.com, 1-800-483-6449

Cover and interior design by Sally Bancroft, Bancroft Graphics

Manufactured in the United States of America

10 9 8 7 6 5 4 3 2 1

Library of Congress Cataloging-in-Publication Data is available

ISBN 978-0-940889-71-2
ISBN 978-0-940889-72-2 (ebook)

# Dedication

This book is dedicated to my wife Cindy who has been with me every step of the way for 40 years. She has never wavered in her support and love for me. It is also dedicated to my daughters Ashely and Ambry, who are both good golfers, but even better people. And to Tom Watson whose friendship means more to me than anything I ever accomplished in golf.

—*Ted Bishop*

# Contents

# Introduction

For 23 months, I had the privilege to serve as the 38th president of the PGA of America, the largest working sports organization in the world today. It was the most exciting time of my life. The PGA of America owns the PGA Championship and the American share of the Ryder Cup, two of golf's most prized properties. On October 24, 2014, I was impeached as president for what some considered to be "insensitive gender-based" remarks. *Unfriended* is a chance for me to tell my side of the story and share my journey through golf.

Why are you writing this book? Are you doing it for the money? What are your motives? Are you angry? These were common questions that I was asked when *Unfriended–Power Brokers, Political Correctness and Hypocrisy in Golf* became a reality.

With this book, I was seeking self-validation and the opportunity to tell my side of the story surrounding my impeachment as the 38th President of the PGA of America. The first couple of chapters of *Unfriended* will explore the historic events behind my impeachment. But, the bulk of the book is about my journey through golf.

I had given 25 years of service to the PGA of America. It all culminated with my presidency in 2013-14. I took great pride in being a pro-active president who focused on what was good for the 28,000 men and women of the PGA. During my presidency, we were able to raise the profile and stature of PGA members.

Just as important, I also wanted to have a positive impact on the game of golf.

I felt many emotions after my impeachment. Embarrassment, despair, rejection, betrayal, anger and depression would best describe my mental state in the weeks that followed my unceremonious fall from grace in golf. It was an extremely tough time for my family and me.

In December 2014, almost two months after my impeachment, things started to turn for the better. I was approached by Greg Fisher, a friend from high school. He and the Horizon Planning Group in Indianapolis wanted to plan a dinner and golf tournament to honor my accomplishments as PGA president.

Fisher's group created *"The Mulligan Open–A charity event creating second chances."* It certainly defined where I was at that point in my life. What made The Mulligan Open so very special was that Tom Watson; eight-time major champion; Tim Finchem, Commissioner of the PGA TOUR and Steve Stricker, PGA TOUR star all showed up on my behalf. Alex Miceli, publisher of *GolfWeek,* emceed a dinner and fireside chat with my three friends and me. Over 200 of my members and closest friends were in attendance. We raised nearly $50,000 for various charities.

When Tom, Tim and Steve, three of the most respected people in golf, came to Franklin, Indiana in my honor it spoke volumes. All of these guys had privately reached out to me in the aftermath of the impeachment. Not only did they offer me their encouragement and support, but they made it public when they showed up in Franklin on that Tuesday night in August 2015.

In Tom Watson's case, it didn't stop there. He was notified about a month after The Mulligan Open that he had been selected as an inductee into the PGA of America's Hall of Fame. Watson issued the following statement.

*"While I was flattered by PGA President [Derek] Sprague's honoring me to be inducted into the PGA Hall of Fame, I couldn't*

*accept in good conscience because of how the PGA mishandled the firing of my friend and immediate past president of the PGA, Ted Bishop."*

In my lifetime, this is probably the greatest display of friendship that anyone has ever showed me. If you know Tom Watson, you know that he is a man of great principle. He once resigned his membership at the Kansas City Country Club when he felt the club was discriminating against Jews. Watson's absence from the PGA of America's Hall of Fame leaves a tremendous void.

I have learned a lot about myself and others throughout this tumultuous time in my life. Friendship is everything. However, it can sometimes be fickle. Power and personal agendas can trump relationships. Your closest friends could become your fiercest enemies and you are usually the last to know.

Would I change some things on my end? Absolutely. Who wouldn't want a few mulligans in the game of life? *Unfriended* is my mulligan.

In the days, weeks and months that followed my unceremonious removal as president of the PGA of America, readers of this book should know I was frequently targeted by the PGA of America. Obviously, there were former colleagues within the hierarchy of the PGA of America who were uncomfortable my perspective on events. They had good reason to be uncomfortable, as you will read in the following pages.

I decided to continue publishing this account while knowing full well that I would lose some friends. So be it. I also believe there are stories surrounding my golf career and my time with the PGA of America that readers will find compelling and instructive. There is no way that I can adequately express my thanks to Mike Beckerich at Classics of Golf publishing. When Mike read the manuscript he believed my story needed to be told. I am forever grateful for his confidence in me and my book.

How my term was preempted came about because of my own short-sightedness, followed by what I believe to be a dreadful mistreatment of me by the PGA. I reacted on Facebook and Twitter to some comments Ian Poulter, an English touring professional, made in his book *Off Limits* about Tom Watson, eight-time major champion, and Nick Faldo, a winner of six of golf's major championships. The fallout from my reaction was summed up best by writer Geoff Shackelford as part of *Golf World's* "2014 Newsmakers of the Year."

*"Ted Bishop made a 'lil' mistake. For that, the controversial PGA of America president lost his job less than a month before his term was to end and he was to become a ceremonial-but-respected figure for having raised the association's profile. When responding to Ian Poulter on Twitter and Facebook, Bishop's 'lil girl' reference was seen as a demeaning remark for the head of a group with a less-than-stellar record on progressive matters. Others, though, saw the comment as a silly mistake that the PGA board overreacted to by hastily forcing Bishop out and sullying a body of work that included more energy and previous action than seen from previous PGA presidents.*

*"During Bishop's tenure the organization shrewdly appointed Pete Bevacqua as CEO and picked Tom Watson as Ryder Cup captain (widely praised at the time). Bishop grew close to PGA Tour commissioner Tim Finchem, fostering a new and important relationship between the two organizations. Most indelibly, Bishop endorsed his organization's long-overdue awarding of its major events to public facilities, specifically Harding Park and Bethpage Black.*

*"Though Bishop's mistake added one more social media casualty to a growing list who've erred, his legacy putting the association in better position to influence the game appears destined to grow in stature with the PGA's 28,000 members."*

The title for this book, *Unfriended*, seemed to be a fitting way to describe what the leadership of the PGA of America did to me during and after my removal as its 38th president. In the minutes, hours, days and weeks after my comments on social media I was unfriended by the PGA of America in the greatest controversy surrounding political correctness in the history of golf. This book is a chance for me to finally tell my side of the story and share how the events of my unprecedented impeachment unfolded.

However, if this book was just about my removal, it would be seen as simply self-serving. This is a chance for me to give you an up-close perspective of golf greats such as Tom Watson, Arnold Palmer, Tiger Woods and Phil Mickelson. You will get never-before-told stories of the Ryder Cup. You will also get a unique perspective on the power brokers in golf—and some people you probably have never heard of but who represent the very core of the game.

Many get the PGA of America confused with the PGA Tour. The simplest way to differentiate them is this: The PGA TOUR is made up of professional golfers who play tournament golf for a living, while the PGA of America is comprised of professionals who teach and promote golf. However, PGA TOUR players are also members of the PGA of America.

In my six years as an officer with the PGA of America, I was involved in virtually everything that happened in golf. I became embroiled in the controversial ban on the anchored stroke, used by a few professionals but more notably by thousands of recreational golfers who had reached the end of their patience with putting. This decision created friction between the PGA of America, the United States Golf Association and the Royal and Ancient, golf's largest and oldest governing body. I served two years on the PGA TOUR Policy Board and on six occasions served as a rules official at the Masters Tournament.

It was my privilege to present the Wanamaker Trophy to Jason Dufner at Oak Hill Country Club and Rory McIlroy at Valhalla Golf Club when they won the PGA Championship in 2013 and 2014, respectively. At the Senior PGA Championship, I handed the Bourne Trophy to a couple unique first-time major champions in Khoki Idoki (the first Japanese-born player to win a major, at Bellerive Country Club) and Great Britain's Colin Montgomerie (finally a major champion, at Harbor Shores Golf Club). I announced a Ryder Cup captain on the set of NBC's Today Show. My perspectives on golf have been influenced greatly by a wide array of experiences.

With the advent of Golf Channel, Sirius/XM Radio and social media, my reputation and status in the golf world grew faster than I would have expected. Because of my communications background, I enjoyed these opportunities and performed them with relative ease. While the work I was doing probably elevated my personal profile, most importantly it was enhancing the status of the 28,000 men and women of the PGA.

*Sports Illustrated, Golfweek, Golf World* and Golf Channel all were kind enough to do profile stories on me during my term as president of the PGA of America. The consistent theme from the media revolved around the positive impact the PGA of America was having on its members and golf in general. This exposure came with a price, however. I truly believe it created jealousy toward me from individuals within the PGA hierarchy who saw the stature of a PGA president elevated like never before.

I was a volunteer for the PGA of America for 25 years and was never paid for the time I dedicated to my Association. In my six years as a PGA officer I traveled more than 770 days—not to mention the hours I devoted to PGA business when I was at home. My expenses were covered, but the time away from my family and business was a huge sacrifice that I made for the PGA. I was happy to do it, and very honored, too, but it was also a sacrifice.

When I made my gaffe on social media, my hope was that the PGA of America would use its vast resources to help me through the incident. In return I would have welcomed the opportunity to become a spokesperson for diversity and inclusion—two cornerstones of my golf career. However, the PGA of America took a strange and twisted approach from a public relations standpoint in the hours that followed my social media mishap. That in itself makes *Unfriended* a case study for communications, public relations and political correctness.

After suffering through the embarrassment of my impeachment as the 38th President of the PGA of America, I was standing at the fork in the most important road of my life. *Unfriended* became my platform to help me face the rest of my life. I chose to tell my life story, which happens to overlap with some of the most significant events the sport of golf has seen in recent memory.

As I said, *Unfriended* is my mulligan.

# Chapter One

# Impeached

I was awakened on Saturday morning, October 25, 2014, by a train whistle. It was haunting. I felt like that train was pulling away without me. It was a hollow feeling and one I will never forget. Reality was starting to set in. I had been impeached as the 38th president of the PGA of America fewer than 12 hours earlier.

Lying in bed, I couldn't help but wonder how history would judge me. This certainly would go down as one of the most unceremonious falls in the history of golf. In a matter of hours I had crashed from being one of the most powerful people in the sport to a social media casualty who had fallen prey to political correctness.

Until that moment, I had actually slept well on that Friday night. There was a sense of peace, and I think it stemmed from what had been accomplished in my 23 months as president of the PGA. We fought for the common golfer when we battled the anchoring ban. I still had great pride in naming Tom Watson as a Ryder Cup captain. The PGA took championship events to public courses like Bethpage State Park in New York and Harding Park in San Francisco. We formed a great new relationship with the PGA Tour and Tim Finchem, its longtime commissioner.

Most importantly for PGA members, we found ways to filter millions of dollars from TV rights and business development agreements back to our 41 PGA sections, the PGA's geographical divisions. This change would benefit our members like never before. For the first time in a long time, PGA members felt good about their Association, and I felt like I had played a role in evoking that positive feeling. Many in golf were saying the profile of the PGA of America had been raised to an unprecedented level during my two years as president.

And now, it was all over.

As I rolled out of bed, I noticed an overnight text on my phone from Dottie Pepper, PGA independent director and former LPGA Tour star.

"I owe you an apology. I should never have abstained. I needed to be stronger and vote "NO" to your impeachment. More than I felt yesterday, this was unequivocally wrong. Haste and hatred ruled, not common sense. I am so sorry not to have done a better job. While I voiced my opinion after you left the call, I should have finished my job."

The furor I inadvertently caused was over remarks I had made about Ian Poulter on Twitter and Facebook late Thursday afternoon. Normally, I would start every morning and end every evening by reading Geoff Shackelford's blog, a great clearing house for any news pertinent to golf. I hadn't checked out Shackelford all week because I was at The Greenbrier Resort in West Virginia helping Nick Faldo, former Masters and British Open champ, with his international junior series.

Around 5:30 p.m. Thursday, I read Shackelford's blog on my phone. What struck me most were the snide remarks Poulter had made about Faldo and Tom Watson in his book *No Limits,* which had been released earlier that day.

Faldo had stirred up the European Ryder Cup team during a late-summer Golf Channel interview when he said Sergio Garcia was useless during the 2008 European loss at Valhalla and that he had "a bad attitude." Faldo later explained in an interview with The *Associated Press* that Garcia had emotional and physical problems and at one point told Faldo he didn't want to play.

"Faldo has lost a lot of respect from players because of what he said," Poulter revealed in his book. He noted it was Europe's only loss in the last 15 years, and Faldo was the captain. "So who's useless? I think Faldo might need to take a little look in the mirror."

Poulter, who was one of Faldo's captain's picks in 2008, then went on to hammer Watson. "Tom Watson's decision making (at Gleneagles) completely baffles me. It gave us a boost. I find it utterly bizarre."

Certainly, Poulter has been a stalwart in Ryder Cup play. He is the heart and soul of the modern-day European teams. And he is entitled to his opinion. But on that night, less than a month after Watson had been publicly annihilated by Phil Mickelson's criticism in the postmortem of the losers' press conference at Gleneagles, Poulter's remarks really got under my skin. Mickelson had pointed the finger at Watson, blaming him for the U.S. loss because the captain had not consulted players on decisions surrounding the pairings in team competition.

I felt Poulter had no business criticizing Watson. Why would a European player comment on the American captain? It was Poulter being Poulter, and I probably should have just let it pass, but I expected him to show some respect to Watson, who had won eight majors and compiled a 10-4-1 Ryder Cup record as a player. Tom, like me, was a volunteer for the PGA of America. My first reaction to Poulter's remarks was to defend one of my own PGA members from the senseless attack by a member of the opposing Ryder Cup team.

And in the case of Nick Faldo? Stack up the records of these two Englishmen. Faldo has six major championships and is the all-time European Ryder Cup points leader. Poulter's resume, without a sniff of a major title, pales in comparison. I thought Poulter's remarks were degrading to both Faldo and Watson.

So without any reservations, I sent out two social media posts directed at Poulter. The first appeared on my Twitter account.

@IanJamesPoulter—Faldo's record stands by itself. Six majors and all-time RC points. Yours vs. His? Lil Girl. @NickFaldo006 @pgaofamerica

Restricted by the character limit of Twitter, I then expanded on Facebook.

"Used to be athletes who had lesser records or accomplishments in a sport never criticized the icons. Tom Watson (8 majors and a 10–4–1 Ryder Cup record) and Nick Faldo (6 majors and all-time Ryder Cup points leader) get bashed by Ian James Poulter. Really? Sounds like a little school girl squealing during recess. C'MON MAN!"

In retrospect, I certainly should have used a better choice of words to describe my frustration with Poulter. Some have said that a leader of a major golf organization should not have said anything. Everyone is entitled to his or her opinion, but I felt compelled to defend our Ryder Cup captain and my friend Faldo.

The ire around Watson's captaincy was intriguing. When we were at Gleneagles on the Tuesday before the matches started, I was approached by PGA Chief Executive Officer Pete Bevacqua, who asked: "If we win this thing, why would we not ask Tom to come back and do it again? He has done an amazing job."

Watson had done just that. Never before had the PGA of America asked more from a Ryder Cup captain when it came to media involvement. Tom never complained and did everything he was asked by the PGA. He committed more hours to the job than any captain ever had. Let's face it: Mickelson's critical comments directed at Watson on Sunday night at Gleneagles shifted all of the blame to Watson. And Phil was still torqued from being benched by Watson during Saturday's competition.

What got lost in the Scottish darkness was the 35-stroke loss the U.S. team suffered over the three days to a European team that was clearly more talented.

My relationship with Faldo had grown at The Greenbrier. One night at dinner I sat with Faldo and engaged him in a conversation about the Ryder Cup. It was still a timely topic, given that only a month had passed since the Euros had beaten the Americans at Gleneagles. Faldo talked about foursome play and his partners.

"I think way too much is made of this. Many times it would be over lunch—maybe 30 minutes before my afternoon tee time—that I would find out who my partner was," Faldo recalled. "We may not have ever played a practice round together, and certainly we never worried about what ball we were going to play. It was the Ryder Cup. You just played."

It was an old-school philosophy, and Faldo's mindset was similar to that of Tom Watson's. I couldn't help but ask myself: When did this old-school mindset change? Faldo and Watson had gone from being two of the greatest players of our era to the two most criticized Ryder Cup captains ever.

For me, Thursday, October 23, started like every other day that week at The Greenbrier. I got out of bed well before daylight and waited on the restaurant to open. I had a light breakfast and downed a few cups of coffee. I walked in the darkness to the building that housed the golf shop and waited as the kids arrived in small groups. Matthew Faldo, Nick's son, was always there to greet the kids and help them get organized for the day. This event was the only American version of the Faldo Series, which featured competition during the day and life skills lessons at night. Multiple major champions Rory McIlroy and Padraig Harrington are Faldo Series alums.

The Greenbrier had given me Stuart Appleby's champion's locker to use for the week. It was here where he shot a final-round 59 to defeat my fellow Hoosier Jeff Overton at The Greenbrier

Classic in 2010. Every day when I entered the locker room, I passed a large display case commemorating the career of Tom Watson, who had succeeded Sam Snead as the pro emeritus at The Greenbrier. Ironically, I had also spent two weeks with Snead back in the 1980s when I ran a corporate pro-am in Scottsdale, Arizona. Lots of history was captured at The Greenbrier, and I felt linked to much of it.

On this particular day I would join Nick for an early-morning segment with Gary Williams on Golf Channel's "Morning Drive." Faldo and I huddled in the chilly darkness amid spotlights from the mobile TV truck that had been brought onsite for the interview. We had a sketchy signal, and it was tough to pick up some of Williams' questions.

Several times Gary asked me questions about the week with Faldo. Nick jumped in and answered the questions for me. It was funny, and I joked with Faldo afterward that he had more interceptions during that short interview than most of the NFL's defensive backs had for the season.

All week, I had been struck by Faldo's genuine passion for what he was doing with his series and the impact it had on the kids, especially those from overseas. Three teenaged sisters from Bulgaria who had driven a car across several European countries in the middle of the night to try and qualify for this trip to the U.S. were at The Greenbrier. So was a boy from India who lived with eight siblings in a one-room house and had learned to play golf through the Faldo Series. Nick's people embraced the boy and brought him to America.

I was at the Faldo Series because for more than a year, he and his girlfriend, LeslieAnne Wade, had pressed the PGA to get involved with the series. Nick was subsidizing the entire effort out of his pocket and was looking for financial help from the PGA.

The week presented a different side of Nick Faldo. Like most people's, my opinion of the six-time major champion was based on what I had seen on TV—Faldo, the great player, or Faldo, CBS announcer. Yet in person, Faldo was anything but the introvert-ed, aloof guy most identified him as. Throughout the week, he was sincere and sensitive. Nick spent hours doing hands-on golf instruction, trying to make the kids better players. He was gen-uine and engaged with every single kid. He knew them by their first names, and the kids, in turn, idolized Nick.

On Thursday afternoon, he and I instructed a group of kids who had been brought to The Greenbrier from area high schools—Faldo's way of incorporating a local component into the week while the kids at the Faldo Series were on the course competing.

It was our final day at The Greenbrier. My wife Cindy and I were to attend a reception that evening at Faldo's house before dinner. As we waited for a ride to take us to Nick's new house, which was atop a mountain overlooking The Greenbrier, I pulled out my phone and checked some emails. That's when I sent my fate-sealing social media posts.

We headed to Nick's home for the reception, where about a dozen people had gathered, including Faldo's longtime caddie, Fanny Sunesson. Also in attendance was a local priest, invited by LeslieAnne to officially bless the new house.

As Cindy and I enjoyed the view from Nick's deck, LeslieAnne approached us and said, "Nick is on the floor of the bedroom laughing his ass off at what you said about Poulter."

I told her that I was fed up with modern-day players show-ing the game's icons a lack of respect. Word about my social me-dia posts gradually spread among the guests at Nick's house. Ev-eryone seemed to be getting some humorous satisfaction with the fact that I had called out Poulter. At that point, my comments still seemed pretty harmless to me.

About 7:30 p.m., we headed to The Greenbrier to have din-ner with the kids in the program. I decided to check my phone for any messages before I headed into "the bunker," where we ate each night. That is when I noticed some activity on my Twitter account. I remember seeing two tweets that suggested my "lil girl" remarks were sexist. That was never my intent, of course. In fact, I never even gave that inference a thought.

One of the tweets I noticed was from Keith Hirschland, formerly with Golf Channel, who sarcastically said something to the effect that "surely his account must have been hacked." It was clear I had a problem on my hands. I immediately removed both posts from Twitter and Facebook.

As I was walking into "the bunker," my phone rang, and it was Julius Mason, senior director of communications for the PGA of America. He was in a pretty jovial mood and said, "So, you and Poulter are just having a good back and forth?"

I responded, "That's what my intentions were, but based on what I am seeing on Twitter, it doesn't appear other people are taking it that way. I think we could have a problem."

Mason told me to relax and said the PGA would be sending me a statement for approval. He informed me that Golf Channel wanted to interview me on "Morning Drive," but he was advising against that. Mason said, "Let us come out with a statement, and this will go away in 24 hours."

Julius and I had a great working relationship. I trusted him completely. I entered the dining room and sat down with LeslieAnne and Nick. I told them Mason had called and explained what he said. I also said I was disturbed by what some people were saying on Twitter about me being "a sexist."

"You know you are going to have to apologize," said Wade, who had been a senior vice president of communications for CBS Sports. "It's not a big deal. You will just need to say you used a wrong choice of words. Emphasize how important you think women are to golf, just like you did last night with the kids. Julius is good, and it sounds like he has the situation under control."

Ironically, less than 24 hours before I had addressed the Faldo Series participants and told the girls about the great opportunities golf presented to them. I encouraged the girls who couldn't play at the next level to seek out other avenues in golf- club professionals, instructors or administrators.

Cindy and I retired to our room about 8:30 p.m. I was still checking my phone to gauge the reaction to my remarks, and it was mixed. A few were calling me sexist, but most were actually lauding me for taking on Poulter.

I received a text from my daughter Ambry, who coaches the women's golf team at St. John's University in New York. She was at a New Jersey Golf Foundation Awards dinner. While she was at the dinner her women's team had sent her a text saying, "It was awesome your dad called out Poulter."

At 8:45 p.m., I received an email from Julius saying, "Ted …this is how I will respond to those inquiring about your tweet: 'Ted realized that his post was inappropriate and promptly removed it.' End of story. Cool with You?" PGA of America CEO Pete Bevacqua was copied on the email.

I read that to Cindy and I said, "This is what the PGA came up with. I'm kind of surprised that it's not a direct quote from me and that it doesn't contain some kind of apology."

"Julius told you it wasn't a big deal," she replied. "It must not be."

At that point I called Julius at 9:06 p.m. and asked him if he thought the statement was strong enough. He assured me this was not a big deal and instructed me to do no interviews—especially with Golf Channel.

At 9:18 p.m. I received my first correspondence from Bevacqua in the form of an email, "Talked to Julius. Know he's reached out. I agree with his plan. Sounds like you do as well. I'm at an FBI dinner of all things. Around at any point if you need me."

At 9:27 p.m. Mason emailed me, "Please make sure that they have been removed from your Facebook and Twitter."

I responded, "I did but I can't stop the Tweets that took place before."

Then I checked my emails for the first time in several hours. I saw one from Doug Ferguson, the golf writer for the *Associated Press,* that was sent at 6:11 p.m. "I have to ask...what was the intended tone of that tweet calling Poulter a 'lil girl?' Because this could become a story coming from the president of the PGA of America."

I felt compelled to at least respond to Ferguson's email and did not see that response as violating Mason's request to refrain from any interviews. "Doug—Obviously I could have selected some different ways to express my thoughts on Poulter's remarks. Golf had always been a sport where respect was shown to its icons. That seems to have gone by the wayside..."

I thought my response to Ferguson was consistent with the tone of the PGA's statement. The PGA would later say that I disobeyed their orders not to do any interviews. I never viewed this brief email answer to Ferguson as an interview. That is why I didn't call Doug; I did not want an actual conversation to be quoted and viewed as an interview.

A few minutes later, I forwarded the PGA's statement to Wade.

At 10:09 p.m. Mason emailed me, "Just a reminder...please don't accept any media interviews on this topic. I am saying no to Golf Channel who wants to have you on tomorrow. If they come directly to you, PLEASE say no. They have our statement."

Bevacqua followed up at 10:15 p.m. "Agree. We need to say no, Ted. I believe that is critical."

To which I responded, "No one has asked me."

We turned the lights off and went to bed about 10:45 p.m. Although it was a restless night, at this point I had no idea how catastrophic the situation was going to be for me personally. My phone was nearby on a table. I could hear the buzzing from Twitter activity throughout most of the night.

The next morning I got up about 6:30 a.m. I didn't have a good feeling about the day. I took a quick shower, tried to collect my thoughts and told Cindy I was going down to grab a quick breakfast and that I would bring her back something to eat. The jet Faldo had arranged for our travel was supposed to leave about 9:30 a.m. from Lewisburg, West Virginia.

At 7:16 a.m. I received a text from Dottie Pepper: "Word of advice from a friend who has been through this before. Get out with an apology and personal reach out as soon as you can. It sucks but you are stronger than this."

Pepper was referring to some remarks she had made on NBC while broadcasting the 2007 Solheim Cup, the LPGA's version of the Ryder Cup. After watching the Americans continually miss crucial putts, she called them "choking freaking dogs," thinking she was off the air. The only problem was, somebody had failed to hit the "off" switch. Pepper's blast of the U.S. team became controversial in LPGA circles and caused her to be ostracized by many of its players. Without question, Pepper is one of the greatest players in the history of the Solheim Cup. She has never been chosen as a captain because of this incident.

I also got a text from my daughter Ambry, who said I was getting killed on Golf Channel's "Morning Drive." I resisted the temptation to turn on the TV and headed to the dining room with my iPad.

A few minutes later, Pepper texted again and said: "People will criticize everything but knowing you made every effort lets YOU breethe (sic) freely again."

Another Pepper text a minute later, "Some of the '07 USA Solheim Cup team have not spoken to me since and will never again but I know they rejected my efforts to reach out. That then becomes THEIR problem."

At 7:21 a.m. I responded to Pepper, "What should I apologize for. Don't mean that sarcastically. What would you say?"

I had no appetite to eat. I stepped outside the dining room and called Dottie. The purpose of the call was to discuss the correct choice of words for an apology. "I don't want to make the situation worse by using the wrong words again," I explained to Pepper. "Help me craft my words. I think saying it from a woman's perspective would be good. Please help me."

She agreed to, and about 7:30 a.m. Dottie texted instructions: "Only thing you need to apologize for is hitting the 'send' button before really thinking about it. I KNOW that's not your heart. You got caught up in an emotional and personal attack on the legacy of those in and around the Ryder Cup and that is totally understandable. I did the same with players I did not have much respect for on a variety of reason. Apology for being human and not perfect…Guess what? That's all of us."

At 7:35 a.m. I called Mason and asked him how bad it was. He said it was bad. I told him Pepper was saying we needed to apologize now. He asked when I was going to the airport and when I would land. He said he would "circle the wagons" and get back to me.

At that point it was obvious the PGA's statement from the evening before had not accomplished what it wanted. This situation was spiraling out of control. I felt helpless but resigned myself to the fact that I needed to follow the PGA's advice.

At 7:57 a.m. I forwarded the Pepper text to Mason. Then I texted Pepper and said, "Thanks I forwarded it all to Julius."

A few minutes later I got an email from Wade, who must have been watching Golf Channel, "As I said in my little clinic last night. An apology must be complete and simple—I knew they would go with sexism. I think in the shortest way ever it must be quickly addressed to simply pulling it down. Julius knows that. Easiest when it's one move but was leaving it to your professionals and Julius is among the best."

More correspondence from Pepper at 8:09 a.m.: "Something along the lines of 'I used a very demeaning phrase, got caught up in the emotions of the subject matter and was very unprofessional. For that I apologize. Certainly not verbatim but that should give you an idea."

Immediately I responded to Dottie, "I wanted to go on Golf Channel this morning as they asked. But Pete and Julius said no."

Pepper replied, "Not too late for Golf Central tonight."

I texted back, "Yes."

It was apparent that an apology was long overdue. I knew it was needed the night before. Hopefully, it wasn't too late, and I assumed when Julius said he "would circle the wagons," the PGA was going to craft an apology for me, given that they had put a gag order on me with the media. Surely he was working on that now? I also thought it was very strange, however, that I had not heard directly from Bevacqua or Derek Sprague, the vice president of the PGA.

At 8:15 a.m. I sent Mason another text, "I think the longer we wait the worse it gets."

No response.

At 8:24 a.m. I texted Mason again, "Can you get me a cell for Poulter?"

No response.

Cindy and I made the 15-minute drive to the Lewisburg airport. As we sat in the tiny terminal I told her I was getting the feeling I was being shut out of all communication by the PGA of America. Julius wasn't returning my texts, and I was not receiving any PGA emails. It shouldn't take this long for Mason and Bevacqua to draft an apology for me, I told her.

A few minutes later I was mistakenly forwarded an email chain by Bevacqua. The email originated from Jim Richerson, PGA District 6 director. It was sent to Bevacqua, Sprague and PGA Secretary Paul Levy. I was clearly omitted. The email read, "I for one think our only option is to take swift and decisive action. Derek, Paul, Pete—I look to you to help us do the right thing!"

To which Bevacqua replied, "We hear you loud and clear. We're on this."

Wow. That was a much different reaction than I had received from Bevacqua the night before, fewer than 12 hours earlier. I knew the tables had flipped on me. At that point, I should have taken my phone out and called Golf Channel Executive Director Geoff Russell and volunteered to go on "Morning Drive." But again, I was trying to obey the PGA's instructions to do no interviews.

As I read down the email chain I could see Richerson originally had reached out to Mason at 6:34 a.m. and said, "Have we confirmed the statements/posts? If so, what are the plans and next steps in the media? Official apology? Statements from Pete? I'm assuming we are not going to sit on our hands and that we will take action regarding the situation?"

My heart sank. I told Cindy, "It's over. They are going to ask me to resign."

She said, "Don't jump to conclusions. You haven't even talked to Pete or Derek."

I said, "Exactly. They have shut me off, and that is why I know I'm done."

My phone rang, and it was a New Jersey number. I let the call go to my voicemail and it was a message from District 1 Director Dan Pasternak of New Jersey. He said he was thinking of me and my family and couldn't imagine how hard this situation was.

We got on the plane and headed back to Indiana. It was a sunny and clear day. My mind was racing, and I thought about the number of times I had looked to the ground from the window of a plane and wondered about life below me. I knew my life was never going to be the same. It was a sickening feeling.

When we landed at the airport in Greenwood, Indiana, I had two messages from Sprague that had evidently been sent while I was in the air.

The first, a text message, said, "This is serious Ted. We need to hop on a call with you at noon. I'm in the air until 11 am. Will noon work for you?"

Then an email, "Ted—I sent you a text but maybe you are in the air too. I'm coming back from the PGA Jr. League. Can we hop on a call at 12 noon today to discuss the seriousness of this situation we are in? We need to speak about this."

In the meantime, I had also gotten an email from Lisa Cornwell at Golf Channel. "Hey Ted—I hate that all of this is going on. We all say things that we regret...I have done that way too many times. I know Golf Channel invited you on this morning. But, I am here this afternoon and tonight working Golf Central. If you wanted to come on our show, now might be a good time since you have a friend in me and I would do the interview. Obviously, it's up to you. Just wanted to reach out. Hope you are doing well otherwise...All the best, Lisa."

I responded to Cornwell at 11:25 a.m. and said, "I appreciate that Lisa. If I had my way I would have done Morning Drive today but PGA not letting me do interviews. I would like to apologize. Let's see what unfolds."

And Cornwell replied, "I totally understand...and figured that was what was going on. Let me know if anything changes."

At 11:34 a.m. I responded to Sprague's request to do a noon conference call. "I can't do noon. Needs to be 1:30."

"OK I'll send call in Number," Sprague texted back.

I attended a noon meeting with my business partners to sign some documents. The time that led up to the conference call was surreal. Around 1 p.m. I called Neil Oxman, who heads The Campaign Group in Philadelphia. I needed to talk to someone. Neil is one of the foremost political minds in the country, and he also is Tom Watson's caddie. I felt Ox could give me the advice I was not getting from the PGA.

He had no idea what was going on with my situation. Oxman was in the thick of campaigns and had not been paying attention to anything about golf. I told him I thought I was going to be forced to resign my position. He told me to send him the exact wording of my social media posts. I did, and he called me back.

"Ted, this is not resignation material," he said with a comforting laugh. "Sure, you need to apologize for the little girl remark. That was stupid. But you don't owe Poulter an apology. The PGA can't be so stupid as to ask you to resign.

"A simple apology on your part will make this a two- or three-paragraph story buried in next week's golf publications," he continued. "A resignation makes it a cover story that lingers for months, and the PGA is not stupid enough to let that happen."

So maybe there was some hope?

At 1:30 p.m. the conference call began. Sprague, Levy, Bevacqua, PGA Chief Operating Officer Darrell Crall and I were on the line. Sprague read a prepared statement informing me the group was 100 percent in agreement that I needed to resign. When I asked for the grounds of resignation, Sprague said it was because of negative media reaction, potential sponsorship fallout and PGA member complaints.

I asked Sprague what my status with the PGA of America would be if I did agree to resign. His response still rings in my ears: "You will have no status. You will not serve as honorary president, and you will not be recognized as a past president. You will be only be a PGA member."

I replied, "Well, it doesn't seem like I have any incentive to resign. What are the consequences if I don't?"

Sprague said, "You don't want to do that. We have the board votes needed to remove you."

"You mean you called a board meeting without the consent of the sitting President?" I asked.

"No, we solicited the Board by phone, and we have their support to remove you," Sprague chirped. "You need to avoid further public embarrassment to yourself and resign immediately. We will prepare a release, and it will contain a statement on your behalf."

I told him I had to think about it. I wasn't in a position to make a decision at that moment. I added that if I did resign, I would write my own statement.

Bevacqua then chimed in and said these were unfortunate circumstances and that I needed to do what was best for the PGA and resign. He asked Levy and Crall if they had anything to add, and neither did. We concluded the call with me saying I had to think about my decision and would get back to them.

Shortly after at 2:12 p.m. I received an email from Christine Garrity, PGA legal counsel. "Ted: I'm contacting you to confirm your decision that was relayed to Derek, Paul, Pete and Darrell a short time ago. I've attached a press release regarding the resignation, and we would like to include a quote by you in the release. It is of the utmost importance that we receive your confirmation via return email and your requested quote no later than 2:45 p.m. this afternoon. Absent that, it will be necessary to convene a Special Meeting of the Board this afternoon for the removal process. Due to the sensitivity of this issue, time is of the essence for the best interest of the PGA and its members."

This email was strange because I had not agreed to resign. It was obvious the PGA was trying to pressure me into doing what it wanted.

At 3:06 p.m. Garrity sent me another email with a revised release that deleted the prepared quote the PGA had done on my behalf. "The Press Release is scheduled to be published at 3:30 p.m. In an abundance of caution and for my records, please send me a message via return email that you have in fact resigned your position as PGA of America President immediately. Please send me a "Yes" you have resigned or "No" you have not resigned message."

Immediately I called Pepper and said, "Look, Dottie, if you don't want to talk to me I totally understand. But can you tell me what was going on this morning with the Board of Directors?"

"I am still beside myself. I got a call from Paul Levy around 9:30 this morning, and he informed me that the impeachment proceedings had already started, and he wanted to know if I would support this," Pepper said. "I asked him if anyone had even talked with Ted Bishop, and he said no. I told Paul that it was my understanding an apology was in the offering. I then informed him that I wanted no part of this."

I thanked her and said, "That makes my decision easy. I am not going to resign. I'm going to force the PGA to go through due process."

Garrity called my golf course while I was speaking with Pepper and remained on hold for about 15 minutes while I wrapped up my conversation with Dottie. I spoke to Garrity at 3:22 p.m. and informed her that I would not resign, and I requested a special meeting with the board.

I then reached out to Pasternak, the District 1 director from New Jersey who had left the consoling message for me a few hours earlier, but he wouldn't answer my call. The tide had definitely shifted against me.

At 3:36 p.m. Crall distributed an email setting up a special meeting of the Board of Directors for 4 p.m.

Moments later things got crazier for me when I received a phone call from Donald Trump. Over the past year I had developed a good friendship with Trump. I firmly supported a business relationship with him that would involve the PGA Grand Slam of Golf, the Senior PGA Championship and the PGA Championship. He and I had played golf together at Trump Bedminster a few weeks earlier.

"Ted, I am just calling to tell you that all of this stuff is nonsense. Don't worry…it will blow over. I have watched the Golf Channel all day, and this is absolutely ridiculous," Donald said.

I informed him of the 4 p.m. conference call and told him that in a matter of minutes I probably would be removed from office. It was the only time I have ever known Trump to be speechless. We all know what Donald thinks about political correctness.

At 3:52 p.m. I received a text from Sprague asking me to call him before 4 p.m. When I did, he once again pleaded with me to resign. I said I would not. I also asked him if I could address the board at the beginning of the phone call, and he agreed to let me do that.

At 4 p.m. I dialed in. A roll call was taken, and everyone was accounted for. Sprague gave me the opportunity to speak to the board for what would be my final time. I apologized and admitted that I had misused my platform as president of the PGA. I told the board I felt total remorse and asked for its forgiveness. I said I hoped my 25 years of volunteer service to the PGA would be worth some consideration for forgiveness. I also emphasized that I had wanted to offer a public apology, but the PGA prevented me from doing so. No one spoke or asked any questions when I finished. That was the true indication that my fate had already been decided.

At 4:16 p.m. I got a text from Pepper, "Proud to be your friend."

My response, "Thanks for that. I'm so sorry."

"I know you are," responded Pepper. "I abstained from impeachment."

"At least I had the opportunity to address the Board and force them to decide after deliberation," I texted back.

"Exactly," said Pepper.

More than an hour passed before I finally got a call from Sprague at 5:14 p.m. He once again offered me the chance to resign. When I refused, he asked why I was being so stubborn. He told me that heads of corporations make mistakes all the time. They resign and move onto other opportunities. The same could be true for me.

My response was simple, "What am I going to move on to? You gave me no incentive to resign. You said I would have no privileges and never be recognized as a PGA past president. In your words I would be only a PGA member. I don't think the punishment fits the crime, and I think PGA members as well as the general public should know what process was used by the PGA."

My head was spinning. In the next few hours I started recalling many things that had happened over the past couple of years that made my Poulter comments seem minor. In particular, I couldn't help reflect back to an incident that took place during a round of golf with a high profile business partner. Bevacqua, Sprague, Levy and I were playing golf with this person when on the front nine Levy missed a short putt and at the top of his lungs screamed, "Cocksucker!" Paul might deny this, but this is what I heard.

*It was one of the most embarrassing moments of my presidency. Here was a national officer making a crude and profane remark in front of a valued business partner. I tell this story not to embarrass Paul Levy – plenty of people have had occasion to lose their temper on the golf course. There were other incidents involving Levy, Board members and staff. To the point, the PGA had turned its back in the past to remarks far more crass than mine. It would point to the hypocrisy the PGA exhibited in the months to come.*

It had been the most bizarre day in my life. My family took the events tougher than I did. Cindy knew the outcome was inevitable, and she stayed home to isolate herself from the outside world. My oldest daughter Ashely and her husband Ted work at The Legends Golf Club, and they were stunned by my removal. Ambry, the PGA member, had a range of emotions, from anger to tears. My staff watched on Golf Channel as it unfolded, and they were speechless. Golfers at my course were bewildered.

When I surfaced from my office around 5:30 p.m., I smiled and used the Tom Watson line from the 2009 British Open: "Hey, nobody died here."

At 6:45 p.m. I was finally able to issue a formal and written apology. I sent it to Doug Ferguson of the *Associated Press* because I figured it would get the widest distribution. I told Doug I would be sending it to other media outlets at 7 p.m.

The statement read:

"I want to apologize to Ian Poulter and anyone else that I might have offended with my remarks on social media that appeared on October 23, 2014. Particularly, I have great remorse that my comments contained the words "little girl" because I have always been a great advocate for girls and women in golf.

"My two children, both girls, have made their careers in golf. I have a 4-year-old granddaughter who I hope will someday play the game. In my 37-year career in golf, I have worked with many women to grow the sport, and I have been a champion for inclusion and equal rights for women in golf.

"However, this is a classic example of poor use of social media on my part, and if I had the chance to hit the delete button on the things I sent out yesterday, I would without hesitation. The PGA of America asked me to avoid any interaction with the media in the past 24 hours, and that is why I did not issue a formal and public apology, which I have wanted to do since early this morning.

"This afternoon I was asked by my fellow officers to resign my position as President. I declined because I wanted to speak to our PGA Board of Directors, offer a personal apology and let due process take place in this matter. The Board heard me out and then voted to impeach me as the 38th President. That is the due process and I respect that, as painful as it might be.

"The PGA has also informed me that I will not become the Honorary President nor will I ever be recognized as a Past Presi-

dent in our Association's history. These, along with the impeachment, are drastic consequences for the offense that I have committed, but I must live with them. I take great pride in what we
were able to accomplish in the last 23 months. Hopefully, we laid
the groundwork for a successful future for the PGA of America.
Today, all I have left is my PGA membership and that will always
mean the world to me."

Cindy and I headed out for a quiet dinner. I felt "unfriended" by the PGA of America—and, worse, by colleagues with
whom I had worked closely for a number of years—and those
indescribably painful emotions would be confirmed in the next
few days.

# Chapter Two

# Haste and Hatred Ruled

In the days following my impeachment, I tried to isolate myself from the golf world, particularly the media. I felt I had to in order to maintain my sanity. However, I knew it would be challenging for me to move on from the PGA of America. I had dedicated more than 25 years of service to the Association. It had consumed me, particularly in the 23 months I was the president.

At the same time, I was still dumbfounded by the PGA of America's haste in removing me from office. To be honest, before October 24, 2014, my interpretation of the term "PC" would have been personal computer, not political correctness. This subject is one we never addressed or devoted much time to at the PGA of America. We didn't have any written policies or procedures for dealing with PGA officers or directors when it came to the fallout from political correctness.

In the aftermath, I never received any formal notice in writing from the PGA of America as to what the full ramifications of my impeachment were. Given the magnitude of the situation it was a very cavalier way for the PGA to handle the situation. It was only through my own questions to the PGA of America's legal counsel and membership department that I was able to piece together the full impact of my "lil girl" comments. Even then, it was ever changing.

In early October 2014 I had asked PGA Chief Operating Officer Darrell Crall for a chronological recap of my term as president in order to begin preparing for my outgoing speech at the PGA Annual Meeting in late November in Indianapolis. Crall responded with a five-page, single-spaced document listing the accomplishments of 2013–14. It was pretty humbling to see what had transpired during my term. I had always felt teamwork was an important component of my leadership style, and I think teamwork was the key to getting things done. That only made what I felt was a betrayal so painful and troubling.

Someone described my ouster by saying the PGA of America had given me the death penalty for shoplifting. Interestingly, after October 24, 2014, the PGA of America would turn nearly all of its focus to diversity and inclusion—one good thing that came from my mistake. This had always been a huge priority for me personally, but it hadn't been much more than a superficial priority for the PGA of America. When I held a committee summit meeting after my election as president in November 2012, I took a different approach with the PGA Diversity and Inclusion Committee.

In the past, we had relied solely on that committee to enhance our position, an approach that had been ineffective. I conferred with John Jacob, a past PGA independent director who had guided the National Urban League, a prominent civil rights organization. It was decided we would challenge the other dozen or so PGA committees to incorporate a diversity component into their mission statements. This avenue had never been undertaken before.

During my term, the PGA of America entered into a partnership with auditing firm KPMG to salvage the LPGA Championship, which was heading toward defunct status because it was losing its sponsor. When Pete Bevacqua, CEO of the PGA, approached me with the idea of an LPGA partnership, my first question was: How will this benefit PGA members?

His response was that it would send a statement to the golf world that the PGA of America was dedicated to providing opportunities for women in golf. Bevacqua suggested we would also host a symposium for female business leaders and other events that would take place the week of the tournament and celebrate women in golf. I told Pete I would support the KPMG PGA/LPGA Championship. My job was to convince my fellow PGA officers and the PGA directors that this decision was the right one, even though it involved a huge financial risk to the PGA of America if KPMG decided to drop its sponsorship.

In 2013, I had been critical of The R&A, golf's international governing body for rules outside the United States, for its exclusion of women as members at clubs where Open Championships were played. My question to Peter Dawson, chief executive of the R&A, was: How can you claim to grow the game when you don't have women as members of the R&A or at the clubs where you play your most prestigious championship?

At The Legends Golf Club I coached our PGA Junior League team, which was made up of many young girls and several minorities. I started the Indiana Women's Open and hosted the event for 10 years. My course held the Indiana High School Girls State Finals for 15 years, along with many other events for women including the Indiana Women's State Am and the Indianapolis Women's City Championship. My daughter Ashely and I co-founded the Central Indiana Executive Women's Golf Association. For seven years I was volunteer coach for the Franklin High School girls' golf team.

To be identified as a sexist for my remarks about Poulter was contradictory to everything I had done in my golf career. And the PGA of America knew this.

What really bothered me was knowing I should have apologized immediately for my stupid choice of words, but I didn't because the PGA forbade me to speak with the media. In the end, following their directions got me fired.

Two days after my impeachment, I checked the voicemail on my office phone. There was a message from Bevacqua, who had called at 8:10 p.m. the day of my impeachment. For two years Pete and I had talked multiple times each day, almost always on my cell phone because he knew he could reach me there. But this time Bevacqua took the easy way out. He left his message on a phone he knew I would not answer. It was the first time in two days that Bevacqua had even attempted to reach me in person.

"Hey, Ted. It's Pete. I know you probably don't want to hear from me. Today was an unbelievably hard day. You know how much I think of you. I hope that we can be friends for life because you know how I feel about you."

That message is still saved on my office phone. It is one that I won't ever forget because it came in a very impersonal way from someone I had considered a trusted friend. We had teamed up to successfully drive the PGA of America forward. My first order as PGA president was to announce Bevacqua as the new CEO. Less than a year later, Pete asked me to carry the ball for him regarding a contract extension and a pay increase. Both were approved. I figured I could always count on Pete, but I now feel that his lack of loyalty in return played a major part in my demise. It was truly a classic case of being "unfriended."

They always say that you really find out who your friends are during the worst of times, and that was certainly true for me in the days following my impeachment.

Tom Watson, one of the first in the world of golf to reach out, sent me an email late Saturday afternoon, two days after the board's vote to remove me. It was a poignant six-paragraph message that opened by saying: "Nothing more can be said of what has happened to you other than the pettiness of a lot of people has reached a level of absurdity never seen before in our lifetimes."

Around 5 p.m. that afternoon, I received a phone call from PGA Tour Commissioner Tim Finchem. He and I had formed a strong professional working relationship that benefitted both of our organizations. We had also become friends.

Tim had issued the following statement after my impeachment: "We understand and respect the PGA of America's decision regarding Ted Bishop. During Ted's presidency, he accomplished many positive things, and the PGA of America and the PGA Tour have worked in a much more collaborative and positive way as a result of his leadership. While his remarks on social media were unfortunate and inappropriate, Ted's apology was heartfelt and sincere. We will always appreciate Ted's commitment to the game of golf."

The purpose of Finchem's call was to see how I was doing. He asked if I had seen the Tour's statement. Tim went on to say he felt the PGA of America had overreacted. He said 20 seconds of poor judgement on my part shouldn't wipe out an entire body of work. Tim also said my social media posts made me look like a choir boy compared to some things PGA Tour players had posted.

Tim's call meant a lot to me. He also told me I had a lot of support among his players. He concluded by asking if I had seen Davis Love III's comments.

"Ted Bishop has been a great supporter of golf, the PGA of America members and the PGA Tour during his presidency," said Love, the 2012 Ryder Cup captain. "I have said things in my passion for the Ryder Cup that I wish came out differently. We all make mistakes on social media. I consider Ted a friend and will not remember his presidency for this incident, but for his support and passion for helping me through my captaincy, and for his role in setting the team up for future success. I have sat in board meetings with him trying to get more women involved in golf."

Later that night I received a call from Billy Kratzert, a television announcer for CBS Sports and Turner Sports. Kratzert is from Indiana, and we have developed a great relationship, and he simply said that he totally disagreed with what the PGA did to me. "It's just wrong," said Billy.

Hundreds of emails started pouring in from all over the country. Most were from people I did not know, including PGA members who were offering tremendous support. Many of those messages were from women. In the next few weeks I would receive more than 1,000 pieces of correspondence. Here is a sampling.

"I can tell you from a personal standpoint, the three ladies in my immediate family were appalled by the miscarriage of justice. "Jerry Tarde, *Golf Digest* Editor-in-Chief

"It's not what we accomplish in life, it's what we overcome. You'll overcome this. It'll pass in time. I've said many things I'd like to take back and it all goes away in time. I understand you were being a good friend and trying to stick up for two of your friends who were being attacked. You could have been more strategic, but your heart was in the right place." Member of the 2014 United States Ryder Cup Team.

"I can only imagine what you had been going through. I wanted to send a short note to simply say hang in there. You have done too much good for the game of golf to let this setback negatively affect your whole body of work. ...Don't let this get you down—things in time will settle down, and you will indeed be remembered for all your fine work." Former executive of a leading golf organization.

"Big overreaction at the expense of a good, dedicated man who sacrificed a lot of time for family and business. This is speculation on my part, and perhaps ill-founded, but it makes sense to me that the people who resented you saw this as an opportunity to hurt you. Hard to believe politics didn't play a big role." One of the most respected golf writer's in America.

"I've known you for 30 years, and you are a champion for girls and women golf. So sorry to read about this today. Thanks for your work and service to all of us in the PGA." Jeanne Sutherland, PGA

"Never did it occur to me that you are a sexist. In fact, I always felt you were quite the opposite. I wasn't offended by your comments. As a PGA member, I am appalled but not surprised at how your situation has been handled. I am truly sorry. I have been a PGA member for 22 years. Many of those the PGA was insensitive to females, including to me as a member. However, recently there have been changes made, and I am sure you had a lot to do with that. Thanks for your service. Your punishment didn't fit the crime." Vici Pate Flesher, PGA; Head Women's Golf Coach Highpoint University

"The biggest reason I am so upset with the PGA's decision is the fact that this knee-jerk reaction totally discounts a women's strongest asset—her huge loving, loving and forgiving heart. I see this reaction as worse than anything you or anyone could have said because it basically is saying that women have no sense of humor and are in need of revenge or some perverse sense of justice." Sharon Fletcher, PGA

"You don't deserve what has happened. I want you to know that I think it has been exaggerated and silly, and I'm thinking of you and how kind you were to me and always have been." John Hopkins, *London Times*, 2013 Recipient of the PGA of America Lifetime Achievement Award in Journalism.

"By any reasonable measure, the punishment didn't fit the crime." Alex Miceli, Publisher of *Golfweek*.

Obviously, there were also those who were highly critical of me.

Poulter said he was "disappointed in Bishop's tweet. Is being called a 'lil girl' meant to be derogatory or a put down? That's pretty shocking and disappointing, especially coming from the leader of the PGA of America."

In its public statement, the LPGA noted: "The PGA of America's quick and decisive action sent a strong message, reinforcing a constant belief that with so many positive gains being made among golf's leading organizations, there is simply no room nor willingness to take a step backwards."

In addition, Christine Brennan, a sports columnist for *USA Today*, tweeted the following: "A top male sports official is busted over sexist remarks. First time I've ever written that sentence."

She also told Golf Channel: "I would now say that golf is now a leader in the fight for women and sports. And we couldn't have said that 48 hours ago. That's how big of a watershed moment this is."

Rex Hoggard of Golf Channel: "Still reeling from the heat he took for his gamble with Watson, Bishop lashed out. It was signature Ted, unapologetic and unedited. The moment exposed Bishop's central weaknesses, the lack of a pause button and an unwavering belief in his own course. History will not be kind to Bishop, not his principled stand against the USGA's move on anchoring, not the olive branch he extended north to the PGA Tour that has brought the two organizations closer than they have been in years, and certainly not his attempt to wrest the U.S. Ryder Cup team out of a slide that has now been extended to eight losses in the last 10 matches. He was Ted to the very end."

Over the next few days, myriad things would be said and written.

*Sports Illustrated's* Michael Bamberger: "In this needless fiasco that led to Ted Bishop's removal as president of the PGA of America, he will be derided as a clown, as a man in constant need of attention but unsure what to do with it, and as a sexist, for his ridiculous comment about Ian Poulter, whom he likened to a 'lil girl."

"In reality, he was none of the above. His two daughters work in the golf industry: Ambry is the women's golf coach at St. John's University in New York, and Ashely works at The Legends Golf Club in Franklin, Indiana, the public course Bishop co-owns. The Legends G.C. has a thriving junior program under

Bishop's direction that stresses the importance of being inclusive of women, minorities and kids from modest economic circumstances. He comes at golf as a populist."

From John Feinstein: "Ted Bishop was an activist president who opened people's eyes. In the end what cost him his job was the non-apology apology. He was an aggressive leader and Ted is a bright guy. He took the Ryder Cup loss very personally and it's just like something snapped in him.

"His legacy will be similar to Bill Buckner, who had over 2,700 hits and was a Gold Glover. Ted will be remembered for the debacle at the Ryder Cup and one unfortunate tweet."

Tim Rosaforte of Golf Channel reached out to my daughters.

"I'm 32 years old, and never once in my 32 years has he ever hinted or made a derogatory comment or suggestion about women," Ambry said. "This is a tough day. He's done nothing but empower me and promote me to be the most successful person, type of person I'm trying to be."

Said Rosaforte: "It was a tough day for Ambry Bishop more as a PGA member than golf coach. She learned of her father's posts through members of her team, all of whom she said were supportive. She talked about her father's support of girls' junior golf, her high school team and the college team she coaches."

"This is a tough pill to swallow," Ambry said. "Yeah, looking back on it, he could have chosen better words. It's important for people to know that it's not the type of person he is. He's not a sexist person.

"I love my dad, and I know he is an honest man that sometimes says things that later he's sorry for—and I'm sure he feels that way now. But he does care what people think, and this kind of stuff tears him down."

Alex Miceli of *Golfweek*: "Bishop's past accomplishments or failures should not be part of the decision-making process. The single incident regarding Poulter was all that should have been judged. By any reasonable measure, the punishment didn't fit the crime. Foolish—even stupid—statements need to be addressed. And there is no question that the reference to Poulter as a little girl was both, but to strip a person of his office and legacy was too harsh."

Geoff Shackelford at GolfDigest.com: "I noted the peculiar double standard in Bishop's ouster, considering that Ian Poulter referred to a 'girlie shaft' in a March tweet, among his many Twitter mishaps. The inconsistency of responses could have something to do with Bishop's position as a volunteer leader of the PGA (4,371 Twitter followers) versus Poulter, a mere professional golfer that children and Ferrari addicts around the globe look up to (1.77 million Twitter followers). Some might conclude from this that Bishop's removal was anything but a victory for rooting out sexism in golf and a mere power play that is hard to view as a 'watershed moment' for women's rights."

Karen Crouse of *The New York Times:* "When Bishop chose to disparage one man, the English golfer Ian Poulter, on Twitter by calling him a 'little girl,' he effectively demeaned all women, including his own two daughters and granddaughter."

Shackelford pointed out this story by Crouse, entitled "Playing Like a Girl? It's About Time: Ted Bishop's Comments Demonstrate Golf's Persistent Sexism" was the *Times'* first original story on the matter even though my fatal missives had taken place four days earlier.

Said Shackelford: "So what does this make *The New York Times,* then?"

Jay Coffin made a similar observation on GolfChannel. com, pointing out the number of women who were refusing to affirm the decision by the PGA of America to remove me as president. Coffin pointed out that on a list of sexist moments in golf, mine came nowhere close to Fred Funk once donning a skirt in a tournament or Wilson putting out blatantly sexist ads to sell golf balls. Or the R&A taking until 2014 to vote to accept women.

"Golf Channel made attempts to reach several of the most respected women in the game, and nearly all did not feel comfortable enough to comment," Coffin said. "Mostly, though, what I really wanted were strong women's voices for my daughter to hear. I wanted her to have a chance to find a new role model because someone stood up to a powerful organization to say enough is enough. It's an important issue to me as a father, and it makes me wonder if it's a big deal to women. Right now, I'm not certain. Perhaps my moral compass needs to be recalibrated, but I expected more from women's leadership."

These Coffin remarks prompted Shackelford to say in his blog: "Actually the silence could be seen as a reaffirmation of leadership, regardless of gender. Could it be they are quietly saying this isn't the right incident and right target to eradicate blatant sexism?"

*Golf Digest's* Stina Sternberg had the weekend to contemplate my ouster, and the former *Golf for Women* editor put my crime into perspective compared to the real issues in golf: "I'm offended that I can't play in most of my own club's tournaments because women's events take place on Thursdays while men's events are played on the weekends, as if women don't work just as hard as men do during the week. I'm outraged that the women's locker rooms at most clubs are a fraction the size of the men's locker rooms and rarely come close to having the same amenities. I resent that my girlfriends and I are never allowed to play through a group of slower-playing men, or tee off before a group of guys, simply because of our gender."

One woman who was quick to weigh in on my circumstances was Suzy Whaley, who on Friday, October 24, 2014, was hoping to become the first female ever elected as secretary of the PGA of America.

"I was extremely disappointed. For me to hear comments that are derogatory about young girls, or insulting, just because you are a girl is offensive. They were definitely sexist. I'm of 100 percent belief that we need to empower young girls. The PGA of America took incredibly swift action and are taking this extremely seriously. Obviously, it's critical that we are inclusive."

Whaley had served on the PGA's Board of Directors while I was an officer. We had worked together on many important things to benefit women and girls. I had appointed her as a tri-chair to my PGA Growth of the Game committee. Ironically, her daughter, Kelly, was in the room at the Faldo Series less than 24 hours before my fatal remarks, when I encouraged the girls to pursue careers in golf. Many viewed Whaley's comments on that Friday to be opportunistic, and she came out with a softened version a few days later.

"I worked with him for three years; he has two daughters; he has a great family; he's worked really hard to make golf inclusive," Whaley said. "There is no doubt in my mind that Ted is not a sexist. I think women in the PGA are trying to balance and understand. They know Ted as a PGA member and what he has done, how he's brought initiatives to make golf inclusive. They know him as a person, and they know he's not a sexist."

On Sunday, October 26, I finally made that call to Geoff Russell, executive director at Golf Channel. The purpose was to tell him that in retrospect, I really wished I had called him Friday morning and offered an apology on "Morning Drive." It wouldn't have made any difference in the outcome of my circumstances because I'm sure the PGA would have used that to further its case against me. But, at least for my peace of mind, the apology would have been out there a lot sooner.

Russell and I had spent some time together. We had played golf at Baltusrol in a PGA of America media day. He had accompanied a Golf Channel film crew to Indiana in October 2013 to start filming a segment on me with Jimmy Roberts and Matt Ginella. Russell was also a member of a task force I had created to come up with new ways to grow the game of golf. We shared the same propensity for out-of-the-box concepts such as FootGolf and relaxed rules for the game.

When I explained to Russell why I was reaching out, he said, "Why don't you come down and do the show tomorrow?"

Russell thought it needed to be an in-studio interview, not via satellite, and I agreed. Making it to Golf Channel studios in Orlando by Monday morning, however, wouldn't be possible, so after a few minutes of discussion, we agreed the interview would be Tuesday morning.

Soon after our phone call this release appeared on Golf Channel: "FORMER PGA OF AMERICA PRESIDENT TED BISHOP LIVE ON MORNING DRIVE TUESDAY IN FIRST INTERVIEW SINCE REMOVAL FROM OFFICE."

My family was nervous about the interview. They thought I was stepping into a trap and that Golf Channel might use the interview to provoke me into going down a negative path regarding the PGA of America. I trusted Russell and believed this interview was an opportunity, not an obstacle.

In my opinion, this conversation would be a chance to sincerely show my contriteness and once again apologize for my actions. At the same time, it would be an opportunity to tell my side of the story and expose some inconsistencies that were starting to surface in the PGA of America's messaging.

I had been told by Derek Sprague, the PGA vice president, that my impeachment was based on three reasons:

- My remarks invoked negative reaction by the media;
- There was potential fallout from sponsors who were offended by my remarks;
- Many PGA members were offended by what I had said.

Over the weekend there had been considerable discussion by the media about the magnitude of my penalty. Was it too severe? Should my record and accomplishments be recognized?

On Monday, October 27, an expansive PGA of America public relations document entitled, "Governance Statement on Removal of PGA President Ted Bishop," was sent to all 41 PGA sections and their officials.

"Due to Mr. Bishop's removal from office, the PGA Bylaws prohibit him from serving on the Board of Directors in the role of Honorary President. Mr. Bishop will always be recognized as the 38th President of the PGA of America, and his record of service during this time will remain intact.

"Mr. Bishop also retains his status as a member of the PGA of America, therefore enabling him to enjoy the same rights and privileges of all PGA members, including the ability to attend any events put on by the PGA."

What the statement did not say was that I was stripped of the rights and privileges accorded to a PGA past president. Even though I would be recognized as the 38th president, I would not be classified as an A-5 member (past PGA president). This sanction would mean I am the only PGA past president ever required to pay dues and still earn his recertification requirements. As Sprague had said, "I was ONLY a PGA member."

Also, in a bizarre move, I was told I could never again hold any PGA office and that I would never be allowed to vote at a PGA national meeting. However, I could still vote locally at the section level. It's like saying you can vote for your mayor, but not the president. Preposterous.

The statement went on to say, "Just last week, the PGA hosted the 3rd annual Sports Diversity & Inclusion Summit, with eight other major sports organizations in attendance. To have led such an important gathering and, within 24 hours, not have acted the way we did through the removal of our president, would have made the PGA look hypocritical and completely out of touch. We likely would be facing intense scrutiny far beyond the world of golf had we not moved at a rapid pace."

Some of the key "push buttons" in the document were:

Q. Why did the Board of Directors take this action?

A. The Board felt that the comments made through social media violated the PGA of America Code of Ethics Bylaws.

That was the first time the PGA of America said that my social media posts violated the PGA Code of Ethics. That was never part of the rationale for my removal as president. Furthermore, this was a ground-breaking precedent set by the PGA of America. Were they going to institute "Social Media Police" to ensure none of the 28,000 PGA members or apprentices ever violated the Code of Ethics with an offensive tweet or Facebook post? The PGA of America was setting a high standard for the future.

Q. What gives the Board of Directors the authority to take such action?

A. The Constitution of the PGA of America is very clear with regard to the Board of Directors authority to take action due to an emergency situation in the best interest of the Association.

I had to pull out my PGA Constitution to get the definition of an "emergency meeting." Anything legislated in an "emergency meeting" was final and there was no appeal process available if the member affected did not agree with the sanction by the Board of Directors. For example at a lower level, even a PGA member convicted of a felony could appeal his or her PGA penalty. Not that I intended to appeal, but my fate was exclusively decided by the Board of Directors with no opportunity to appeal the severe penalties imposed on me.

In my nine years as a PGA director and officer, I had never heard of or been exposed to an "emergency meeting." We had gone through some personnel issues with staff that warranted an emergency meeting, but we never resorted to that.

Legal fingerprints were all over my impeachment. A few months later, Sprague would tell *Sports Illustrated* that Bevacqua, an attorney by trade, "made sure we followed protocol at every turn and we gained a lot of feedback from in-house and outside."

Q. Was this the last straw? Is this one of many moves Ted made that angered the Board?

A. Ted has always been an outspoken President that has not changed. The Board's decision was based solely on the insensitive gender-based comments Ted made on social media.

All of this was forwarded to me by several PGA members. Obviously, the PGA of America was starting to take some heat from its members. But what bothered me most was that the PGA leadership was starting to backtrack and change its story on why I was impeached and what the full extent of the penalties were. It started with my status as a past president.

I reached out to Christine Garrity, PGA legal counsel, at 9:09 a.m. Monday. "Did the PGA of America keep a record or text of my conference call last Friday with the officers?"

Her response: "No."

My email back to Garrity: "I would have thought given the magnitude of what was happening the PGA would have done this."

I never received a response from Garrity. Going forward it would be my word against the PGA of America's on the interpretation of what transpired in that conference call with PGA leadership. The media was starting to question the expunging of my record, which had clearly been stated to me by the PGA of America. A point that confused me was how I could still be recognized as the 38th President and not be classified as a past president.

I flew to Orlando Monday night for the Golf Channel interview. Upon my arrival around 10 p.m., I recorded an interview with Matt Adams of the "Fairways of Life" show on Sirius/XM Radio. This interview was scheduled to run the next morning simultaneously with my interview on Golf Channel's "Morning Drive." Adams and I had done a weekly segment on his show, and it was important for me to give Adams the same opportunity as Golf Channel. Adams agreed to hold the interview until Golf Channel started its interview.

Russell met me early Tuesday in the darkness of the hotel parking lot, and I followed him to the Golf Channel studios. Gary Williams would do the live interview, and he was waiting for me. Williams was very prepared, and it was evident to me from the minute we started prepping that this interview would accomplish what I had hoped. It would give me the chance to apologize in front of a national audience and, at the same time, shed some light on some of the PGA of America's questionable actions.

The interview lasted about 30 minutes. The most dramatic moments came in the final minutes of the interview, when I bluntly summed up what my comments would probably mean for my legacy in golf. "The remorse I feel is because it potentially wipes out a lot of really good work I've done over my career with women. It's painful because it's taken a lot of things that I've done and put them down the drain," I told Williams.

"When I wake up at 2:30, 3 a.m. and I can't sleep, it's because of the things I feel like I've done in my career, for my girls, for women from Day One, and I think these things, they're flushed down the toilet. And that's going to be my legacy. That's it. That's the situation I created for myself," I said, my voice cracking with emotion.

With cameras off, I stepped down from the "Morning Drive" set. Williams shook my hand. He had done a fabulous job with the interview. Ironically, the first person to greet me was Kelly Tilghman, Golf Channel's first female anchor, who had been suspended early in her career for suggesting young players who wanted to challenge Tiger Woods should "lynch him in a back alley."

Kelly greeted me with a heartfelt hug. She and I had done several interviews over the years. She assured me the interview "was perfect." Countless people at Golf Channel congratulated me on a job well done, including many of their talent who was at the studio on that day.

I had a short farewell meeting with Russell and his wife Molly Solomon, who was the first woman to serve as an executive producer in her role with NBC Sports. Today, Solomon is the executive director of Golf Channel.

As I drove to the airport, my phone and emails were blowing up with messages from family, friends and people all over the country, including many PGA members. They were unanimously telling me how well the interview with Williams had gone. In particular, the words from LeslieAnne Wade, former executive vice president of public relations for CBS Sports, were gratifying. She had helped me prepare for the Golf Channel interview.

"You could not have been better or shown more dignity or intelligence. Ticked every single box perfectly. Breathe. Your family has to be so proud of you. We are! There is more for you! You will continue to do great things for golf! This is historic. Will be talked about in communications classes. They (PGA of America) blundered it," Wade said in an email.

In some ways the accolades on "Morning Drive" were bitter. I couldn't help but ask myself the question: What would have happened if I would have done this interview with an open apology on Friday the week prior?

The positive reaction to my interview with Williams carried over to Wednesday, when the Metropolitan PGA Section conducted its fall meeting in Long Island, New York. It was the first PGA section meeting since my ouster, and I was originally scheduled to speak at it, but the Met PGA and I jointly agreed not to go through with it. Bevacqua offered to speak in my absence, but the Met PGA turned him down. In attendance was Dan Pasternak, District 2 PGA director.

Mark Herrmann from *Newsday* covered the meeting. "The rank and file are steamed and riled that PGA of America President Ted Bishop was fired. Local golf pros, at their annual fall meeting at Bethpage State Park Wednesday, decried what they saw as unfairness of their leader losing his job over a social media faux pas," Herrmann reported.

At one point in the meeting while Pasternak was speaking, the entire Met PGA delegation stood to show its support for me.

"The more I thought about it, the more upset I got," said Greg Hurd, the North Hempstead Country Club pro. "There had to be a different way to handle it. For all of the time and effort and service that he had put in, I just didn't feel the punishment fit the crime."

"The punishment really went over the top," said Rick Meskell, head pro at Meadow Brook Club. "He did a lot of great things for the PGA and was a great voice."

Said Bobby Heins of Old Oaks in Westchester and one of the section's most experienced head pros: "This seemed like everybody got in a room, and there was no outside voice saying, 'Slow down.' My members didn't even know there was a PGA president until Ted Bishop came along because the others always toed the company line."

Southhampton Golf Club pro emeritus Bob Joyce said: "As soon as I heard this news, I emailed him: 'Ted, so many home runs, then one strike and you're out. Nothing is more unfair. Thank you for your service to the membership and the game.'"

After the Golf Channel interview, my support was increasing on an hourly basis. Mike David, executive director of the Indiana PGA, helped me send a letter to the 41 PGA sections, thanking many of them and their members for showing their support. That was sent on Thursday.

On Friday Derek Sprague, the new interim PGA president, sent a letter of his own, trying to again explain the PGA of America's position and rationale regarding my impeachment. His letter made six references to diversity and inclusion or gender equity.

This defensive approach by the PGA of America would continue in the weeks leading up to the PGA Annual Meeting in Indianapolis scheduled for November 18–22. Conference calls were conducted with PGA districts and sections. I felt the PGA of America was trying to build a case ex post facto. Many PGA members were not accepting diversity and inclusion as an adequate reason for my impeachment.

For me, this was like being tried in a court of law and not being able to hear the charges nor offer a defense against them. Some information was relayed to me by those who witnessed what the PGA was saying. Several erroneous accusations got back to me. Similar to the PGA's backtracking on my status as a past president, the reason for my impeachment was now also changing.

I was told by a PGA insider that PGA of America leadership was saying I purposely skipped the Diversity and Inclusion Symposium so I could hang out with celebrities at the Faldo Series. In fact, the Faldo Series had been on my schedule for a year. I was supposed to help Nick in 2013 but had to cancel when Bevacqua and I needed to interview NFL Hall of Famer Lynn Swann in Pittsburgh for the position of PGA independent director. When the PGA of America set the dates for the 2014 diversity symposium, I was never asked to attend. In fact, no PGA officer was present.

In January 2014, I tweeted about my new TaylorMade irons. I had been on staff with Titleist for 32 years before I switched to TaylorMade. The reason for my staff change was because TaylorMade CEO Mark King and I were aligned philosophically about where golf needed to go in the future in order to grow. I had come to believe that Titleist, on the other hand, had a conservative and almost elitist approach to the game. After the tweet about my new irons, a top Titleist official complained to the PGA of America. What the PGA did not tell its members in trying to justify my removal was that after I changed staffs, TaylorMade and King committed to a major five-year sponsorship of the PGA Junior League.

Another insider told me the PGA was also saying I refused to attend the press conference announcing the KPMG sponsorship with the PGA/LPGA Championship in 2014 in New York. They said that absence was my way showing I did not support the PGA of America involvement in the event. As I wrote previously, I was in full support and served an instrumental role in making that event happen. I felt Bevacqua deserved to be out front on this because he did the bulk of the work in getting a deal done with KPMG and the LPGA. My travel schedule had been crazy at that time, and I needed to be at my course when the press conference took place in New York.

In mid-November 2014 I did an interview with Bob Bubka on Sirius/XM's "Grill Room." Bubka asked me some general questions about the PGA's Ryder Cup Task Force. A few days later I received a caustic letter from PGA lawyers telling me I had violated the confidentiality of my oath of office. There was nothing Bubka and I talked about that hadn't been discussed previously by many in the media.

The PGA of America hoped I would be dead and buried after my impeachment. That wasn't going to happen. As I told my family, "When the day comes that I can longer have an opinion and express it, then you might as well shoot me." That's probably not politically correct either, but you get my point.

Many times I have been asked the question: "Why did the PGA of America take such a drastic action against you?" Honestly, I am not sure I can answer that. Since my impeachment the PGA of America has been inconsistent in how it has prioritized its commitment to diversity and inclusion, and I will address that.

Part of me thinks my impeachment was directly related to a shift in power at the top of the PGA of America, although the PGA claims otherwise. I may never know. I do believe that if the PGA had let me address the Poulter comments more quickly, the public controversy might have quickly passed.

Regardless, I had been encouraged by many to bring the PGA of America back to its members when I became the president. Over the years we had become an association that was more corporate and staff driven than member-oriented. At least in 2013–14, I feel like the PGA seemed to be headed in a more member-centric direction.

The PGA of America gave me great independence, but it also set up nearly all of my interviews and media appearances. Most weeks, the PGA asked me to perform five to 10 television, radio or print media interviews, sometimes more.

With my demise, the power inside the PGA of America again shifted away from the president and back to the executive staff. In my opinion, this was a power struggle between the president and staff. A "staff driven" PGA of America has been a source of heartburn for PGA members for decades. I tried to change that and it cost me dearly.

From the minute I became the president of the PGA of America, my priorities were always focused on my 28,000 PGA members and apprentices. Although I sometimes put myself in the crosshairs, I never worried about it as long as it was in the best interest of my PGA of America constituency. I realized too late that I was dead-center in the kill zone, and it was those inside the PGA of America who actually had me in their crosshairs.

I knew PGA members needed to be at the forefront of the fight to make golf better and more accessible. I always followed my heart, and some would call that blind ambition, intuition or even stupidity.

For decades, leaders in golf have been full of lip service with selfish agendas that preserved the status quo. I never wanted to be like that. I set out to shake up the system. Clearly, there are many who thought I shook it too hard. But I did so for the benefit of the thousands of PGA professionals who devote their lives every single day to golf. For that I offer no apology.

# Chapter Three

# An Unlikely Rise to the Top

My dad Jim used to say that Logansport, Indiana, was an hour south of Notre Dame and an hour north of the Indianapolis 500 Mile Race. I was born there in 1954. The town was a repair hub for the Pennsylvania Railroad, a blue-collar community of 21,000 people situated between the Wabash and Eel rivers. The railroad influenced a major part of the Logansport culture. A diverse collection of whorehouses were located on Biddle's Island, a small tract of land in the middle of the Wabash River. That was an attraction for many travelers.

I grew up at 2125 Otto Street in the east end of Logansport. We lived in a modest flat-top house that had a full basement with a pool table that could be converted to a ping-pong table. The walls were blanketed with cover photos from *Sports Illustrated*. The first edition I ever received as a young subscriber featured Detroit Tigers outfielder Al Kaline, and it was one of several hundred *Sports Illustrated* covers that would grace the concrete block walls of the basement.

That basement was my escape. There were many Saturdays when I would invite a bunch of my buddies over for round-robin ping-pong tournaments. When my dad put a black-and-white TV in that basement, I also had a place to escape with my teenaged girlfriends while my parents were in the upstairs living room watching their own shows. One of my favorite things in that basement was a dart board, where I conjured up all kinds of games.

Competition and games were what I lived for. When I was 9 years old I made up a dice game and played a 162-game baseball season as manager of the Houston Astros. I picked the Astros because I didn't care if they won or lost. It was all about compiling the stats, making player moves and doing the play-by-play for each game.

My real childhood love was the New York Yankees. The first Major League game I attended was in September 1961, when my dad and grandfather yanked me out of my first-grade classes and took me to Chicago to see New York at Comiskey Park. Roger Maris had 58 home runs at the time. The Yankees didn't sign autographs but I got to shake the hand of closer Luis Arroyo, the '61 "Fireman of the Year" according to *The Sporting News*.

I would lay in bed at night with a 9-volt transistor radio and listen to the Yankee games on New York's WCBS-AM radio. Many mornings I would wake up and see that my dad had taped a piece of typing paper to my bedroom door with the Yankees line score on it. As a kid the Yankees were—and remain to this day—my biggest love in team sports.

My dad was a devoted Yankee fan but actually named me after Ted Williams, the legendary Hall of Famer with the Red Sox, because he met him while serving in the U.S. Navy. In fact, he wanted William to be my middle name and tried to persuade my mom, noting that his dad was also William. Marge, a no-nonsense home economics teacher, would have nothing to do with it, and I became Ted Michael Bishop.

Bishop's Barbershop was a Logansport institution for sixty years. Opened in 1935, it was run by father and son Bill and Jim Bishop. Located at the corner of 17th and Smead Streets, the barbershop was a hot bed for sports and politics. The Logansport Berries were in the North Central Conference—arguably for many years, the toughest high school conference in Indiana. Any

Logansport team or individual athlete who won the NCC in a Berry uniform had the honor of having their picture appear on the walls of Bishop's Barbershop.

It was a three-chair barbershop. In the "pre-Beatles era" flat tops or crew cuts were cranked out every 15 minutes. Saturdays and most days after work, "the shop" was packed. If I stopped in after school for a 10-cent soft drink, my dad made me stand so I wouldn't take a seat from a paying customer.

Over the years Bishop's Barbershop featured unique things such as a talking mynah bird and a pet monkey. There was no better place to hang out than the barber shop because the discussions that took place around sports or politics were more educational than anything I ever learned in school.

Bill and Jim Bishop were the epitome of entrepreneurs. They always had something going on and swore the 13-run baseball pool started at their barbershop. There was a weekly contest for high school basketball games; everybody had a team, and if yours scored 66 points, you won the pot. You paid $10 and drew a driver in the Indy 500. On and on. You could bet modestly on anything at Bishop's.

Basketball and baseball were the kings in Logansport. Every kid wanted to someday wear the Red and Black for the Berries. A stuffed Felix the Cat was our mascot, and he was actually the first physical high school mascot in Indiana. Our school song is an original written by an LHS grad. No other school in the nation can lay claim to it.

I made the varsity team in baseball, basketball and tennis in my junior year of high school. Back then we had to play a fall sport in order to try out for the basketball team, and after doing cross country my freshman year, I bought a used tennis racket because running bored me.

As a three-sport athlete I was never a star, but I started and played full-time on every team with which I was associated. My junior year, I set all of the Logansport High School free-throw records. I hit all 15 attempts in a single game and made 22 in a row over several games. As a senior I pitched a no-hitter in front of eight Major League scouts who were watching a couple of my teammates. I discovered there was no demand for a pitcher who had a 70 mph fastball with good command. I was the No. 2 man on the tennis team.

Before becoming a full-time barber, my grandfather ran an athletic club in the nearby town of Peru. Boxing was a big deal there. Neither he nor my dad played golf when I was growing up. My first experience with the sport was watching it on TV. Quite honestly, I loved the way the pros dressed, and I just thought it would be cool someday to be a golfer.

When I was a teenager I went to a local hardware store and bought a George Fazio 7-iron and a sleeve of Faultless golf balls. I would meet some friends at Tower Park, which was three blocks from my house. We would hit golf balls from lamp post to lamp post, and that was the first golf course I ever played.

During summer 1971, before my senior year in high school, I got a job working at the Rolling Hills Par 3 course on the east edge of Logansport. My boss was Dick Herr. He was a PGA pro who gave a lot of lessons, and he was also responsible for taking care of the golf course grass. I spent the next five summers working for Dick. He encouraged me to change my major after my freshman year at Purdue University from radio, television and journalism to turf management.

My love affair with golf really started during those five wonderful summers at Rolling Hills. Caddyshack could have been filmed there, as there was never a dull moment. Dick and I formed a great friendship. He gave me a lot of responsibility, and I was basically a one-man grounds crew from Memorial Day to Labor Day.

I started playing a lot of golf without taking lessons—a mistake I would later regret. I was the secretary for all four leagues that Rolling Hills hosted. Soon after high school, I drifted away from basketball and softball. Golf became my passion, and my dad even started playing with me on Sunday afternoons.

Dick Herr would later go on to become the superintendent at Jupiter Hills Country Club in Florida and was working with George Fazio when the course hosted the United States Amateur Championship won by Billy Mayfair in 1987. It was pretty incredible to look back on those summers at Rolling Hills and think that a golf course superintendent who hosted a U.S. Am and a future President of the PGA of America were together at that Par 3 course for five summers from 1971 to 1975.

In January 1976, a few months before my graduation from Purdue, I was offered a position as the pro/superintendent at the Linton Municipal Golf Course in southwestern Indiana. At first I turned down the job because I was going to make my money doing what a golf pro does, and my college education taught me to be a golf course superintendent.

Then, one night that winter, I got a call from Frank Henry, the PGA pro at Dykeman Park Golf Club in Logansport. He had been in the barbershop and heard that I turned down the Linton job. Frank told me I could learn the business part and that I had the turf skill they needed. He told me I should reconsider. I was going to own the golf cars, golf shop and snack bar concessions. It was some of the best advice I ever received, and I wound up going to Linton after graduating from Purdue.

While at Purdue, I met Cindy Ellingwood in 1974 and we dated for two years. She had long blonde hair, was athletic and a physical education major. For me, it was love at first sight. We were married in June 1976 at the Fairmount Friends Church in Fairmount, Indiana, the hometown of James Dean. The actor's funeral, in fact, had taken place at the same church more than 20 years earlier. I took only two days off work for my wedding and honeymoon. Like most couples who have made it through

40 years of marriage, Cindy and I are survivors. We have not had a perfect marriage by any stretch. She has been my biggest critic and my most loyal fan.

In 1979, one of Linton's most beloved sons started coming back to his hometown to raise money for a scholarship in his name at Linton High School. Phil Harris, the legendary entertainer, was born in Linton in 1904. Today, Harris might be best known for his voiceover of "Baloo the Bear" in the 1967 animated movie *The Jungle Book*. Part of the weekend's festivities was a celebrity golf tournament at the course, which was renamed the Phil Harris Golf Course.

My relationship with Phil Harris blossomed. He was loved and respected by many of the early PGA Tour players. Over the years in Linton, we hosted golf greats such as Jack Burke, Jay and Lionel Hebert, Dave Marr, Mike Souchak, Toney Penna and Doug Sanders. Phil would attract entertainers such as Jimmy Dean, Forrest Tucker, Pete Fountain, Frank Sinatra Jr., Roy Clark and many others to a variety show he hosted in the high school gym the weekend of the tournament.

By the mid-1980s, Phil's tournament had grown to 600 players. We had shotgun starts on Saturday and Sunday at 7:30 a.m. and 1:30 p.m. Each shotgun had 25 six-man teams. We had 18 holes on 83 acres, and we should have given hard hats as tee favors. Dick Taylor of *Golf World* called it the largest pro-am in the United States. The celebrity field included Johnny Unitas, Ernie Banks, Neil Armstrong, Eugene Cernan, Bob Knight, many former professional baseball and football players, and dozens of standout college athletes. Linton had one small motel, so many of the celebrities stayed in private homes. Cindy threw parties in our backyard for hundreds.

Doors in golf started opening for me because of my association with Phil Harris. In the late 1980s, I started working for three weeks each March at the Nabisco Dinah Shore Tournament in Palm Springs. Dave Marr was the tournament director when

I first started. He was later replaced by Mike Galeski. I learned a lot about tournament operations from those guys.

The Nabisco Dinah Shore Pro-Am was one hell of an event. Team Nabisco in those days was made up of guys like Frank Gifford, Bobby Orr, Joe DiMaggio, O.J. Simpson, Jack Nicklaus, Ben Crenshaw, Ray Floyd and other top names in sports. The celebrity field at Dinah's pro-am included former President Gerald Ford, Bob Hope, and Frank Sinatra, along with many other Hollywood stars.

One of the side gigs I got in the 1980s was directing an exclusive corporate pro-am called The Fedigan in Scottsdale, Arizona. Each year we would honor a golf legend, and the list included Jimmy Demaret, Sam Snead, Byron Nelson and Claude Harmon. The professional field had Tour players from the 1950s and '60s, including Miller Barber, Gardner Dickinson, Johnny Pott, Fred Hawkins, Jerry Barber, Tommy Jacobs, Bob Goalby, Johnny Bulla, Souchak, Marr, Burke, Penna and the Hebert brothers. Glen Campbell joined Phil Harris each year to do the entertainment.

The Fedigan experience was one of the most memorable of my life. At night the pros would sit in the bar and tell war stories. The amateurs played with a different pro for three days. It was the quintessential pro-am featuring golf, food, drink and great camaraderie. It was a week where friendships were formed for life.

The pros were paid $5,000 as an appearance fee, plus their travel expenses. The pro-am competition was all team-based, but there was also a pro purse. The old pros loved it because they didn't have to card their own score.

Jay Hebert had the task of helping Jack Fedigan select The Honoree. When Snead was asked in 1986 to be the honored guest, he told Hebert that he would come, but that he wanted the $5,000 in cash and a different woman every night. Mr. Fedigan replied, "Tell Sam we are not in the cash business, and I am not a pimp."

As a result, Nelson became the '86 Honoree. It was my privilege to be Byron's shadow for the week. I would eat breakfast with him every morning. I drove him 90 minutes round trip each day from the Carefree Inn to Orange Tree Golf Course. Without question, Nelson was one of the finest gentlemen I have ever met.

On one of those late afternoon drives back to Carefree, I asked him about his relationship with the legendary golfer Ben Hogan. The two had grown up together in the same caddy yard in Fort Worth, Texas. Nelson recounted a story about an interview he and Hogan did one night at a radio station in their hometown.

"The host asked each of us what we thought about the other as a player," Nelson said. "I spoke first and said that I thought Ben was the greatest ball striker I had ever seen.

"When he asked Ben about me, Hogan said that he didn't think I ever reached my full potential because I didn't practice hard enough," Nelson continued. "I was never a player that needed to hit hundreds of practice balls like Hogan did. In fact, I worried more about hurting my swing through fatigue if I over practiced." I could tell Nelson was still stinging from Hogan's words. "I didn't like Ben's answer," he said, "and never forgot it."

In 1987, Snead did agree to be the Honoree, and this time it was under Fedigan's terms. Sam was truly "a man's man" and someone all of the guys gravitated to. He was also unquestionably the greatest joke-teller that I have ever been around, although most of his stories were not fit for a mixed crowd.

Snead was 76 years old when we honored him, but the man could still play golf. I had the pleasure of joining him for a practice round in 1987 at Orange Tree. The scorecard is framed and hangs in my clubhouse today. He shot a 69—bettering his age by seven strokes—and that included one bogey on the ninth hole, where he misjudged the layup on his tee shot and inadvertently knocked it in the water.

In those days, Snead was on the Wilson Sporting Goods golf staff and doing a lot of TV commercials touting their Ultra golf ball. I thought it would be appropriate if I played that ball during this round with Snead. On the first tee I saw Snead pull a Pinnacle golf ball, made by Titleist, out of his pocket. I was shocked—and told him so.

"Son, when that Ultra ball gets to the top of its flight it starts fluttering like a quail," Snead quipped. "Hell, I would never play that ball. But if they pay me enough, I will tell others to play it."

One morning I was driving Harris, Snead and Penna to the golf course when a conversation broke out about Lloyd Mangrum and his time in the military. Mangrum, who won the 1946 U.S. Open, received two Purple Hearts and was wounded in the Battle of the Bulge. Penna was telling a story about Mangrum capturing some German soldiers while on patrol, but Snead had another version of the story.

"The story I heard was there were six or seven Germans who voluntarily surrendered because they were unarmed. Mangrum told the rest of the guys in his platoon to go back to their camp, and he would bring them in by himself," Snead recalled.

"A few minutes later there were gun shots, and when the guys ran back to find Lloyd, all of those Germans were laying on the ground dead," Snead continued. "Mangrum told his guys that they tried to escape, and he had to shoot them. The truth is, Lloyd hated Germans and just shot them. Hell, they were unarmed and didn't try to escape. That Mangrum was a mean son of a bitch."

Penna went nuts and called Snead "a lying sack of shit." He was in the rear seat of the van, and Snead was in the front seat. Phil was in the middle seat and became the referee. Snead just laughed it off and swore his version of the true story was true.

Snead came back to The Fedigan in 1988 when we honored Claude Harmon. The event took place in November, and Harmon was in poor health. His son, Billy, accompanied him. Unfortunately, Claude passed away a few months later.

During the roast of Claude on the final night, Snead said he was playing against Harmon back when the PGA Championship was match play and Claude was rattling change in his pocket while Sam was trying to make a critical putt. Claude rose up from the head table and grabbed the microphone away from Snead. "Sit down, Sonny, and let me tell the story the way it really happened. I laid a perfect stymie on you, and you took forever to hit that shot, and I wound up beating your ass."

Harmon brought the house down. Even Snead was laughing hysterically. Claude was a phenomenal honoree. Some of his former assistants at the exclusive Winged Foot Golf Club in Mamaroneck, New York, included Burke, Souchak and Marr.

"I remember the old pro (Harmon) telling me that if I couldn't give him one a side at Winged Foot and beat him, I had no business playing the Tour," Marr said.

Burke jumped out of his chair and chimed in, "I worked for Claude in 1947, and he never had a round out of the 60s that summer. I don't think I ever cashed a paycheck."

Years later I would make copies of the video from that Fedigan roast and send them to all of the Harmon sons—Billy, Dick, Craig and Butch.

Had it not been for Phil Harris, these experiences would never have taken place. Phil was truly one of the kindest men I have ever known. He was a good golfer in his day and actually won the 1951 Bing Crosby Pro-Am with Dutch Harrison as his pro. After Phil made a 90-foot putt on the 17th hole at Pebble Beach to seal the victory, he proclaimed, "I wish I owned that much frontage on Wilshire Boulevard."

There were many stories about Harris and his drinking exploits. One year at the Crosby he announced himself as the pro from the Jack Daniels Country Club. He and Crosby were in Scotland filming an episode of ABC's American Sportsmen when they drove past a distillery one night after dinner.

"See, Phil, they can make that stuff faster than you can drink it," Crosby said.

"Yeah, but I got them sons of bitches working nights," Phil replied.

On the last night of one those Fedigans, Phil got ready for bed and told me he had a driver picking him up at 4:30 a.m. the next day. He was going bone fishing in the Florida Keys, and Phil said, "It won't be easy, but make sure I'm up because I have to be on that flight in the morning."

My bedroom was down the hall. I had invited a guy named Russ Smith to help me with some of my tournament duties. We had twin beds in our room, and Russ was snoring like a freight train. I couldn't sleep and moved out to the couch in the front room near the kitchen. About 2 a.m. I was awakened by the rattling of silverware. I rose from the couch and saw the image of Phil in the kitchen and asked him what he was doing.

"I'm dying of thirst. Do we have anything to drink in here?" Phil asked. The next thing I knew, he had grabbed a bottle of beer out of the refrigerator, popped it open and gulped it down. He then shuffled on back to his bedroom.

A couple hours later I went in to wake him up. He soon surfaced in the kitchen, bare-chested with his pajama pants on. "Do we have any milk in this place?" he asked.

I told him it was in the refrigerator. The next thing I know he grabs a tall glass and a spoon. There was a bottle of Crown Royal on the kitchen counter. Phil filled the glass with half milk and half Crown Royal. He stirred it up and drank the glass empty. After putting the glass on the counter he looked up, grinned and said, "Now, that's a glass of milk!"

The greatest Phil Harris saying was, "It doesn't cost anything to be nice to people. There is no tax on it."

After 17 years at the Phil Harris Golf Course, I had the chance to build my own facility in Franklin, Indiana, and be a part owner. The Legends of Indiana Golf Course was designed by Jim Fazio, and 18 holes were opened on August 29, 1992. We later expanded to 27 championship holes plus an 18-hole Par 3 course. We have a superior practice facility, and the offices of the Indiana Golf Association and Indiana PGA are located on site. The Indiana Golf Hall of Fame, into which I was proudly inducted in 2013, is also located at The Legends.

Owning a golf facility can best be described by the old adage "Be careful what you wish for." After we expanded our operation in 1995, there were 24 new golf courses built in Central Indiana. Most were done by residential developers with no regard for the demographics of golf. The result was a complete oversaturation of golf in Central Indiana.

The Legends went through a tough time and in 2010 became the first of many area courses to file Chapter 11 bankruptcy. We rebounded with new ownership in a matter of months, but the public golf business still remains a huge challenge for us and many around the country.

Today, after 25 years, I remain the PGA general manager at The Legends. It's now a family-owned business, and I love what I do every day at my facility. I could never have been able to fulfill my volunteer duties as a PGA officer had I not been in an ownership position at my facility. Even then, the time I spent away from work was tough on our business.

My whole family is in golf. Cindy runs the food and beverage operation at The Legends. She was an outstanding high school girl's golf coach at Franklin High School, taking five of her teams to the state finals. Ashely, my oldest daughter, handles memberships and outside events at the Legends. My son-in-law, Ted Davidson, is the assistant general manager at The Legends, and members of his family are my business partners.

My youngest daughter Ambry is the women's golf coach at St. John's University in Queens, New York. Ambry is also a PGA member and the assistant pro at St. Andrew's Golf Club in Westchester County, which was founded in 1888 and is the oldest golf club in the U.S.

Both of my girls played college golf. Ashely graduated from the University of Kansas, where she played in every tournament during her four years. She was the Most Valuable Player her senior year and graduated as the only athlete in KU history to be named All-Academic Big 12 eight times. Ambry played four years at Indiana University, where she had individual runner-up finishes in tournaments at Baylor University and the University of Michigan. She won the Indiana Women's Match Play as well as the Indianapolis Women's City Championship.

Golf has been our life.

As I close this chapter, I want to share one of the most poignant moments I experienced as the 38th president of the PGA, because it represents the essence of golf. It was at the 2014 Champions Dinner at Valhalla Golf Club in Louisville, Kentucky. Jason Dufner was the defending champion so he hosted the dinner, picked the menu and was the focus of the evening.

As PGA president I determined the seating arrangement for the event. At the head table was my wife Cindy; Tim and Holly Finchem; Phil Mickelson; Jason and Amanda Dufner; TJ Oshie and his soon-to-be-wife Lauren Cosgrove. TJ was a 2-handicapper who now plays for the NHL's Washington Capitals. He had scored four game-winning shootout goals against the Russians at the Sochi Olympics. TJ and Lauren were my guests.

Phil got the dinner conversation started by asking everyone at our table to tell a story about someone who had significantly impacted each of our lives in golf. When it got to Dufner, usually a man of few words, his story moved the entire table.

"When I was a kid growing up, my dad would take me to this beat-down nine-hole public course. We walked because we couldn't afford to ride a cart and the course was never in good shape," Jason said. "I always liked playing with my grandfather more because he belonged to the local country club. The course was a lot nicer and we always rode in a golf cart. But, if I had one round left to play—I would want to play with my dad on that beat-down nine-hole public course." Frank Dufner had passed away in 2001 at age 50 from cancer.

We all knew exactly what Jason meant. Those were eloquent words from one of golf's newest major champions. I was fortunate to experience that moment. But when it comes to golf, I've been a lucky guy.

# Chapter Four

# Rebuilding a Relationship with Arnold Palmer

On Wednesday, March 27, 2013, Pete Bevacqua and I met in Orlando with Arnold Palmer to discuss the United States Golf Association's proposed ban on anchoring. The meeting took place in Palmer's second-story office in the clubhouse at his Bay Hill Club and Lodge.

Bevacqua and I were greeted by Janet Hulcher, Palmer's longtime Orlando secretary. We sat in a small waiting area for a few minutes. The door to Palmer's office was being guarded by his dog, Mulligan.

Palmer had been a vocal supporter of the USGA over the years, as you would expect from a former U.S. Open champion who has the utmost respect for the rules and the traditions of the game. When it came to anchoring, the act of gripping a club (most notably the putter) against one's body to enable a golfer to make a supposedly easier stroke, he was very much in support of the USGA's proposed ban. My intent was to merely try to explain why the PGA had taken an opposing stance. I had no intention of trying to persuade Arnold Palmer to change his mind.

When we were finally summoned to Palmer's office for the 1 p.m. meeting, "The King" greeted us quietly with a handshake and motioned for us to be seated in two chairs directly in front of his desk. He spoke no words, just motioned for us to sit. That didn't quell my nerves any.

It was three days after the Arnold Palmer Invitational, and the 84-year-old host still showed signs of fatigue from the big week. His office reminded me of mine—cluttered with lots of memorabilia scattered everywhere, especially on the floor.

I started the meeting by introducing Bevacqua and thanking Palmer for his time. I explained to him that we were not there to try to change his mind about anchoring, but simply wanted him to hear first-hand why the PGA had taken an opposing viewpoint from the USGA. He gave a stern nod. I continued.

"In our opinion, anything that happens in golf right now that would lessen the enjoyment of the game for even one player is a mistake. We see no positive reason to ban the anchored putting stroke, which will have a negative effect on many golfers, particularly older men."

As I continued to run through a couple of other reasons why the PGA opposed the anchoring ban, Palmer had positioned two of his signature umbrella lapel pins on his desktop, and he was moving them around with both of his index fingers. He was looking down at the desk, but I could tell he was intently listening to every word I was saying.

When I finished my brief presentation, he looked at me, slowly raised his arms in the air and said, "I think the worst thing that could happen to the game right now is to have two sets of rules. That's where I fear this is headed."

To which I instinctively replied, "With all due respect, Mr. Palmer, in 2000 you endorsed a non-conforming Callaway ERC driver for amateur play, but not on the professional tours. That's bifurcation of the rules, and I don't see how that is different."

Palmer shrugged his shoulders and said, "That's just how I feel."

I figured that was Arnold's cue that this meeting was over. I stood, and Bevacqua joined me. I extended my hand to Palmer. He didn't shake it and said, "What's your hurry? Sit down."

He began proudly showing us pictures of his family and his grandchildren. It lightened the tension, but then all of a sudden Palmer pointed his finger in my direction and pierced me with a somber look.

"Now I'm going to tell you some things about the PGA you probably don't know," he said.

Palmer repositioned his fingers on the umbrella lapel pins and once again started moving them around his desktop. He began talking about his father, Deacon. His tone was serious, and it was apparent that he had pent-up anger with the PGA of America.

"My father was a cripple. He had infantile paralysis. For years he was not allowed to join the PGA of America because of it. The PGA had a membership policy that excluded people with handicaps," he said in that foghorn voice. "And the PGA had that policy where you had to be a member for five years before you could play in a Ryder Cup. That cost me two Ryder Cups."

It was very apparent that Palmer had a few bones to pick with the PGA. The Ryder Cup frustration didn't surprise me, but I was taken aback by what he said about his father being denied PGA membership because he was handicapped. The PGA's darkest times came prior to 1961 with its Caucasian-only clause, but the exclusion of the handicapped as members was something I didn't think Palmer was correct about. However, that afternoon was not the time to argue the point.

Bevacqua and I shook Arnold's hand and thanked him for the time. The meeting had not ended the way I had hoped, but it cast a light on an issue that was far greater than my desire to have Arnold Palmer understand the PGA's position on anchoring. He is the game's greatest living icon, and the PGA needed to repair this relationship. Somehow I had to figure out how to make that happen.

Bevacqua and I were still pretty much in shock when we went to the grill room at Bay Hill for a quick bite to eat before heading our separate ways. I laughed and told him, "I was really hoping we would at least get one of those umbrella pins."

Bevacqua grinned and said, "I was thinking the same thing when he was pushing those things around the desk, but that's not going to happen. He is really upset with the PGA."

When I got to the Orlando International Airport I called Tom Brawley, the senior director of membership services for the PGA, and asked him if we ever had a policy that would keep a handicapped person from being a member. As I suspected, Brawley said no. I asked Tom to dig up everything he had on Deacon Palmer and get it to me.

A couple weeks later, I sent Palmer a two-page letter detailing what I had learned, much, of course, of which he already was well aware. But I wanted him to know that I was looking into his father's case in earnest. As a teenager, Deacon was on the construction crew that built Latrobe Country Club in the early 1920s. He became the greenskeeper in 1926 and Latrobe's pro in 1932. That would have made him eligible to join the PGA of America in 1937, after the required five-year waiting period. But Deacon did not become a PGA member until 1946.

In my letter I told Palmer that my daughter, Ashely, has a large picture of Arnold and Deacon that hangs on her office wall at The Legends. I wrote that when I pursued my PGA membership in the 1980s, I was often looked down on by my PGA members in the Indiana section because of my background as a greenskeeper. And I also told Palmer the PGA never had a policy that restricted handicapped people from joining.

A year went by, and I never heard from Arnold. I had seen a Golf Channel documentary on him in March 2014 that talked about how Palmer religiously answered all of his mail over the years. They actually showed a storage barn at his home in Latrobe that contained thousands of letters he had received. I didn't know if my letter had alienated Palmer to the point where he refused to answer it, or maybe he just didn't receive it.

When I went to the Masters in early April to work as a rules official, I was partnered with Palmer's longtime friend, Dow Finsterwald. We worked the ninth green on Friday. I had a chance to tell Dow about the letter I had written Palmer. He was shocked that I had never received a reply. Dow told me he was having lunch with Palmer the following week, and he would inquire about my letter.

On the Monday after the Masters, on my way back to Indiana, I stopped at Reynolds Plantation and played in an outing that TaylorMade Chief Executive Officer Mark King was hosting that featured 15-inch holes instead of the regulation 4 1/4. It was a true pleasure to join PGA Tour champions Sergio Garcia and Justin Rose in helping King promote his Hack Golf concept, designed to introduce unconventional ways to grow the sport. When the outing was over, I continued driving to Franklin and purposely stopped before 10 p.m. so I could see the second part of Golf Channel's documentary on Palmer, which was about the major championships.

I laid in bed and watched the final 15-minute segment devoted to the PGA Championship. It was disappointing to hear narrator Tom Selleck open by talking about Palmer's hard feelings for the PGA because of the policy it had excluding his handicapped father from membership. Selleck went on to talk about the painful frustration Palmer felt because the PGA Championship was also the only major he never won. I immediately notified Bevacqua that we had to demand a correction of some type from Golf Channel regarding "the exclusion of the handicapped" before the segment could be re-aired.

The following afternoon I got a call from Finsterwald, who said, "Arnold has your letter in the top drawer of his desk. He's trying to figure out how to respond to it. I told him that he owes you a response, and I would hope that you hear from him soon."

At that point I reached out to Golf Channel President Mike McCarley and told him how much it bothered me that Palmer felt the way he did about the PGA. I told McCarley about my letter to Palmer and what Dow had said. As we talked, McCarley came up with a suggestion. Why not create a new PGA award that would be named after Deacon Palmer, signifying the qualities that made him a great father and golf professional?

I loved the idea. The award could be presented to a PGA member who had overcome a serious personal challenge to serve the game and the community in which he or she lived. That PGA member needed to be a teacher and promoter of golf, just like Deacon Palmer was. It would be a person who was not a self-promoter. After all, Deacon's signature line was, "Don't tell people what you can do. Just show them."

In less than two weeks I was able to get the backing of my fellow PGA officers and the approval of our Board of Directors to move forward with the Deacon Palmer Award. The next step would be another meeting with Arnold Palmer; there was no guarantee that he would even agree to do it.

I made a call to Cori Britt, vice president of Arnold Palmer Enterprises, and told him what I had in mind. He spoke with Arnold, and a meeting was set for Wednesday, April 30, 2014. I then called Finsterwald and told him about the meeting. We agreed to meet at Bay Hill for dinner on the Tuesday night before to discuss my strategy in making the presentation to Palmer.

The Bay Hill Club & Lodge is a step back in time. Built in the early 1960s, the entire complex remains much the same as it was 50 years ago. Bay Hill is well-kept, and there is a certain quaintness to its retro look. The Palmer family owns it and operates it.

I made this trip alone. After I checked into Bay Hill early Tuesday afternoon and enjoyed a late lunch, I went back to my room to do some work and turned on the TV, which offered a continuous loop about Arnold Palmer's life and career. I found it fascinating, particularly the part about his relationship with his father.

Dow and I enjoyed our dinner together. I told him the specifics of what the PGA had in mind with the Deacon Palmer Award. He thought Arnold and his family would be "very pleased." Dow was an instrumental piece in not only making the Deacon Palmer Award a reality, but he was also responsible for giving me the thought of awarding Ryder Cup rings to all those players who had played in the competition before 1981 who had nothing to symbolize their participation for the U.S.

The eighty-five year old Finsterwald had won the 1958 PGA Championship. He won 11 PGA Tour titles from 1955–63 and finished fifth or better 55 times. He played on four Ryder Cup teams and served as the 1977 U.S. captain. As a club professional at The Broadmoor in Colorado, he lost a bid to be elected president of the PGA in the late 1970s. Being a close friend to Palmer is as important to Dow as anything he ever accomplished in golf.

When I returned to my room that night, I watched the Bay Hill Arnold Palmer tribute for the third time. I was fixated on the Deacon Palmer segments. Hearing Palmer talk about his dad was very compelling. I was really excited to be there and to be able to present the idea of the Deacon Palmer Award to Arnold the next morning at 10 a.m.

Arnold Palmer began that morning by meeting and greeting a group of disabled veterans, who had ventured to Bay Hill to meet The King. Palmer had served a three-year stint in the U.S. Coast Guard from 1951–54 and had been a devout supporter of the U.S. military throughout his career.

I headed up to Palmer's office and was greeted once again by Janet Hulcher, his secretary. Soon Amy Saunders, who is the younger of Arnold's two daughters and instrumental in the Bay Hill operation, showed up in the alcove outside Palmer's office. Next it was Britt, who handles Palmer's day-to-day affairs in Orlando. Then Palmer appeared and welcomed us all to his office. I could tell he was still very emotional from the meeting he had just had with the veterans.

He spoke about it as we sat down. Several of the guys were missing limbs from their service to our country and faced major obstacles in their daily lives. Palmer's voice cracked as he talked about it. Soon he shifted the conversation to the purpose of our meeting. He told me he wanted the three women in the room to also hear what I had to say.

I began my presentation by talking about how important it was for the PGA of America to have a positive relationship with Arnold Palmer. In addition, I was convinced that something had happened between 1937 and '46 that prevented Deacon Palmer from receiving his PGA membership. There was no handicap exclusion by the PGA that would have prevented it, but maybe his dad couldn't get the two signatures he needed on his application from Tri-State PGA members. Who knows?

I explained that the Deacon Palmer Award would be given annually to a PGA member who had overcome a serious personal obstacle in their career to serve the game and his or her community. It would be a way to recognize a PGA member who, like Deacon, was more dedicated to service than recognition. The award would embody all of the positive qualities of Deacon Palmer.

Arnold looked at me with tears rolling down his cheeks and said, "Pap would be proud."

Saunders, Britt and Hulcher agreed. The Deacon Palmer Award was born around 10:20 a.m. April 30, 2014, at Bay Hill, where Deacon had, ironically, passed away in 1971.

In the months that followed, the details of the award were ironed out. It was decided that a bust of Deacon would symbolize the physical award. The Deacon Palmer Awards would bestow special recognition upon a PGA Professional who personally displays outstanding integrity, character and leadership in the effort to overcome a major obstacle in his or her life. And it was decided that the first recipient of the award would be Deacon Palmer.

On November 22, 2014, Arnold Palmer and his family came to the PGA Annual Meeting in Indianapolis to accept the Deacon Palmer Award for his father. That meeting was supposed to be my final one as president, but my impeachment wiped that out. It should have been a celebration of my two years as president, including tributes and a dinner in my honor that would be attended by nearly 1,000 people. Missing that event was painful, but not being there to personally present Arnold Palmer with his dad's award was the worst consequence of my termination by the PGA. Nothing hurt more me than that.

The week after the annual meeting, I received the following letter dated November 24, 2014:

*I wanted to personally and sincerely thank you for your involvement in the creation of the Deacon Palmer Award. The presentation on Saturday was very emotional for me and I'll never forget that it was because of you Pap was recognized in such a prestigious way. If he was still with us, he wouldn't have approved of all of the fuss, but it was a very nice tribute to him.*

*I can't tell you how disappointed it was for me to watch the events around your departure from the PGA of America unfold knowing the efforts on your behalf to create this award. I was immediately cognizant of the fact that you would not be there to present it and what a blow that would be for you. I'm truly sorry that you were not able to see your idea become reality.*

*Again please know what this award means to my family and me. We are all very grateful to you for having the vision and initiative to create this lasting memory of my father. Thank you, Ted.*

*Sincerely— Arnold Palmer*

On November 11, 2015, Brad Clayton of PuzzleDuck Golf in Oxford, North Carolina, became the second recipient of the Deacon Palmer Award. When Clayton accepted his award at the PGA Annual Meeting in Palm Beach Gardens, Florida, he in-

formed the audience that when notified of receiving this prestigious honor by the PGA of America, he "cried like a little girl."

Fortunately for Clayton, the PGA did not revoke his award.

# Chapter Five

# Anchors Away

In midsummer 2012, PGA of America officers were made aware of the fact that the United States Golf Association was seriously considering a ban of the anchored putting stroke. In August, we scheduled a conference call with Mike Davis, executive director of the USGA, and during that call it was apparent the USGA was going to seek a change in the Rules of Golf that would ban the anchored stroke with a long putter.

Just one year earlier, Keegan Bradley had won the 93rd PGA Championship at Atlanta Athletic Club. Webb Simpson had won the U.S. Open at the Olympic Club. Ernie Els had just beaten Adam Scott at the Open Championship at Royal Lytham. All were using anchored strokes with long putters.

It seemed apparent that the angst felt by the USGA and the Royal and Ancient over this issue was heightened when players such as Simpson and Els won championships with anchored putters. When Bradley won the PGA in 2011, nobody made much of the fact that he anchored his long putter.

I had immediate concerns about how this might affect the game for recreational players. Golf professionals and teaching pros around the country have seen many players, mostly older golfers, go to an anchored stroke with a long putter because they suffered from putting yips. The yips occur when a golfer's nerves affect their ability to control muscle movement. This causes them to miss short putts. Anchoring the butt end of the putter against the body offers stability that can eliminate muscle trembling which causes the yips.

In addition, the anchored putting stroke had been around for 600 years in some form or another, so why change it now? There wasn't much public discussion about a proposed rules change in August and September. Mike Davis was scheduled to attend the PGA TOUR Policy Board meeting at Sea Island on October 15, 2012, and he would be making a presentation on the proposed anchoring ban. This would also be my first PGA TOUR Policy Board meeting.

In the beginning, the USGA did not like the way the anchored putting stroke looked and it took the opinion that the game was never intended to be played employing any anchoring method for any stroke. As I listened to Davis' presentation it was obvious the decision had been already made by the USGA. It didn't look to me like Mike was there for feedback. He was there simply for support.

I remember having a discussion early the next morning at the airport with John Cook, a Champions Tour Policy Board member. Cook talked about the tough spot the Champions Tour Board was going to be in because of the number of players who anchored on that Tour—most notably Bernhard Langer and Fred Couples. Cook said a decision banning the anchored stroke could have a negative impact on the quality of the Champions Tour product and that it could cause fallout from fans and sponsors. It could hurt the Champions Tour.

After hearing the USGA's reasons to proceed with the anchoring ban, the PGA officers decided that we should ask Davis to make a similar presentation to our PGA board at the upcoming Annual Meeting on November 8 in Baltimore.

In the meantime, I called PGA President Allen Wronowski and suggested the PGA conduct a survey of our membership on the anchoring ban. "Why would we do that?" Allen asked.

"It will help our board know where the membership stands on the issue," I said.

"What if our members feel differently than we do? No, we aren't doing that," Wronowski said.

"Well, wouldn't that be a novel idea if we actually listened to what our members said and then did it?" I responded. I found Allen's response to be mind-boggling, so the idea of a PGA survey on anchoring went down the drain—at least temporarily.

When Mike made his presentation to the PGA board, the reaction was similar to that of the PGA TOUR Policy Board's. The meeting was probably less confrontational, but the objections were the same. Our board didn't agree with the USGA. Dottie Pepper, an Independent PGA Director, was the most vocal opponent of the proposed ban. Never short on opinions or courage, Pepper took on Davis.

The PGA of America's opposition on anchoring stemmed from how it would adversely affect the enjoyment of the game by recreational players. We had just received a consumer study from the Boston Consulting Group in 2011 indicating the game needed to be more fun and inviting. A ban on the anchored putting stroke conflicted with where we wanted to take our grow-the-game efforts.

My election as PGA president came two days later on November 10. It was apparent that the PGA board opposed the ban on anchoring. I really wanted to conduct a membership survey and instructed our new CEO, Pete Bevacqua, to make it happen on PGAlinks.com. This survey would be distributed to our entire membership. We pushed out the survey during Thanksgiving week. Ironically, while the survey was live, we found out the USGA and R&A had scheduled a joint announcement for the following week, so the timing was good.

The survey was simple:

With regards to anchoring a golf club:

- Yes, I would favor a ban on anchoring a golf club
- No, I would not favor a ban on anchoring a golf club

A total of 25,638 surveys were emailed to PGA members and apprentices. Of the 4,228 responses received, 63 percent did not favor the USGA's proposed ban on anchoring. I felt this was a great response given it was Thanksgiving week and the PGA typically got about 1–3 percent participation from its surveys. In this case the PGA got a 16 percent response rate. We passed the information on to the board. Bevacqua and I began working on a letter to the USGA expressing the official position of the PGA of America.

When Pete sent me the final draft, the letter called for his signature and mine. In my opinion that was a mistake because Bevacqua had worked for the USGA for 11 years. He had been passed over as David Fay's replacement as USGA executive director, and Mike Davis was given the job. Shortly thereafter, Pete left the USGA. It was my concern that if he appeared to be in the middle of the anchoring fight, some people—particularly at the USGA—would say the PGA's plea was sour grapes on Pete's part. That could detract from the essence of the PGA's heartfelt position, which was related to the enjoyment of the game by the recreational player.

The USGA received our letter opposing the ban on Monday, November 26. Included with the letter were the results of our survey. The USGA's official anchoring announcement was scheduled for the following day on Golf Channel. During the announcement the USGA said it was opening a 90-day comment period on the proposed anchoring ban.

The USGA totally ignored the PGA's letter. The battle lines had been drawn. This was the first time in the history of golf that two major bodies such as the USGA and the PGA of America had publicly disagreed on something of this magnitude.

Later in the week, Bevacqua called Davis. Pete informed me that Mike said the USGA was really bent out of shape because he believed that Joe Steranka, former PGA CEO, and my predecessor Wronowski had indicated that the PGA would support the USGA position on banning the anchored stroke.

This news was both shocking and disconcerting. My initial reaction was that the USGA should not have assumed any position from the PGA given the fact that Steranka was no longer our CEO and Wronowski was not the president. But, if the USGA had been informed by Wronowski and Steranka of such a stance without first speaking to our Board of Directors, then the PGA had a huge problem of its own. Bevacqua and I agreed I needed to have a conversation with Glen Nager to investigate Davis' story.

Nager is a highly intelligent guy who had appeared in front of the U.S. Supreme Court on 13 occasions. My first impression of Nager was that he was very self-assured and slightly arrogant. Nothing would happen during the phone call that would change my mind. We had a brief and terse conversation. Glen talked about his disappointment in the PGA's stance. He criticized our survey, saying it had no credibility. I tried to explain that in my role as president I had a responsibility to get input from my constituents. He implied that we were using the survey to portray an inaccurate perspective on how PGA members actually felt. Nager felt that way because he said the 4,000 PGA members who responded to the survey didn't represent the membership as a whole.

Why have a 90-day comment period if you don't want comments? I asked Glen.

Then Nager dropped the same bomb on me that Davis had the night before on Pete. Glen was really disappointed because he contended that Steranka and Wronowski had assured the USGA the PGA would support the anchoring ban. Nager, like Davis, felt the PGA had backtracked and betrayed the USGA.

The following day I reached out to Wronowski to get his side of the story. Allen had been in Nager's presence on several occasions during the past year. They played golf together to

promote Tee It Forward in summer 2012. There were other occasions when their paths would have crossed. When I told Allen
what Nager had said, he denied ever making any insinuation to
Glen that the PGA would support anchoring. I told Allen that
Davis had said the same thing to Bevacqua. But, Wronowski was
adamant that it never happened.

It was a bizarre set of circumstances. There is no doubt this
had led to much of the initial conflict between the PGA and the
USGA. I certainly had no knowledge of any conversations between the USGA and PGA prior to hearing Mike and Glen's story.

PGA TOUR Commissioner Tim Finchem and I began having frequent conversations about the anchoring ban in late November 2012. It was apparent that the Commissioner shared the
same opinion I had. He was in a more ticklish position because
his players were divided on the anchoring issue. Obviously, some
player's careers would be affected if the ban was instituted. Ini-
tially Tiger Woods, Jack Nicklaus, Arnold Palmer and Tom Watson all supported the USGA, though later Watson changed his
mind and would oppose the ban.

More PGA TOUR players started speaking out against the
anchoring ban as the 90-day comment period unfolded. Keegan
Bradley was, naturally, very vocal and praised the PGA of America for its stance. Others did, too. Steve Stricker and I had several
conversations on the subject, and he opposed the ban despite using a conventional putting method himself. Stricker was one of
the best putters on the PGA TOUR. He opposed the ban because
of its impact on golf at the recreational level.

Even though Finchem had strong opinions against the proposed ban, he stayed in the background publicly during the comment period. It was decided that the PGA TOUR would discuss
anchoring at a required players meeting on the evening of January 22, 2013, at Torrey Pines Golf Course in San Diego during
the Farmers Insurance Open. This was also the week of the PGA

Show in Orlando, but it was imperative that I attend and Pete went with me.

The meeting grew contentious early. Many PGA TOUR players departed that evening saying, "Why do we need the USGA? Let's create our own set of rules to play by."

"It's kind of an interesting thing, and it's a difficult thing," Finchem said the next day. "If the governing bodies had said in 1965, like after Sam Snead came out and putted croquet style, and a week later they changed the rule or whatever it was—if they had said 'You know, this isn't consistent with historically the way you swing a club, so we're not going to allow it.' Nobody would have been affected except for maybe two players. But 40 years later—and the amount of play there is with that method, amateur and professional—it does affect a lot of people. So it's a very difficult kind of issue, and it stirs a lot of strong feelings. So, consequently, it's a difficult situation."

When I returned to the PGA Show, we had a panel discussion on the state of the game. Finchem joined Dottie Pepper, TaylorMade CEO Mark King, Golf Channel President Mike Mc-Carley, former USGA Executive Director David Fay and me in the discussion. Damon Hack from Golf Channel moderated. We had invited Mike Davis with the intent of letting him explain the USGA position on anchoring, but he elected to not attend the PGA Show.

The 90-day comment period had started November 27, 2011, and it would end in late February 2012. I always felt if the PGA had done another survey in January 2013, the opposition to the anchoring ban would have been at least 80 percent from PGA members. A day never went by that I didn't receive an email or letter from a PGA member supporting our position.

The suspense surrounding the PGA TOUR's position came to a close when Finchem announced February 24 that the TOUR would officially oppose Rule 14-1b. This was tremendous validation for the PGA of America. We had been the first to oppose the ban and now, some three months later, the TOUR joined us. It was a landmark decision for the PGA of America and the PGA TOUR to both oppose the United States Golf Association.

"We hold the USGA in highest regard as a key part of the game of golf," Finchem said in a press conference. "We don't attempt to denigrate that position in any way whatsoever. It's just on this issue, we think if they were to move forward they would be making a mistake.

"I think the essential thread that went through the thinking of the players was that in the absence of data or any basis to conclude that there is a competitive advantage to be gained by using anchoring, and given the amount of time that anchoring has been in the game, that there is no overriding reason to go down that road," Finchem added.

Finchem emphasized that he was only responding to the USGA's request for a comment and that it did not represent a donnybrook with the USGA. Immediately, there was ramped-up speculation that the PGA TOUR would formulate its own set of rules governing its competitions. The USGA was now in a position of going through with the ban or backing down because the PGA TOUR opposed it.

Finchem had said in the final weeks of the comment period that while slightly different rules for the PGA TOUR are acceptable, he did not think anchoring would be one of them. And he didn't indicate which direction the TOUR would go if the USGA followed through with the ban.

"I haven't spent much time worrying about that," Finchem said. "That would be speculation, and I haven't really thought about it. I've thought more about some areas of bifurcation, whether it would work or not. But I think the focus here ought to be, if possible, to go down the same road, everybody go down the same road on anchoring, and that's certainly where we are now.

"We just hope they take our view on it," he said. "We'll see. We have to look at it from the standpoint of is it good, bad or indifferent for the game as a whole—professional level, amateur level—and we conclude that it's not a bad thing."

The USGA issued a statement saying, "As we continue the various perspectives on anchoring, it has always been our position that Rule 14-1b aims to clarify and preserve the traditional and essential nature of the golf stroke, which has helped make golf a unique and enjoyable game of skill and challenge."

The USGA said it would decide on the proposed rule later in the spring.

Two days after the PGA TOUR announcement, I flew to Augusta National Golf Club for meetings with The Masters Foundation and the USGA on a proposed junior golf initiative called Drive, Chip and Putt.

On the short flight from Atlanta to Augusta, I was seated behind Nager. As soon as we lifted off I moved up and sat next to him. I became more impressed with Nager during our conversation because he actually showed some compassion to the recreational golfer. It was clear that he understood the ramifications to the amateur game if the ban was instituted.

I pointed out to him that many PGA facilities were already discussing the prospect of instituting a "local rule" which would permit anchoring. He seemed surprised by that, which shocked me. How could the USGA not anticipate local backlash to Rule 14-1b? Nager was quick to point out the intent of "local rules" which were for things dealing with abnormal playing conditions and the physicality of the golf course—not the actual Rules of Golf.

Nager also brought up the idea that a potential compromise in the anchoring debate could be with the addition of a "Condition of Competition" to the Rules of Golf.

These conditions include many matters such as method of entry, eligibility, number of rounds to be played and other details.

It is not appropriate to deal with these matters in the Rules of Golf. The fact that Nager even brought up the idea of anchoring being a Condition of Competition was a very positive sign that the USGA might be considering some compromise.

If this did happen, the PGA of America would have to make a decision and in all likelihood be the only major championship to allow anchoring. The PGA TOUR could do the same and that would mean that only three weeks out of the year—the Masters, U.S. Open and British Open—players would not be allowed to anchor long putters. This would drive golf purists crazy, but it was a possibility with either a Condition of Competition or bifurcation of the rules by the PGA and the PGA TOUR.

I would say that my relationship with Glen Nager took a turn for the better during those two days at Augusta National. The Masters had given us all rooming assignments. Nager and I would stay in the same cabin with Club Chairman Billy Payne and Jimmy Dunne, the Augusta National member who was the liaison for Drive, Chip and Putt.

That evening, Payne insisted on giving us all a sneak preview of Berckmans Place, the new hospitality area that would open at the upcoming Masters. Payne had tremendous pride in the facility, and he gave us a detailed behind-the-scenes tour. As darkness fell we loaded up in vans and headed to the retreat near the 13th hole for dinner.

I was seated in the middle seat of the van, and Nager was behind me. As I departed the vehicle I had my right hand on the back of the seat. When I stepped down my hand came up and hit Nager in the face, knocking his glasses to the ground. It was one of those spontaneous moments when something happens before you know what hit.

Glen reached to the ground and recovered his glasses. He looked up at me with a grin and said, "Wait until the media gets a hold of this. Ted Bishop strikes Glen Nager in the face and knocks his glasses to the ground."

Nager, the high-powered attorney, showed a human side. Everyone in the van got a great laugh.

Early the next morning I got dressed and took a cup of coffee to the living area in our cabin. Soon Glen joined me. The television was tuned into Golf Channel's Morning Drive. The only awkward moment of the two days came when Nager and I watched a report dealing with the likelihood that golf could be headed for bifurcation because of the PGA TOUR's stance on anchoring. Nager and I watched what was being said, but neither of us commented.

He and I joined Dunne and Tony Sessa, the co-head pro for golf at Augusta National, while Payne rode along in a golf cart because his back was bothering him. Our foursome won the team competition, and it was a great day on the greatest course in the world. I clearly remember thinking how valuable the time that I spent with Nager was. Each of us had a better understanding for the other. It was the beginning of an unlikely friendship.

Talk of bifurcation and two sets of rules in American golf was starting to heat up. In mid-March I was headed to the PGA TOUR Policy Board meeting. Before that I had informed Finchem of the straw poll at our PGA Spring Leadership Conference, where our PGA Section and national leadership indicated it would support another set of rules developed by the PGA TOUR. Tim was still noncommittal on where the TOUR might wind up because he was waiting for direction from his players.

During that Policy Board meeting I became even more impressed with the sincerity of the PGA TOUR and its players on the real essence of the anchoring argument. While the players were concerned with their own issues, they were actually just as engaged on how an anchoring ban might affect the amateur game.

It was obvious to me that Finchem was listening. He was still not advocating that the TOUR institute another set of rules. In my private discussions with Tim I knew that in addition to opposing the ban, Finchem also felt that bifurcation might be good for golf. Finchem had drawn a correlation between the difference in college and professional football rules. He said it was still football. I felt that if the players eventually mandated that another set of rules were needed, Finchem would support it.

I was at the Masters as a member of the Rules Committee. The first official function of the Rules Committee would take place Wednesday of that week with an early-morning meeting in the Magnolia Suite. There are over a hundred members of the Masters Rules Committee. They come from all over the world.

Immediately after the Rules Committee session, I was scheduled to have a meeting with Finchem, Bevacqua, Davis and Nager in a private room at the Magnolia Suite. Only a handful of rules officials were still in the Magnolia Suite as I waited for that meeting to start.

I spotted Peter Dawson, chief executive of the R&A, standing across the room, and I approached him. I extended my hand and said, "Peter, I hope in no way you take our differences on anchoring in a personal way."

Dawson looked me right in the eye, refused to shake my hand and said, "I most certainly do take it personally. You and others in this country have grandstanded during the past few months and, in my opinion, it has set golf back."

I was completely taken back by Dawson's hostility. We had never had much interaction with each other, but I genuinely admired and respected Peter.

"Peter, I am sorry you feel that way. In this country we feel that an anchoring ban is detrimental to the growth and enjoyment of the game," I said. "The PGA of America feels like it has been cast in the role of representing the recreational amateurs in this country."

Dawson snapped back and pointed his finger at me, "That is not your job. It's the job of the USGA over here and the R&A around the world."

I said, "Well, I don't agree with that, and I guess we have nothing else to talk about."

This was my most contentious encounter up to that point on the anchoring issue. Moments later, I met Finchem in the hallway outside our meeting room and told him about my exchange with Dawson. Tim chuckled, patted me on the back and told me not to worry about it. Our meeting with the USGA simply confirmed that an announcement on anchoring was forthcoming.

Later that evening I attended the Chairman's Reception at Augusta National hosted by Billy Payne. I was still bothered by my confrontation with Dawson. I spotted Peter entering the reception, which took place under the big live oak tree on the lawn behind the Augusta National clubhouse. He headed toward me, and my heart started pounding.

As Dawson approached me, he smiled, extended his hand and softly said, "Ted, I want to apologize for this morning. I guess the frustration of this whole ordeal had been building up over the past few months, but that doesn't excuse the tone in which I addressed you."

I really appreciated that and told Peter so. We had daily encounters throughout the week with our rules duties, and all was well. My confrontation with Dawson was a vivid example of the tension that existed between the people who were really deeply entrenched in the anchoring controversy.

Bevacqua attended numerous meetings during Masters week. He told me it appeared to many that Dawson and the R&A were actually driving the anchoring ban. Bevacqua still had his sources inside the USGA, and he was hearing that Mike Davis was growing increasingly frustrated over the fervor in America and starting to question the USGA's position. The inside word was that the USGA had supported the R&A on anchoring hoping to improve its own relationship with the R&A.

During The Players Championship in May, the USGA told us that they were going to proceed with Rule 14-1b. There would be no changes to the rule and no compromises such as creating an additional Condition of Competition, as Nager and I had discussed in February.

A curious thing happened during the meeting when a terse exchange broke out between Davis and Nager. "Can I get a word in?" Davis snapped at Nager. It was my first indication there might be some problems inside the USGA. It was an awkward moment.

The official USGA anchoring announcement came on Tuesday, May 22, 2012, during the Senior PGA Championship at Bellerive Country Club in St. Louis. Rule 14-1b would proceed. Many of us at the PGA were perplexed by the timing of the USGA announcement as it came during one of our two major championships. The USGA would later maintain that Jack Nicklaus had pleaded with the association not to do it the following week during his Memorial Tournament. Jack obviously had more clout with the USGA than the PGA of America did. I felt there was a lack of respect shown to PGA by the USGA with the timing of the announcement.

Finchem and I continued to talk over the next few weeks with the main issue being whether or not the TOUR would devise a new set of rules and move away from the USGA. He still held steadfast in the belief that there was no reason why Rule 14-1b could not be "grandfathered" in over the next 10–15 years for amateurs. This would be similar to how the change in the rule on grooves for irons was handled by the USGA. Bifurcation was still a possibility, but it was obvious to me that Finchem viewed it as a last resort.

The commissioner and I stated our case on "grandfathering" to Davis and Nager on the Sunday morning of the final round of the U.S. Open at Merion Golf Club. Nager did most of the talking that morning. It didn't appear that the USGA was interested in any sort of a compromise.

When the PGA TOUR Policy Board met, it was evident that the players were still fired up on the issue. They clearly looked to Finchem for direction. Tim did not think it was in the best interest of the game for the TOUR to create a second set of rules. The players were insistent that either the USGA "grandfather" the rule for amateurs, or they would pursue their own rules of the game.

I left the meeting and headed to Washington, D.C., to throw out the first pitch at the Nationals-Brewers baseball game that night. My emotions were twofold. The ban on anchoring was becoming a reality. But, if we could succeed with the "grandfather" concept, then it was still a victory of sorts for the recreational player.

The relationship between the USGA and the PGA of America took another turn for the worse early on Wednesday night of PGA Championship in early August. Minutes before the PGA would honor Lee Trevino as its Distinguished Service Award Winner and on the eve of the start of the PGA Championship at Oak Hill Country Club, the USGA announced its multi-million-dollar television contract with FOX. Once again, the USGA was attempting to upstage one of our championships.

As soon as I walked into the reception honoring Trevino in downtown Rochester, New York, Bevacqua informed me of the USGA/FOX announcement. He had a forlorn look and was shocked at the timing. I smiled and said, "Cheer up. This is the best thing that could happen to the PGA of America. NBC now needs the Ryder Cup more than ever."

Nager was an invited guest at that Distinguished Service Award ceremony that evening. He sat in the back of the room and left as soon as the presentation was over. The media backlash to the timing of the FOX announcement was overwhelmingly sympathetic to the PGA of America. We didn't have to bash the USGA because everybody else was doing it. But I could not resist in sharing my disappointment with Glen the following day. I sent him a text message concerning the lack of respect the USGA had once again shown the PGA by virtue of the timing of this announcement.

The USGA would claim FOX was a publicly traded company and the announcement had to be made immediately.

As it turned out, I was spot-on about NBC. The PGA and NBC would finalize a 15 year extension of the Ryder Cup TV rights on September 17, 2013, slightly more than a month after the USGA dumped NBC. It turned out to be a landmark deal for the PGA of America. On top of that, the PGA and NBC waited until October 10 to announce the extension, demonstrating that confidentiality can be maintained when both parties see to it. But make no mistake: The PGA of America would never have gotten the deal that it did without the USGA/FOX deal.

Finchem had asked me to compose a document that we would jointly present to the USGA. We would ask that Rule 14-1b be "grandfathered" for amateur play until 2025. It was a five-page document. We gave it to the USGA in early September. Tim and I felt the timing of our presentation was important, and we hoped we could see the USGA Executive Committee sometime in late September or early October. Several weeks went by until we were finally told by the USGA that it would hear the presentation in six months at its 2014 Annual Meeting. That was extremely disappointing, and it sent a clear message that the USGA had no interest in the "grandfather" clause.

Tim and I eventually headed to Pinehurst Resort on February 8, 2014, to do nothing more than go through the motions of giving the "Grandfathering" presentation on anchoring. At that point it was all anticlimactic. Our presentation that morning had been nothing more than a futile formality. The anchoring controversy was officially dead that wintry Saturday at Pinehurst—438 days after it officially started with the USGA's announcement of the 90-day comment period.

The anchoring ban went into effect on January 1, 2016. It will have an impact on the enjoyment of the game for many players—particularly older men who suffer from the yips or who have tremors. Many have talked about quitting the game or refusing to abide by the new rule.

On the PGA TOUR players have been forced to find alternative methods of putting. How the anchoring ban affects the careers of players such as Bradley, Els, Scott, Couples and Bernhard Langer remains to be seen. Many PGA club professionals feel the new rule is too vague when it comes to what actually constitutes an anchored stroke. Our ability to police and enforce Rule 14-1b in club events could be arduous.

The only positive thing that came out of the anchoring controversy for me was the budding relationship that I formed with Tim Finchem. We developed a great friendship as we worked closely through all of the anchoring details. That resulted in a partnership between the PGA TOUR and the PGA of America that had not existed since the two split in 1968. We eventually collaborated together on major championship sites, purse increases, playing spots for club professionals and other issues that benefitted the members of both our associations.

A little-known fact is that Tim and I knew we needed to take the lead in patching the relationships that had been damaged during the anchoring controversy. The two of us worked together to organize a series of quarterly meetings between the PGA TOUR, PGA of America, USGA, Masters and LPGA. The intent of these meetings was to create a cooperative collaboration among the top golf entities in the United States.

And today, golf is in a better place because of our efforts.

# Chapter Six

# Power Brokers

Ask any PGA member to prioritize his or her member benefits, and at the top of list will be the access that they have to the Masters Tournament. For decades, Augusta National Golf Club has allowed PGA members to simply show their membership cards at a special gate and they will be a welcome guest during Masters week. You never know if that could change, but I'm confident as long as Billy Payne is Chairman of the Masters, PGA members are in good hands.

Billy Payne became chairman of Augusta National Golf Club in 2006. Before that he had the idea of Atlanta hosting the Olympic Games. He was able to gain the support of the local community and convinced the International Olympic Committee to award Atlanta the 1996 Summer Olympics. After winning the bid, Payne remained as the head of the Atlanta Committee for the Olympic Games, serving as the chief administrator to organize the Olympics.

Since he became chairman, Augusta National has undergone a multitude of transformative changes. In 2008, he implemented a new TV contract with ESPN that allowed for unprecedented coverage of the par-3 tournament. Also in that same year, a junior patrons program was instituted, allowing one Masters patron to bring a junior at no cost.

Payne drew a lot of attention in 2010 when he criticized Tiger Woods during the week of the Masters for not serving as a role model. In 2011, Payne and his fellow members sanctioned a video game featuring the Masters name, logo and golf course. The proceeds from the sale of the game benefit a nonprofit foundation that promotes junior golf.

In 2012, Payne announced that former U.S. Secretary of State Condoleezza Rice and business executive Darla Moore would become the first female members of Augusta National after 75 years of all-male membership.

During Payne's tenure, Augusta National has continually expanded its infrastructure. This includes a new practice facility for Masters contestants. In addition, many permanent hospitality areas have been constructed such as Berckmans Place, a luxury VIP area that features four restaurants as well as scaled replicas of the No. 5 and No. 14 greens where patrons can test their putting skills on Masters-like surfaces. Next up for Payne and Augusta National will probably be a new state-of-the-art media center.

In 2013, Payne was the driving force behind the formation of Drive, Chip and Putt, which is a competition for boys and girls age 7–15. The DCP competition involves the Masters Foundation, the USGA and the PGA of America. The finals are held at Augusta National on the Sunday prior to the start of the Masters and the contestants display their driving and chipping skills on the contestants' practice area. The putting contest actually takes place on the famous 18th green at Augusta. Payne even made sure that a new group of patrons would be able to gain access to the course in order to watch the Drive, Chip and Putt competition on Sunday.

I started getting nervous about the access that PGA members had to the Masters in 2012 when I was Vice President. There were some rumors that PGA member access was being discussed at Augusta National. For decades Augusta National Golf Club had extended unlimited access privileges to members of the PGA of America. It was a privilege we were very grateful to have. The PGA had a good relationship with the Masters, and this was especially so given the critical importance of PGA members in the execution of the newly formed Drive, Chip and Putt competition in 2013.

If The Masters ever decided to limit PGA member attendance this could have created a firestorm within the ranks of the PGA membership. And in reality, it was up to Augusta National whether to extend this privilege. The PGA of America and its members have absolutely no recourse if that is the direction things ever go. The scary thing was that these reduced access rumors were definitely out there.

In 2013 while I worked the 14th hole at the Masters I was approached by a couple of former PGA board members, Michael Kernicki and Jim Manthis, and they asked if this would be the last year they would be allowed to attend the tournament? This was just one of many inquiries I had gotten from concerned PGA members.

I also received a phone call from Mike David, Executive Director of the Indiana PGA. Mike was the chairman of the PGA Executive Director's Committee. "Is there any truth to this thing about the Masters taking away PGA member access? I have been contacted by several executive directors who are saying that access is going to be severely limited for PGA members."

I told Mike that I was hearing a lot of the same type of rumors and I assured him that I was on top of the situation. Some were saying that the PGA's position on anchoring might be a factor. But, I knew from my time with Payne in February of 2013 that he was trying to maintain a neutral position on anchoring and that Augusta National would stay completely out of that fray. Another legitimate issue could be PGA member behavior at the Masters. It's a well known fact that people who violate the sanctity of their Masters credentials are banned for life and there are PGA members who are on the banned list. I was also aware of situations where PGA members showed up at the Masters expecting to get their spouse into the tournament. When they were informed by gate officials that it was "member only" access, some PGA members reacted with rude behavior and this didn't sit well with the people at the Masters.

For several weeks I stewed over the possibilities of this access issue. I knew the devastating effect it could have on PGA members. Masters access is such an important perk to PGA members and most incorrectly assumed it was a "right of membership." Quite frankly, I did not want to be the PGA president who had to deliver news that would create a firestorm within the ranks of PGA membership. There were already lots of rumors floating around PGA member circles about the possibility that we might lose some Masters access.

Eventually, I felt it was imperative that I leverage my friendship and relationship with Billy Payne and speak to him personally about this issue. For my part, I put a lot of preparation into the phone call with Payne. I had gotten to know Payne fairly well through Drive, Chip and Putt. He seemed to be a reasonable man and I wanted to have the opportunity to thank him for the access the PGA had at The Masters and at the same time let him know I had some concerns.

When we spoke, I pointed out to Billy that when the Masters started as the Augusta National Invitational in 1934, it relied heavily on the participation of PGA club professionals to bolster its field. The first two Senior PGA Championships were also played at Augusta National in 1937 and '38. Over the years, members of the PGA of America Rules Committee had been critical assets to the Masters when it came to volunteering to officiate the tournament. PGA officers had also served the Masters as volunteer rules officials for decades. The PGA and Augusta National had a unique longstanding relationship, maybe more so than any other allied golf association.

With the advent of Drive, Chip and Putt, Augusta National was now relying heavily on PGA club professionals to run local and regional qualifiers plus serve as volunteers at the finals.

Payne listened intently and told me he was not aware of any discussions at Augusta National that would limit PGA access to the Masters, but he assured me that someone would get back to me with an update. This was indicative of the new leadership style at Augusta National established by the current chairman. My dealings with Billy were always open and he was responsive on any topic. Payne had tremendous ability to see the big picture.

A few days later I received a call from the Masters saying that there was not going to be any changes in PGA member access. In my opinion as long as Billy Payne is Masters' chairman, PGA members will always be able to enjoy a dream shared by all golf fans of attending the world's greatest tournament on golf's most hallowed grounds. That's why Billy Payne will always be one of the most important power brokers in golf to me.

* * *

Paul Miller is the PGA pro at the Newtown Country Club in Connecticut. As you recall, Newtown was the site of the tragic shootings at Sandy Hook Elementary in December 2012 that killed 20 boys and girls ages 6 and 7, as well as six adults. Miller had the idea to host a day of golf for the 70-some Sandy Hook first responders.

"The first responders didn't receive much attention," Miller told me. "They have to live with what they've seen. We wanted to give them a day when they could hopefully escape that."

Michael Breed, PGA teaching instructor and host of Golf Channel's "The Golf Fix," joined me in spending the entire day hitting shots on the eighth hole, a par-3 147-yard hole. Breed and I had a chance to talk with all of the first responders. Michael Kehoe was the Newtown police chief when the Sandy Hook shooting took place, and he summed up the gravity of the situation: "We have people on the police force who were the first to arrive at the scene. Unfortunately, many have not been able to come back to work."

Newtown Country Club gave up its course for the day. Miller secured a sponsor who provided a free lobster dinner for all who played in the outing. With the help of Newtown native Joe LaCava, who caddies for Tiger Woods, Miller made sure no first responder left empty-handed when he conducted a raffle of memorabilia that went well into the night. I left Newtown that night feeling extremely proud to be a PGA member, thanks to Paul Miller.

\* \* \*

Before 2013, there were edicts that were passed down from one generation of PGA officers to another. One such example was certainly the perception that the PGA TOUR was a threat and major competitor to the PGA of America. No doubt there was tension between the two golf organizations since the historic split in 1968, when a group of players formed their own tour and broke away from the PGA of America.

More than forty years after that split, the perception of the PGA leadership was that the TOUR had two major objectives. The first was to have The Players Championship surpass the PGA Championship as golf's fourth major. Secondly, the TOUR was striving to elevate The Presidents Cup ahead of the Ryder Cup in international team competition. The PGA was traditionally very wary of the TOUR and jealously guarded its two biggest financial assets.

I attended my first PGA TOUR Policy Board meeting in late October 2012 at Sea Island, Georgia. It was my "shadow" meeting in which I received a quick orientation from top PGA TOUR officials, who brought me up to speed on their operations. As PGA president, I would be one of nine individuals to sit on the TOUR's Policy Board. After my orientation, I was summoned to a private meeting with Commissioner Tim Finchem. We could be described as no more than casual acquaintances.

"We have an opportunity to change a lot of things. The PGA of America is embarking on a new era of leadership," Finchem said, referencing the fact that Steranka was done as our CEO and we were in the process of hiring his replacement. "The PGA and the TOUR need to work together to make the game stronger. We can accomplish a lot if we do that."

It was clear Tim had an agenda, but it turned out to be much different than what I expected.

"You guys (PGA of America) need to understand that there are only four major championships, and you have one of them in the PGA Championship. That will never change. Forget your egos and get over the fear that The Players is a threat to the PGA because it's not," Finchem said.

"That being said, the tag line that you have given the PGA Championship—'Glory's Last Shot'—insinuates that there is no meaningful golf played after the PGA. It's a slap to the FedExCup playoffs, and I would like for the PGA to consider dropping 'Glory's Last Shot' during its PGA Championship telecast on CBS.

"And The Presidents Cup will never be the Ryder Cup. The Ryder Cup is the biggest team competition in golf. It always been, and it always will be. The TOUR wants the Ryder Cup to be as successful as it can be because our players are part of it. I do have some thoughts from a player's perspective on a few things that can enhance the Ryder Cup, and I would love to share them with you sometime," offered Finchem.

Wait a minute. Was this the same Tim Finchem painted as a potential adversary to the PGA of America? When I later shared my first meaningful Finchem conversation with some PGA past presidents, they said Tim was just setting the table for some big ask. Be cautious, they said—he is going to use you for a greater purpose.

I never felt that way. Tim was sincere in his words. But I also saw opportunities for the PGA of America. So, in that first meeting, I asked Tim to give some thought to the 2014 PGA TOUR schedule, with the possibility of creating a week off between The TOUR Championship and the Ryder Cup. I knew Tom Watson would ask for that in a few weeks, so I might as well get it on the table. Tim listened and at least didn't say no. This meeting launched the beginning of the most historical give-and-take relationship that has ever existed between the PGA TOUR and the PGA of America.

From my standpoint as PGA president, I viewed Finchem to be the most powerful individual in golf. Tim took what he was given by former Commissioner Deane Beman in 1994 and elevated the TOUR to an unprecedented level with purse increases, sponsorship commitments, property acquisitions and television rights. Quite honestly, in an era in which most in golf have struggled, the PGA TOUR has prospered beyond belief because of Finchem's leadership.

If the PGA could have an ally in Tim Finchem, our position in golf would only be stronger. Plus, PGA TOUR players are members of the PGA of America. I always viewed TOUR players as my constituents and that I had an obligation to serve them just as much as any other PGA member. Over the next 23 months, Finchem and I would continually create opportunities that would benefit the TOUR, the PGA and golf in general.

Tim and I drew closer when the United States Golf Association proposed the ban on anchoring. While the PGA of America immediately opposed the ban, Finchem took a more calculated approach. He waited until the end of the 90-day comment period to let the USGA know that the TOUR would join the PGA in opposing the ban. Tim and I talked constantly during this period of time. The TOUR's opposition of the anchoring ban gave great credibility to the PGA's position.

Tim soon got his wish to see "Glory's Last Shot" disappear, and in return, Tom Watson's team got the week off before the Ryder Cup. In addition, the PGA agreed to award Ryder Cup points for the TOUR's Fall Series. This had never happened before, and it gave great credibility to that part of the TOUR's new wrap-around schedule. (The season began with the fall events and ended the following September with the FedExCup Playoffs). Unfortunately, it was short-lived as the Ryder Cup Task Force eliminated the points in the Fall Series for the 2016 Ryder Cup—except for one World Golf Championships event. More on that later.

In 2013, Tim asked to me to consider allowing the TOUR to regain qualifying spots for Web.com Tour events that were being taken by PGA club professionals. Finchem's contention was that because the Web.com Tour had become the stepping stone to the PGA TOUR, club professionals were taking up important playing opportunities. He came armed with statistics showing poor performances by club pros. "These Web.com qualifiers are precious for our players," said Tim.

I completely understood, but PGA professionals would scream if we lost any playing opportunities. What could the TOUR do in return to replace those Web.com spots? Finchem responded by giving PGA club professionals even more playing opportunities in Monday PGA TOUR qualifiers. A TOUR event had more sizzle to our club pros than a Web.com qualifier, so this was a win for the PGA.

In 2013, Finchem and I talked about a purse increase for the PGA Championship. The Players Championship had a $10 million purse compared to the four major championships being in the $8.5 million range. We discussed this at the PGA of America and decided to match The Players' purse making the PGA the richest among the majors at $10 million also.

I went back to Tim and said, "We support the rationale behind raising the purse in the PGA Championship. It's good for us to be able to promote the fact that our championship is the richest major in golf. But in a time when many PGA members are struggling this could be perceived as the rich getting richer. What can the PGA TOUR do for our members if we raise the purse?"

In return, the TOUR wound up kicking in additional dollars in perpetuity to all 41 PGA Sections that could be used for tournament purses. This was another fair trade-off between the TOUR and the PGA. In addition, the TOUR implemented numerous growth of the game PSA's into its telecasts. These promoted PGA member branded programs such as Get Golf Ready. These were things that impacted virtually every PGA pro who played in their section events or who was actively promoting golf at their facility. It was also another example where members from both of our organizations benefitted.

When we announced our joint initiatives at a press conference at Sea Island on November 6, Finchem was asked how he felt about The Players Championship no longer being able to lay claim to golf's richest purse, "Well, we might have to be $10 million and $1," he quipped.

In 2014, the PGA of America was searching for a West Coast site for a PGA Championship. We had exhausted all resources when I approached Tim about the possibility of playing the 2020 PGA at TPC Harding Park in San Francisco. It meant the TOUR would have to modify its agreement with the city of San Francisco, given that The Presidents Cup was already set for 2020 at Harding Park. Finchem made the deal happen. The TOUR extended its agreement with the City of San Francisco and rescheduled the President's Cup at Harding Park to 2025.

Finchem started inviting me to attend the TOUR's mandatory player meetings. Each time, he would introduce me to the players and expound on what our two organizations were doing together. This allowed me to be more visible and accessible to the players. It opened lines of communication between a PGA president and TOUR players like never before. Tim used those venues to share valuable information with TOUR players that helped them better understand the role of the PGA of America and the Ryder Cup to members of the PGA TOUR.

When I was honored at a dinner in summer 2015 at The Mulligan Open at The Legends, Finchem joined Tom Watson and Steve Stricker. Tim summed up our relationship very well that night.

"Ted and I just clicked right off the bat. We proved that our two organizations could accomplish a lot when we worked together. It really was historic in that regard." Finchem said.

During my 23 months as PGA president, Tim became my best ally and, in many ways, even my best friend. I've often been asked what my greatest accomplishment was during my presidency. My answer has always been the improved relationship that was formed between the TOUR and the PGA. The reason was simple. It was a true collaboration that will benefit the members of both organizations for decades. More importantly, we impacted the game of golf like never before.

\* \* \*

In October 2013 I was at the PGA Grand Slam of Golf when Adam Scott and his dad, Phil, approached me about some things the PGA was doing to promote junior golf in America. The impressive thing about this meeting was that Adam recognized the obligation that he had to help grow the game in Australia given his stature as a major champion.

Phil Scott is a club professional in Australia. Adam introduced me to his dad and asked if I could spend some time with Phil and share how PGA Junior League and Get Golf Ready worked. What impressed me most was that Adam had taken the time to understand the intricacies of PGA Junior league and Get Golf Ready.

Phil Scott and I remained in communication and had a lengthy meeting at the 2014 Masters. I hope the Scotts have been successful in their efforts in Australia. This certainly gave me a new appreciation for what a truly great champion Adam Scott is.

\* \* \*

It's impossible to write a chapter about golf's power brokers and not include Donald Trump. Without question he has been the world's most successful golf course developer in the past decade. His lineup of courses has hosted championship events for the USGA, PGA TOUR, LPGA and PGA of America. Hopefully he will have the same opportunity with the Royal & Ancient as well as the European Tour.

Tom Watson might have summed up Trump's impact on the golf industry when he told Donald: "The best thing that ever happened to Turnberry was you buying it."

Cindy and I had the privilege to stay at Trump International Golf Links, Scotland, during the 2014 Scottish Open, which was being played at nearby Royal Aberdeen. Trump International in Scotland features a stunning 18-hole golf course built along the North Sea. The course is situated among some of the oldest and largest sand dunes in Scotland. The Hawtree design looks like it has been there for hundreds of years.

Also located on the grounds is the MacLeod House & Lodge, offering a small and exclusive lodging and dining component. Trump has one of his helicopters parked on-site, and he offers guests complimentary rides. The pilots hang out at MacLeod House and are there when the guests beckon. We enjoyed a spectacular ride down the coast to Cruden Bay.

We actually stayed in the carriage house with Rory McIlroy and his contingent. The carriage house is located a couple hundred yards away from the MacLeod House. The Bishops were given the Trump Suite, and when we checked in there was a handwritten note on our bed from Donald.

Ted-

*I just left town because I couldn't get a room in my own place. You have it!*

*I hope you both have a great stay at what some are saying is "the greatest golf course ever built" —Play the course often!*

*Have Fun—*

*Donald Trump*

Our week at Trump International Golf Links, Scotland, was incredible. We were joined on property by Phil Mickelson, Rickie Fowler, Jimmy Walker, Justin Rose, Ernie Els, Padraig Harrington and Jose Maria Olazabal. They were all staying in the MacLeod House. On several nights we all wound up having dinner together in the quaint dining room.

Cindy and I played Trump's course Tuesday afternoon. While I have played many but not all of Scotland's great courses, I did feel Trump International Golf Links, Scotland, was one of the best I have ever played anywhere in the world. When Cindy and I finished golf, we had dinner in the small clubhouse. While I was eating I noticed that I had a missed phone call from a New York number. After dinner I discovered the call was from Trump's office.

"Hey, I'm sorry I missed your call. I was actually eating an order of fish and chips in your clubhouse," I explained to Donald.

"Are those not the best fish and chips you have ever had?" queried Trump. "I don't know what we do to them, but many people have said they are the best in the world. What did you think of the golf course?"

I told Trump it was great and it had even exceeded my expectations. I also told him many of the touring pros and their caddies had come back from the Scottish Open and played the course. Jimmy Walker had set a new course record that week. All of the players were raving about it. Trump was delighted. The pride that Donald had for his course in Scotland was so genuine—and rightfully so.

Alex Miceli of *Golfweek* and I played the course a few days later. We enjoyed an early morning two-ball in total solitude. As we approached No. 18, we noticed a waiter and waitress standing near the back of the green. They held a sterling silver tray with a decanter of Trump-branded Scotch. They poured Alex and me a shot of the Scotch after we finished our round at 10:30 a.m. It was another impressive detail orchestrated by Donald Trump.

I have always found Trump to be a generous and kind man. When my kids attended the Ryder Cup at Gleneagles, Donald made sure that Ambry, Ashely and their dates played Turnberry as his guests. Ambry coaches a women's golf team in Queens. Trump National Golf Club Ferry Point is located near the campus. Donald has always welcomed Ambry's team to Ferry Point.

In summer 2015 the PGA of America decided not to play the Grand Slam of Golf at Trump National Golf Club in Los Angeles after Donald made the following remarks about Mexicans: "They're bringing drugs. They're bringing crime. They're rapists. And some, I assume, are good people."

Shortly thereafter, I received a call from Brendan Prunty of *The New York Times*. He expressed dismay that no one at the PGA of America would comment on the Trump situation, and he asked me if I would answer a few questions. Brendan knew I had been the president when the PGA/Trump business relationship was formed.

When Prunty's story came out in *The New York Times*, it was misreported that former PGA of America CEO Joe Steranka and I wanted nothing to do with Trump or his growing grip on the sport. Once Pete Bevacqua took over for Steranka, Prunty said, he pushed the two sides to do more business.

The true story was that Joe never allowed the PGA to have any discussions about doing business with Trump. I told Prunty that I had no feelings one way or the other about Trump before Pete became the CEO. Bevacqua had introduced me to Donald. I was 100 percent in favor of doing the PGA business deals with Trump then—and I am still am now.

After I read Prunty's story I called him and told him he had misrepresented me. He denied it. I insisted he send me the audio of the interview. Later that night he did, and it confirmed my claim. Prunty refused to cooperate with my request for a correction and said, "It's pretty much an insignificant sentence in the middle of the story."

I told Prunty it would not be insignificant to Trump if he saw it. Still, *The New York Times* refused to oblige my request for a correction. It left me no choice but to call Donald's office on July 7.

Not only was he in, but he accepted my phone call. For the first few minutes I listened to Trump rant about what he had read in the newspaper. Donald said he was extremely disappointed because he thought we were friends, and my remarks indicated otherwise.

When I could finally get a word in, I told Donald the purpose of my phone call was to let him know that I had been misrepresented. I wanted to explain what I had really said and meant. I reminded Trump that he, above anyone, should understand the media can screw things up.

Trump finally calmed down, and we had a civil conversation. In *The New York Times* I had accurately been quoted as saying, "I think a lot of people are surprised that it wasn't all or nothing. I don't know what kind of statement the PGA of America makes by saying, 'We're not going to do this for one year, but we're going to go back for all these others.'"

What I meant was that based on the PGA's no-tolerance policy dealing with my "insensitive remarks" about Ian Poulter, I was surprised the PGA didn't stay consistent with how it dealt with me and just wipe Trump completely off the slate of events. However, I went on to emphasize to Trump that I didn't feel his comments warranted any action by the PGA of America.

I could sense Donald's frustration with the PGA. He told me the same thing he had told Prunty in the story. If golf wasn't going to return his loyalty, then he had alternatives, such as making more money by not hosting high-profile events. "I don't need the Grand Slam. I have plenty of better things to do with that money."

The human side of Donald Trump was also exposed in our phone call. He asked me to do two things. He wanted me to summarize our conversation with an email that he could show his wife, Melania. "My wife was devastated when she read the article in the paper because she always really liked you and thought so much of our friendship," he said. Secondly, Trump asked me to write a letter to the editor of *The New York Times* expressing my dismay over its decision not to run a correction. I did both.

I mentioned the round of golf I played with Trump at his course at Bedminster, New Jersey. While we were playing I remarked about how good the hot dogs at the golf course were. I ate one for lunch. When we finished our round, we went to the men's grill room. Donald lamented the fact that he was going to have to leave soon in order to take his wife to a Steven Tyler concert at The Meadowlands. But he insisted on ordering a platter of hot dogs for our group. The kitchen brought a couple dozen hot dogs for the five of us!

"Are those not the best hot dogs you have ever eaten?" Trump said. Actually they were outstanding. The next week I received a box from Trump National Golf Club. It contained a case of Best's Kosher Beef Franks—the hot dog we had enjoyed so much at Trump National. Another case of Donald focusing on the details.

Donald Trump, the golf course developer, was welcomed with open arms when the sport's leading organizations thought he had something to offer them. Now, Donald Trump, the presidential candidate, is receiving a different level of treatment from some of those same people. Trump golf properties hire thousands of people, including many minorities. His golf facilities generate millions of dollars in revenue and taxes. Quality is the cornerstone at every Trump golf course. I would argue golf is far better off with Donald Trump in it.

*    *    *

The PGA of America is divided into 41 territories called Sections. Executive directors lead the day-to-day operations of these Sections. Most PGA pros would tell you that the executive directors are the lifeblood of local golf.

Charlie Robson hung it up in 2016 after 43 years as the executive director of the Metropolitan PGA in the greater New York City area. Robson is a PGA legend, and he has been a mentor to nearly every executive director in America. Robson might be one of the most influential people in the history of the PGA of America.

"Charlie has positively impacted the lives of PGA professionals and apprentices. He developed one of the country's strongest section tournament programs and set the standard for developing relationships with sponsors. Charlie has always been true to the traditions of the game and set consistently high standards for all of us. We are all better because of his presence and caring," said John Kennedy, longtime PGA professional at Westchester Country Club.

"A general consensus of Met PGA members would be that the extraordinary communications skills of Charlie Robson place him in a class by himself. In the late 1960s, he wore a tie to class at Washington-Lee University, and he continues to do this today, even in 97-degree heat. His most important work has been serving as a valued private advisor to many Met PGA members for five decades." said Nelson Long, from Century Country Club in Purchase, New York.

Charlie gave my daughter Ambry her first job in golf. His wisdom and advice helped serve Ambry as a surrogate father when she left Indiana for New York City. She owes her career to Charlie Robson—a power broker and a "pro" in his own right.

\* \* \*

What a privilege it is to live in the same era with Jack Nicklaus. Now that it appears no player will ever top Jack's mark of 18 major championships, the myth and legend of the man will only grow in time. I had the unique opportunity to get to know Jack when he was at a point in his career where he was really focused on giving back to the sport that had given him so much.

Nicklaus agreed to be a spokesman for the PGA of America, and he assisted us in growing the game of golf. One of the platforms Jack created was a concept of playing six- or 12-hole rounds versus the traditional nine- and 18-hole rounds. Nicklaus felt by playing fewer holes, people would be more able to fit golf into their busy schedules.

"Besides saving time, 12 holes is about all I can handle at my age anyway," Jack said. Here was a novel concept. The greatest player of all time advocating a six- or 12-hole round.

The thought of Jack's six-hole concept was something that Ian Baker-Finch and I discussed as a way to change the format at the Grand Slam of Golf. We had this idea of playing three six-hole round robin matches with the four major championship winners during each of the two 18-hole rounds. The players would receive points instead of a score.

"This would be so exciting for the players and the viewers," Baker-Finch said. "It brings risk and reward into the competition and takes the focus off total score."

Baker-Finch and I met with Jack on the idea. Nicklaus loved the concept, and he even agreed to be the honorary host of the Grand Slam. Unfortunately, we could never get the logistics hammered out with the television production. We also had fears that the format would confuse the casual viewer from a scoring standpoint. But here was Jack Nicklaus, one of the most traditional people in golf, being totally on board.

I had the pleasure of joining Jack at some of growth-of-the-game meetings. Certainly I loved operating out of the box, and it was great to see someone like Nicklaus not being afraid to venture out there as well.

One such meeting involved the people from U.S. Kids Golf and Snag Golf. In the case of U.S. Kids Golf, they offer a concept in which a golf course installs blue and gold markers in the fairways to create a shorter set of tees for kids. Snag Golf produces large lightweight plastic golf clubs and tennis-sized balls, making it a great entry point for kids.

Jack loved both ideas. He pledged that Muirfield Village and The Bear's Club, two clubs he owns, would install the U.S. Kids Golf markers. In addition, he started working with Snag Golf to find ways to use their equipment in limited spaces such as public parks in hopes that it would be a way to introduce a new demographic of juniors to the game.

In that meeting I offered the thought to Jack that the U.S. Kids Golf program was also a friendly way for beginner women to enjoy the game with their spouse or friends. "The great thing about it is that the guys can actually hit their tee shot and second shots before the woman ever tees off. It eliminates that tension when beginner women are trying to play from the regular ladies tees, and it takes them a bunch of shots before their husband can ever hit his second shot," I said.

"Oh, I don't know about that one," Jack said.

"You have to see it to believe it?" I joked.

As part of Labor Day activities at Muirfield Village, Nicklaus hosted 12-hole tournaments in which the hole was 8 inches in diameter instead of the traditional 4¼ inches. To encourage faster play, participants were required to complete the round in two and a half hours. They were penalized one stroke for every five minutes over the allotted time.

When it came to player development, Jack got it, although he was still more of a traditionalist than I. "I'm not sure I am in favor of this soccer golf that you promote," Jack once told me, regarding my endorsement of FootGolf.

We also disagreed on the anchoring ban. I got a call one day from Jack, and he was insisting that as PGA president I make a pitch to Mike Davis and the USGA that a rollback of the golf ball was needed. I told him I was having a real hard time with that one. "I'm not sure how hitting tee shots a shorter distance is go-ing to help the average golfer," I responded to Nicklaus.

I was also heavily involved with Jack during the massive renovation project the PGA of America undertook at Valhalla Golf Club in Louisville, Kentucky, before the 2014 PGA Cham-pionship. The PGA owned the course, and Jack had been the de-signer when the course opened in 1986. We wanted to rebuild all of the greens, expand the practice area, redo some bunkering, re-grass the roughs and install a new irrigation system. I was the liaison for the PGA of America on the project because my degree from Purdue was in agronomy, and I had built 81 holes of golf in the 1990s.

The Valhalla project turned out great, and Jack spent quite a bit of his own time making sure that happened. The par-3 eighth green at Valhalla had been rebuilt multiple times and had been a continual source of aggravation for the PGA and Valhalla su-perintendents. The most recent problem with the green was that its severe contours really limited where Kerry Haigh, PGA Chief Championship Officer, could place pins during a championship week. We needed at least 10 pin locations, and the severe undu-lations that the Nicklaus group created on No. 8 never gave us anything close to that.

Haigh and I were determined to flatten out the green. We had some small battles with Jack's group during construction. On the day Jack came to Valhalla for the final walk-through, Kerry and I anxiously awaited his arrival to the eighth green.

Jack walked up on the green and stood. He looked in all di-rections and shook his head. His lips were drawn, and there was a frown on his face. It was obvious he didn't like what he saw. He glared right at me.

"Ted, what do you think of this green?" Jack asked in his terse high-pitched voice.

"Jack, I think it's just perfect. Kerry has a lot of pin place-ments. It's good," I responded.

Nicklaus threw his arms up in the air. He grinned and cracked, "Well, if you like the look of a pancake with one small blueberry in the middle, then you like this. Let's go to No. 9."

The PGA was the customer, and like any good businessman, Jack respected our wishes.

During that day at Valhalla I asked Jack about a letter Byron Nelson had written him while watching the 1986 Masters unfold on Sunday afternoon.

"Jack, Byron Nelson once told me that he started writing you a letter as you began play on the back nine during the 1986 Masters. Byron said that he intended to tell you how great it was that you could still compete at Augusta at your age. As that final nine holes unfolded, he just kept writing a hole-by-hole description of what he saw. That has to be one of your greatest keepsakes," I said.

"I never received that note," Jack said in a dejected voice. "I never got that."

To this day I wonder about the whereabouts of Byron's note to Jack. It was obvious that Nelson was so proud of what he had said to Nicklaus. He would be just as disappointed as Jack to know the note never saw its final destination.

Being in the presence of Jack Nicklaus is the equivalent of being with Babe Ruth. I'm not sure there would be another sports figure that you could throw into the conversation. My involvement with Jack was obviously in a non-playing environment. I can't include him as a power broker without pointing out some things about his playing record that you may have forgotten or not know. The following were pulled from *Golden Twilight* by Dave Shedloski.

"If you count his two U.S. Amateur titles, he has 20 major championship wins. He was runner-up 19 times in the majors and was third on nine occasions. He finished in the top five 54 times and in the top 10 on 73 occasions. The next best total of 46 belongs to Sam Snead. Nicklaus is the only player to win the

U.S. Open in three decades. During the 1970s he did not finish out of the top 10 in the Masters. At the British Open there was a remarkable 15-year stretch beginning in 1966 when he finished no worse than tied for sixth.

Jack won 70 times on the PGA TOUR and 100 events worldwide. In the 100 major championships that he competed in from 1962-86, Nicklaus finished in the top three—46 times or nearly half of his appearances. His most dominant stretch was 1971–77. In 28 majors he never finished out of the top 11 and he won six times."

There will never be another Jack Nicklaus. Today's "big four" consists of Rory McIlroy, Jordan Spieth, Jason Day and Rickie Fowler. Combined, they have won seven major championships. Would you take the over or under of 18 on the number of combined majors these four players will win in their careers? I love all four of these guys, but I would take the under!

The legacy of Jack Nicklaus will be defined in many ways— and they are all positive. The greatest golf champion of all time. A tremendous role model on and off the golf course. A husband, parent and grandparent we could all strive to be more like. A true giver—never a taker.

What an honor and privilege it was for me to spend a few moments with Jack in my time as PGA president.

# Chapter Seven

# Stuck in the Mud at Wales

December 11, 2008, had been an exhausting but exciting day in New York City. Darkness had fallen, and our day was almost finished as I stood in the Manhattan office of NBC Sports President Ken Schanzer and listened to him talk about the Ryder Cup.

"We have been privileged here at NBC Sports to cover the world's greatest sporting events. I've seen it all—The World Series, Super Bowl, Stanley Cup Final, Wimbledon, Kentucky Derby and Olympics, but no sporting event has the drama and the pressure of the Ryder Cup. There is nothing in all of sports like the Ryder Cup," he said.

It was my first official duty as the newly elected Secretary of the PGA of America. I was part of the PGA's official party at the announcement of Corey Pavin as the 2010 Ryder Cup captain for the matches to be played at Celtic Manor in Wales. It had been a whirlwind day in New York. PGA President Jim Remy announced Pavin as the captain during a morning press conference at the now-defunct Tavern on the Green in Central Park. Thanks to the PGA, even the Rockettes from Radio City Music Hall showed up.

We were shuttled all over the city, and it was my job to guard the Ryder Cup, a small gold trophy that represents the fruits of victory in golf's greatest international competition. The PGA of America owns the American stake in the Ryder Cup, which dates to 1927. Ryder Cup Europe owns the other half. After three straight losses, the U.S. had recaptured the trophy in September at Valhalla Golf Club in Louisville, Kentucky, under the guidance of team captain Paul Azinger.

It was a rainy day, and I kept the Ryder Cup under a tan felt cover. Our stops included all of the major media outlets as Pavin did a barrage of national and international interviews.

My first introduction to Corey and his wife, Lisa, came at Benjamin's Steakhouse on the night before the captain announcement. I could tell early on that Lisa was the dominant of the two personalities. She was a 36-year-old Vietnamese woman who was witty, charming and fiery. Lisa was Corey's second wife and 14 years younger than our captain. I liked Lisa Pavin and her Ryder Cup passion from the start.

"The Captainess," as she would soon dub herself, was extremely committed to doing one thing, and that was helping her husband win the Ryder Cup. At dinner that night, she jaw-dropped the table with several F-bombs. It was obvious that PGA Senior Director of Communications Julius Mason and his public relations team would have a full-time job managing Lisa Pavin over the next couple years.

It was explained to me by my fellow PGA officers—Remy, Allen Wronowski and Past President Brian Whitcomb—that Pavin had been promised the Captain's job when Azinger was chosen in 2010. "Keep your nose clean, Corey, and you will be the next guy," was the way it was explained to me by Remy.

Early in my time as secretary I asked Mason about the process for selecting a Ryder Cup captain. He said the criteria was pretty simple—a former major champion in his late 40s who had Ryder Cup experience. He went on to wryly insist that a well-known U.S. player had given him a napkin with names and years written on it, and that served as an unofficial template for the next decade. Mason wouldn't reveal who the player was, but I would say it was either Tiger Woods or Phil Mickelson. I never did see the infamous napkin, but I don't doubt it exists some-where at PGA headquarters.

One thing that stands out from that rainy, wintry day in New York was some unhappiness which got back to the PGA from Woods' agent, Mark Steinberg who expressed his dissatis-faction with the pick of Pavin as the next U.S. Ryder Cup captain. It was hard to say who didn't like the choice of Pavin, Steinberg or Woods. But in 2008, Woods was on top of the world and any opinion from within his camp on any subject would get the atten-tion of the PGA of America. Back then, the PGA seemed to have a constant paranoia that Tiger might at some time decide to pass on a Ryder Cup if things weren't to his liking.

Pavin had been a feisty player throughout his career. He was a bulldog who gained a reputation for being a relentless competi-tor. The former U.S. Open champ had 15 PGA Tour wins and had compiled an 8-5 record in Ryder Cup play. Corey did a thorough job with all of the captain's responsibilities in the two years that led up to Celtic Manor. I found his sarcastic sense of humor to my liking, and I really enjoyed being around both him and Lisa.

Not much ever happens in the year that proceeds the Ryder Cup, and that was true in the case of 2009. But things started to heat up in 2010 at the Masters when Dan Jenkins sent a tweet on Saturday night: "Y.E. Yang is only three shots off the lead. I think we got takeout from him last night."

Lisa was highly offended by Jenkins' remarks about the Ko-rean golfer and made no bones about it. Even though *Golf Digest* issued a formal apology on Jenkins' behalf, she seemed to want more. To Lisa's dismay, the PGA of America took a neutral and noncombative position.

Later that summer at the PGA Championship, Corey and Jim Gray from Golf Channel had a very vocal dispute in the media center after Gray reported that Pavin had told him Tiger Woods would be an automatic captain's pick if he didn't make the Ryder Cup team on points. (The top eight players via a two-year points system based on performance automatically qualified for the team, while the captain selected four "wild-card" picks—one of the most-scrutinized parts of the job.) If Pavin had confided anything about Woods' status as a captain's pick, it was no doubt in confidence.

Pavin denied it. The two got in a shouting match. Gray poked Corey in the chest and exclaimed, "You're going down."

And Pavin replied, "You are full of shit."

As Gray walked away he was also confronted by Lisa, who had recorded the argument on her phone. She waved her phone and said, "It's all right here." All of this uproar happened in front of a sizable audience in the PGA media center at Whistling Straits in Wisconsin.

Golf Channel supported the accuracy of Gray's statement, a move that really ticked off both Corey and Lisa. Ultimately, the PGA never came out with any kind of public statement in support of Pavin. As a result, there was tension between the Pavins and the PGA leading up to the Ryder Cup. In my opinion, the PGA owed Corey some show of support and when it didn't offer any, the authenticity of Gray's comments were validated. I think the Pavins expected undivided loyalty from the PGA of America and felt a lack of trust when that didn't happen.

Leading up to Celtic Manor, Corey handled all of the team details while Lisa dealt with the Ryder Cup uniforms. She selected Peter Millar as the clothier. Lisa developed a Ryder Cup crest that would be used on all U.S. apparel instead of the conventional Ryder Cup logo. It was a retro approach similar to what some of the U.S. teams in the 1950s and '60s had done. I liked it, but many inside the PGA were criticizing her for it.

Lisa's choice of colors for the clothing were not exclusively red, white and blue. The Saturday outfit would feature a lavender cardigan sweater. Again, she got criticized by many inside the PGA for this even though the official European Ryder Cup colors are blue and gold and rarely are their uniforms in that color scheme. Lisa Pavin was putting her stamp on this Ryder Cup. She once confided in me that she hoped the PGA would consider retaining her as a consultant for the 2012 matches at Medinah Country Club outside Chicago. That never happened.

Shortly before we left for Wales, Lisa participated in a photo shoot with *Avid Golfer*. She was draped with only an American flag and wore a cross around her neck. This shoot created a stir in the golf world and particularly among the old guard in the PGA of America, who thought the pose was provocative. They said Lisa was making this Ryder Cup more about herself than the competition.

Looking back at this Ryder Cup, there were definitely things that happened in the lead-up to Wales that would not happen later at Medinah or Gleneagles. It got crazier when we finally made the trip to rain-soaked Wales. It was a team laden with rookies. Bubba Watson, Dustin Johnson, Matt Kuchar and Jeff Overton all earned automatic spots by being among the top eight in the points system. The other "automatics" were Phil Mickelson, Hunter Mahan, Jim Furyk and Steve Stricker. Rickie Fowler, the fifth rookie, joined Woods, Zach Johnson and Stewart Cink as the four captain's picks.

Overton had never met Woods and made the mistake of telling someone that one of the highlights of this Ryder Cup would be his chance to finally meet Tiger. As Overton sat at a table eating at the Renaissance Hotel prior to our departure from Atlanta, Woods entered the room wearing an all-black ensemble. He spotted Overton and sneaked over to a chair next to him and tapped Jeff on the shoulder.

"Oh my God it's Tiger Woods," shouted Overton when he turned around. Everybody, including Woods, got a good laugh out of it.

The PGA had oversized character drawings of all the U.S. team members in the large ballroom where we congregated prior to our departure for Wales. Fowler had his phone in hand and was taking a picture of his own image when he busted out laughing, "I wish I actually had forearms that big."

Once airborne, three of the rookies were seated near Woods. Keep in mind this was less than a year after Tiger had run over the fireplug at Lake Nona, Florida, and been exposed by his wife, Elin, for multiple extramarital affairs. Tiger was in a business-class compartment facing Watson, Johnson and Fowler. The three rookies were hyped up for the trip to Wales, and it was all they could to sit still. Woods sat alone with his headphones doing Sudoku puzzles. Soon the three rookies were pestering Woods, and he tore three pages out of his book and gave each of them a puzzle to work on.

All three took their seats like good students and went to work. One by one they presented the finished product to Woods, who gave them yet another puzzle. Soon all was calm, and the lights were out. Woods had managed to put the rookies to bed with his Sudoku puzzles. It was very apparent that all three rookies yearned for the approval of the player still considered the best in the world.

There was a lot of attention given Woods' presence on the American team. The international media, especially, wanted to make a deal out of the fact that Woods would be with wives of other players. I thought the entire American entourage went out of its way to make Tiger feel comfortable, especially Steve Stricker, who was traveling alone. Stricker's wife, Nicki, had to cancel at the last minute because the family's pre-arranged babysitter had fallen and broken a hip.

We all knew the weather could be bad in Wales, but we didn't realize how bad it would actually be. The practice round days weren't that wet, but once the Ryder Cup started, the weather changed. Early in the week, Pavin assigned a PGA officer to each assistant captain. Our primary job would be to drive a golf cart during the practice rounds and matches, allowing the assistant captain more freedom to be with our players. I was paired with Tom Lehman, who had been our 2006 Ryder Cup captain at the K Club in Ireland.

The PGA officers were located next to the caddies in the small Celtic Manor locker room. Steve Williams, who caddied for Woods, was across from my locker. No caddie ever had a tougher job than Williams, who had taken on the role as Tiger's on-course enforcer, shielding his player from the groping masses and throngs of fans who tried to get a piece of Woods. Williams is from New Zealand and a professional race car driver in his spare time. He was a tough, no-nonsense guy who had also caddied for Ian Baker-Finch and Greg Norman. Today, he caddies for Adam Scott.

When we got to Wales, Williams began lobbying a group of his American peers to boycott wearing the USA caddie bibs during the competition. The bib is worn over a caddie's clothing and identifies who his player is. Williams had a propensity to take his bib off as he walked down the final hole of a tournament when it was apparent Tiger was going to win. He also pulled the stunt on the first hole during the final round of the 2009 PGA Championship until PGA Championship Director Kerry Haigh stopped him in the middle of the first fairway and told Williams that a replacement caddie was standing by if he didn't put the bib on.

On the PGA TOUR, being "bibless" gave Williams the opportunity to promote his own sponsors which were on his clothing. Doing so at the Ryder Cup made no sense because nobody—including players—can wear anything other than the official Ryder Cup uniform, devoid of any sponsors. The Ryder Cup caddie bib featured a red, white and blue USA on the front with the player's name on its back.

By midweek Tiger learned of Williams' ploy to not wear his USA bib. As he stood in the 18th fairway waiting to hit a second shot during a practice round, Woods said to Stevie, "You really are going to wear your caddie bib, right?"

"I'm not planning on it," Williams said.

"You have to wear it so people will know who I am," said a smiling Woods.

"Let me tell you something, pal. If they didn't know you before—they do now," replied a sarcastic Williams, referring to the publicity Woods had received in the past year since his affairs had been exposed.

Earlier in the day Williams had delighted in his ability to fart on command. Several times during the round he would walk up to the tee, set Tiger's bag down, snuggle up close to the gallery rope and rip off a big fart. The players and caddies in the group could hardly contain themselves, and the people in the gallery were pretty much left astonished each time Williams passed gas. It was a combination of Williams being crass and making a feeble attempt at humor.

During the middle of the week at one of the team meetings, Pavin addressed the team regarding the player interviews, which were starting with the assembled media delegation. The format would involve three players from the same team at the same time. Pavin told the team to expect any and all questions, particularly from the British tabloids.

"You need to be ready for anything. This morning I was asked by a reporter if our wives were nervous about being around Tiger this week. I told him absolutely not and that I didn't appreciate the question," Pavin said. There was no reaction from any of the players—just silence. But it was worth the warning, particularly for the five rookies who could face different types of questions than ever before.

On Wednesday evening we attended an exclusive Ryder Cup gala dinner with both teams at the 12th-century Cardiff Castle. The dinner was hosted by Charles, Prince of Wales, the eldest child and heir apparent to Queen Elizabeth II as the next King of England.

The PGA of America had briefed all of us on the proper protocol when meeting British royalty. The first rule was not to touch Prince Charles unless he first offered his hand. The wives were taught the proper way to curtsy. We were also told that Prince Charles reveled in knowing something about his guests and that he took pride in making each guest feel as though the prince knew them.

When Cindy and I met Prince Charles, he asked where I was from. After I said Franklin, Indiana, he said, "You are not far from Medinah. Don't you have a junior golf academy at your course?"

It floored me. At The Legends we do have the Indiana Golf Academy, which is housed at the Indiana Golf Offices located on-site. We were near the end of the reception line, and at that point I was only a junior PGA officer, so it was very impressive that Prince Charles knew anything about us.

What struck me most about Prince Charles was that he was only 5-foot-10 and weighed 178 pounds. Television made him look like a taller man with greater physical stature. The week after we returned to America after this Ryder Cup at Celtic Manor, it was announced that Prince William, the son of Prince Charles, would marry Kate Middleton.

When Friday finally rolled around, Tom Lehman and I were assigned to the first match in the morning featuring Phil Mickelson and Dustin Johnson against Lee Westwood and Martin Kaymer in a four-ball competition. We arrived at the practice range before daylight. There was a light drizzle, and Lehman said, "I will tell you this, if it starts raining hard…we are in deep shit with these rain suits. These things are not waterproof."

The rain suits were made by Sun Mountain and had been designed by Lisa Pavin. The jackets were navy blue, and there was white USA lettering on the front. Each jacket had the player's name embroidered on the back. There was white trim around the bottom of the navy pant legs, and the rain suit looked similar to a college basketball warmup. Top-of-the-line rain suits were made from Gore-Tex, which would keep players dry even in a downpour. These Sun Mountain suits were not destined to perform like Gore-Tex.

The light drizzle soon turned into a steady rain as we accompanied our players to the raucous first tee at Celtic Manor. The rain was not dampening the spirits of the European crowd, which was in typical Ryder Cup form with their customary songs and chants. There is nothing in sports like the electricity at first tee of a Ryder Cup.

Westwood and Kaymer had beaten us to the tee, and the crowd was going crazy. Soon the familiar "Ole, Ole, Ole, Ole" was being flung from the vocal cords of the Euro fans. This stemmed from the Spanish national soccer chant, which had become a staple demonstration of support by European golf fans during Ryder Cup competition. It made the hair stand on the back of my neck as we walked across the bridge to the tee. I shouted to Lehman, "What does it feel like as a player when you hear that?"

"It still pisses me off," Lehman snorted.

It was raining harder by the minute. When we got to the second hole, a par 5, I stood up in the golf car and felt water hitting my calf. I reached inside my rain pants, and my underwear was soaked, with the water dripping off it onto my leg. Tom's prediction about the rain suit was spot-on. To make matters worse, the wetter the suit got, the heavier it became. The Sun Mountain suit was failing to shield the Americans from getting wet.

Mickelson and Johnson were not coping well with the conditions. The Americans were 2 over par and three down when the matches were suspended after six holes.

Lehman took our golf car and hauled some wives and girlfriends back to the clubhouse. I stayed with our players, and we got a lift from a volunteer who had a golf car with a rear seat. Mickelson and I were looking backward as we crossed under a gallery rope, and the driver dropped the rope, hitting Phil and I in the back of our heads. His hat was knocked off in the mud, and he jumped out of the car to retrieve it, much to the amusement of the European crowd. An agitated Mickelson wiped the mud off as we made the trek back to the clubhouse locker room.

As the players and caddies assembled in the locker room, all hell broke loose about the rain suits—particularly from the caddies. Steve Williams and Jim "Bones" Mackay, Phil's caddie, were really pissed, as were many of the players. Tiger said there was no way he could play in the rain suit because it was like wearing a suit of armor.

Steranka pulled out his American Express corporate card and instructed Eric Schwarz, Pavin's longtime caddie and right-hand man, to go to the Ryder Cup merchandise tent and buy 24 rain suits—12 for the players and 12 for the caddies. He said the color made no difference, just get 12 matching ProQuip-brand suits for each group. Sizes were collected, and one of the largest and most unlikely retail purchases in the history of the Ryder Cup took place.

We had a seven-hour rain delay and returned to the course late that afternoon. Before play started, some of the U.S. caddies were saying this could be a break for the Americans because they thought many of the European fans would vacate Celtic Manor during the prolonged downpour. Lehman had joined a group of assistant captains from both sides to inspect the course. As we left the clubhouse for the drive out to the seventh hole, I told Tom what the caddies had said.

"Are you kidding? These people have spent the last seven hours at their nearest watering hole, and they are going to be worse than ever!" Lehman exclaimed. He was right. Many of the fans recognized Lehman as we headed to our destination. A lot of them were drunk, and they shouted at Tom. Some were very close to us, yet Lehman was very accommodating. He shook hands and exchanged pleasantries. It was a pretty classy move by the former Ryder Cup captain.

We played until dark. With the threat of continued rain over the next two days, Ryder Cup officials modified the format. It took all of Saturday and Sunday to complete foursome and four-ball play. We were slated for a Monday finish with the U.S. trailing 9 ½ to 6 ½. We mounted a serious comeback, and ultimately the 2010 matches came down to the last match, America's Hunter Mahan versus Northern Ireland's Graeme McDowell. Europe won the Ryder Cup 14 ½ to 13 ½ when Mahan flubbed a chip shot on the 17th hole.

As the defending champion, the United States needed 14 points to retain possession of the Ryder Cup. While the Mahan-McDowell match might have been the final on the course, I have often thought back to a foursome match in the second session on Saturday between Jim Furyk and Rickie Fowler, who were pitted against Westwood and Kaymer.

Furyk hooked his tee shot into the mud outside the ropes on the fourth hole. Fowler hit the next shot in the alternate-shot match and knocked it onto the front of the green of the par-4 hole. The Euros were about 20 feet behind the pin in two shots. As the four players walked to the green, they stopped in the middle of the fairway. A conversation took place and it turned out that Fowler had incorrectly dropped the ball from his pocket that he was using to tee off with on the odd-numbered holes. He should have used Furyk's ball. (Teammates in alternate-shot play must play the same brand of ball on a hole; a difference in brands can lead to a complicated round full of switching from hole to hole.)

The penalty in match play for playing the wrong ball is loss of hole. After a tie appeared likely on the fourth hole, the Euros wound up winning it. Furyk and Fowler won the final hole of the match to earn a tie and a half-point, but a case could be made that the incorrect drop by Fowler prevented the U.S. from winning 1 up and giving us one full point, which would have then resulted in an overall 14–14 tie, allowing the Americans to take home the cup because they were the defending champions.

In fairness to Fowler, the U.S. team had not given great attention to some of the nuances of the rules of golf concerning match play competition. There was also confusion on when and how to suspend play due to darkness and weather. There was a dispute between Lehman and Paul McGinley, an assistant captain for Europe, concerning advice given to players. These were all things that I made note of with the anticipation of rectifying them before the next Ryder Cup in 2012 in Chicago.

Stricker and Woods each compiled a 3–1 record to lead the Americans at Celtic Manor. On the other hand, Mickelson was 1–3 and suffered through another lackluster Ryder Cup week. If anything, Phil seemed to be trying too hard. That was never more apparent than on Sunday afternoon when his wife, Amy, approached Lehman.

"Phil puts so much pressure on himself at the Ryder Cup. He doesn't want to let the other guys down. Tom, could you please talk to Phil and say something that will help him relax? He needs to get in the same mindset he does when he is competing for himself in the majors," Amy said. It was a poignant moment and it demonstrated that she knew her husband well. The pressure of the Ryder Cup is like nothing else in golf, a fact that was once again proven on that Sunday afternoon in Wales.

I don't know if Lehman ever had that talk with Phil, but Mickelson did close out the matches with a 4 and 2 win over Peter Hanson in Monday's singles play. Phil would then compile a 3–1 record at Medinah in 2012. He was 2–1 at Gleneagles in 2014. What I do know is that after Amy's talk with Lehman, Mickelson has gone 6–2 compared to his previous Ryder Cup record of 8–16–6.

Lehman was highly respected by all of the players at Wales. Many on Lehman's team at the K Club had publicly said he had been a stellar captain even though the U.S. suffered an 18 ½ to 9 ½ beatdown. When it came to the support staff that Pavin surrounded himself with at Celtic Manor, Lehman as a former Ryder Cup captain brought the most experience.

Davis Love III was rumored to be the next U.S. captain. He rolled up his sleeves and did whatever Pavin needed. Love was clearly on a mission at Celtic Manor. He was there to help us win, but also he was making mental notes and learning as much as he could about being a captain. Paul Goydos and Jeff Sluman rounded out the other U.S. assistant captains.

One other thing about Lehman—make no mistake—it was because of him that Fowler was on the U.S. squad. Tom had lobbied hard for Rickie back in September in New York, when Corey was choosing his four captain's picks. At 21 years and 9 months old, Fowler became the youngest American Ryder Cup player ever. He was winless on the PGA Tour and considered by many to be the No. 12 man on the U.S. team.

Lehman and I were assigned to the final three singles matches on Monday. We had Mickelson, Zach Johnson and Mahan. Stricker set the tone for a possible U.S. rally when he beat world-ranked No. 1 Westwood by a 2 and 1 margin in the first match out. "Stricker is like the silent assassin," Lehman said when the first red flag went on the scoreboard.

Johnson won his match 3 and 2 while Mickelson rebounded from a bad week with his convincing win over Hanson. It appeared any chance the U.S. might have would come down to the Mahan match. Hunter won the 12th hole to cut his deficit to two down when Lehman did something that was shocking to me.

He told me to keep the golf car with the Mahan match. Tom said he was going to leave that match and go to Fowler because he said we somehow had to get a half-point in that match. First of all, Fowler was not in our grouping of players. Even stranger was the fact that Rickie had just lost four of his last five holes to Eduardo Molinari and was now 4 down heading into No. 13. As Tom walked away I remember saying to myself, "What is he smoking? Rickie is done."

As it turned out, Fowler won 13 and then won Nos. 16, 17 and 18 to halve his match with Molinari. Lehman was there for all of it. It was one of the most remarkable displays of karma that I have ever witnessed in sport, and one of the many reasons why I have a wealth of respect for Tom Lehman.

Highlights of the 2010 Ryder Cup will always feature Mc-Dowell's victory over Mahan because it was the last match on the course and ultimately decided the outcome. It was absolute madness. There had to be 30,000 spectators crowding into the 211 yards that comprised the 17th hole. People were falling and sliding down the hillside on the left side of the hole. The mud was like an oil slick. When someone went down, it looked like a human bowling ball knocking down human bowling pins.

After Mahan chunked his chip and secured Europe's win, we all got into the locker room, and Pavin held a brief team meeting. Everybody's emphasis was on Mahan, who was unfairly feeling the sole responsibility for the U.S. team loss. Over the course of three days a lot of things happened that could have resulted in a different outcome for the Americans, but at this moment Mahan felt the weight of the world on his shoulders. He was sobbing on a bench in the locker room.

Mickelson walked over to console Mahan, gently placing his hand on Hunter's shoulder and saying how proud everybody was of him. Mickelson talked about how no one in that room had ever been in the position that Mahan was in—on the course during the final round of the Ryder Cup with everything on the line.

With his win over Hanson that day, Mickelson was in a better position to lead the U.S. team. Make no mistake that Mickelson is a natural leader. But my guess is that his Ryder Cup losses prevented him from taking that role. I think this created even more pressure on Mickelson over the years at Ryder Cups. He had to feel like a caged lion with his dominant personality wanting to lead, but in his own mind lacking the credibility until he became a Ryder Cup winner. Phil is a different type of leader than Tiger. Mickelson motivates with words and Woods with action. Regardless, Phil couldn't start leading until he started winning.

When we flew home I was seated next to Bubba Watson, and I asked him what the best part of the Ryder Cup week had been for him.

"Being around Phil," Watson said. "I had never spent much time with him. One night he got the rookies together and talked to us about our responsibility to grow the game and make it better. That was pretty cool."

That would be a sign of things to come from Phil.

# Chapter Eight

# Stop! In the Name of Love

Losing a Ryder Cup like we did in 2010 at Wales was tough because the PGA of America needed to move on and prepare for the next competition. However, there has traditionally been a transition period until the selection of the next U.S. captain to allow the PGA to show its appreciation for the outgoing captain, regardless of the outcome. I had been told that Hal Sutton was upset after we lost at Oakland Hills in 2004 because he thought the PGA wasted no time in naming Tom Lehman as its next captain just a few weeks later in early November.

So, once the PGA's official mourning period was over in early December, we gathered at PGA National Headquarters in Palm Beach Gardens, Florida, to interview Davis Love III for the 2012 Ryder Cup captaincy. Love was the next guy on the list of that infamous napkin held closely by Julius Mason, our PR guy. Allen Wronowski would be the PGA president when the matches were slated for Medinah, and he was a firm believer in Mason's list. No other name beside Love's was on the Ryder Cup radar. When it came to the choice of the 2012 captain, there was absolutely no dissention. Conducting the interview would be Wronowski; Derek Sprague, the newly elected secretary; Jim Remy, PGA past president, and me as the vice president. This interview would be just a formality before we announced Love as the 2012 captain.

Mason and Joe Steranka, PGA CEO, insisted that we conduct the interview behind closed doors in the boardroom outside of Steranka's office. Both took tremendous pride in the PGA's ability to conceal the choice of a captain from the media as long as possible. It had become a game to them, but the choice of Love hardly came with much suspense.

It would be difficult to find a finer gentleman in all of golf than Davis Love III. He was born on April 13, 1964, in Charlotte, North Carolina, to Helen and Davis Love, Jr. Davis III entered this world on the day after his dad competed in the Masters. Love's dad was also a PGA member and a renowned golf instructor before he died tragically in a 1988 plane crash.

Love III won the 1997 PGA Championship at Winged Foot Golf Club in New York. When we conducted our interview, he had 19 PGA TOUR victories. He has since added his 20th in 2015 at age 51 at the Wyndham Championship, making him the third-oldest PGA TOUR winner ever. He played in six Ryder Cups, compiling a 9–12–5 record. Love was presented the 2008 Payne Stewart Award for his character, charity and sportsmanship. There is even a stretch of I-95 near Love's current home in Sea Island, Georgia, that is named after him. Picking Davis Love III as the 2012 Ryder Cup captain really was a no-brainer.

The interview lasted about 45 minutes. We all had a chance to ask questions. In particular, I was curious to hear whether Love might approach the rules preparation at the Ryder Cup differently. It was clear at Celtic Manor that our players should have known more about the intricacies of team match play competition as well as when and how to suspend play due to weather and darkness. I was pleased to hear Love agree this was a priority for him.

Steranka ended the interview by volunteering to take Love on a tour of the PGA Headquarters. That was our cue to decide whether Love was the right guy for the job. Wronowski wrapped up that discussion in a few seconds. We all agreed DL3 was the man to lead us at Medinah.

Joe brought Davis back into the room. Allen informed him that we would like him to be our next captain. Love accepted, and he was immediately overcome with emotion. Davis buried his head in his hands and began to cry. Pretty soon, he looked up.

"I just wish my dad was here to share this journey with me," Davis said in a tearful voice. It was one of the most moving moments I ever experienced in my time with the PGA.

Mason was summoned to the boardroom, and he informed us that he had arranged for a caterer to bring us Davis' favorite meal of Southern fried chicken with all the trimmings. We enjoyed the meal, free from the chance any media might see us at a public dining spot, and the 2012 United States Ryder Cup effort began that night. We decided the announcement of Love as our captain would come in mid-January in Chicago.

When all of us gathered again in the Windy City, we dined at Harry Caray's on the night before the official announcement. The following morning we were shuttled to Medinah Country Club for breakfast and meetings. The official announcement of Love as captain took place late morning in Medinah's expansive clubhouse. We then headed downtown for a reception on Michigan Avenue with Ernie Banks of the Cubs, Dan Hampton of the Bears, Scottie Pippen of the Bulls and the Blackhawks' Denis Savard. Later that night, we headed to the United Center to see the Chicago Bulls play. It was over in a flash.

For the next 20 months, Love and his wife Robin would be organized and easy to work with. Their personalities were much more laid back than Corey and Lisa Pavin. I enjoyed the Pavins and would say these two captainships were different and reflected the personalities of their respective leaders. One wasn't necessarily better than the other, just different.

Davis had a large staff already in place for The McGladrey Classic, the PGA TOUR event conducted each fall at Sea Island,

Georgia. Love plays a primary role in the execution of that event. He volunteered his team of people to assist the PGA in any of the Ryder Cup planning. Love was a Polo Ralph Lauren staff member, so early on it was decided that Polo would provide the uniforms.

There was absolutely no drama whatsoever in the months leading up to the competition. One by one, Love named his assistant captains. They would be Mike Hulbert, Scott Verplank, Jeff Sluman and Fred Couples.

On Labor Day 2012, we headed to New York City for the announcement of Love's four captain's picks, who would round out the 12-man U.S. squad. Eight players had automatically qualified through the Ryder Cup points system conducted in 2011–12. The announcement of the remaining four U.S. players would take place on Tuesday, September 5.

The PGA Officers never before had any input in the captain's picks. But Love, being the ultimate consensus-builder, even took the time to privately ask the four of us who our picks would be. Just for kicks, I had already prepared a detailed matrix, and my four choices were Steve Stricker, Brandt Snedeker, Dustin Johnson and Hunter Mahan. Our only difference would be that Love took Jim Furyk over Mahan. I liked Mahan, who had won twice that year, and I felt like he would be motivated after his loss to McDowell at Wales. But Love was looking to Furyk for some veteran leadership, and it was hard to argue with that.

The BMW Championship was played at Crooked Stick Golf Club in Indianapolis a couple weeks after the U.S. team had been set. Love reached out to me and wanted to set up a team dinner during the BMW at the famous St. Elmo's Steakhouse in downtown Indy. I called the restaurant and made the necessary arrangements and booked a private room. Love and his team attended minus Zach Johnson, who had a previous commitment. Davis was all about establishing team unity heading into Medinah.

The 39th Ryder Cup would be conducted in perfect late September weather. The matches were slated for September 28–30, and Medinah was a massively impressive host. It has a ton of acreage, and the infrastructure was the largest in Ryder Cup history. The Chicago-based fans were enthusiastic and loud. It was a tremendous home venue for the Americans.

The Hilton in Oak Brook was the official Ryder Cup hotel. The Loves had established the biggest and most extensive team room in U.S. Ryder Cup history. There were four ping pong tables, video games, a weight room with a dining area and a full bar. The opening-night dinner featured one long table with the team, captains and official party intermingled together. In Chicago, Cindy and I were seated next to Woods and Stricker compared with individual tables in Wales, where the same people seemed to hang with one another all week. The Loves were all about getting everybody involved and creating a "family atmosphere" for this Ryder Cup.

Jose Maria Olazabal was the European Ryder Cup captain. The Spaniard had been a close friend and teammate of the great Seve Ballesteros, who had succumbed to brain cancer in 2011 at 54. As Ryder Cup partners, Olazabal and Ballesteros racked up an impressive record of 11–2–2 including a 6–1–1 mark in foursomes and 5–1–1 in the four-ball. Olazabal had dedicated his captainship in 2012 to his good friend Ballesteros. The Euros had even asked for Love's permission to wear blue and white on Sunday as a dedication to Ballesteros.

"In his captaincy Seve was obsessive. He wanted to control everything. I share Seve's passion for the Ryder Cup, but I will not be doing that," Jose Maria said early in the week at his Medinah press conference.

"What I will try to impart is his attitude. Perhaps the biggest thing I learned from Seve is to be patient and never, ever give up. He always saw the glass as half-full. It didn't matter if he was in a tough situation and the opponents were in good shape. His attitude was always, 'Make a par. Force the other guys to make a birdie, which is never easy.' That was the mentality I learned just by being around him so much," Olazabal said.

"Other than that, I will let the players play their own games. They know them better than I do. So I will be there if they need me. Otherwise, I will let them be comfortable doing what they normally do," concluded the European captain.

Davis was going to use the same system Pavin had in Wales, in which a PGA officer would be assigned to an assistant captain. I requested that he put me with Couples because I wanted to get to know Freddie better. He was a winning Presidents Cup captain in the off years, and I was intrigued with his leadership style.

Couples was engaged with the players and seemed happy to help his good friend Love at Medinah. His name continually came up as a potential Ryder Cup captain. Insiders at the PGA of America would hold his Presidents Cup duties against Couples almost as though it tarnished him in some way. I personally never bought into that.

In the practice rounds leading up to the start of the matches, Couples was extremely engaged. He had a great rapport with all of the American players. Stricker summed up the Couples mystique best: "Every guy wants to be cool like Freddie."

One morning while we were on the course, Couples and I had a conversation about the activities of the Ryder Cup week. In his opinion, too much was being asked of the players. Fred thought the evening activities were excessive. Just to clarify, there are really only a couple of structured things the PGA of America asks the players to do outside of pressers and practice rounds. There is a Gala Dinner on Wednesday night and the Opening Ceremonies on Thursday afternoon.

After Fred and I had our conversation about the Ryder Cup, we went to the team room for lunch. We were joined by Tiger Woods and Brandt Snedeker along with their respective caddies,

Joe LaCava and Scott Vail. Out of the blue Woods made an interesting comment to Couples.

"You know you will never be a Ryder Cup captain," Woods said.

"Why is that?" Couples responded.

"Because you are a prick and the PGA doesn't pick guys like you," Woods laughed.

Couples was slightly taken aback. He grinned and refused to take Woods' bait.

Later that evening in the team room before heading to the Gala, Stricker approached me and said, "Hey, are you OK? I heard about lunch."

"I'm not sure I know what you are talking about," I told Stricker.

"The guys know you will be the president at the next Ryder Cup, and that stuff about Freddie being a Ryder Cup captain was all for your benefit," Stricker said.

"Really?" I said in a light-hearted way. "No, I didn't think anything about it. I just thought Tiger was busting Fred's balls."

The 2012 U.S. team was stronger on paper than the Europeans. The Americans had an average Official World Ranking of 12.2 compared to 18.9 for the Euros. Woods, who was ranked No. 2, led the U.S. team while Europe's Rory McIlroy was the No. 1 player in the world.

Joining Woods on the U.S. team were Ryder Cup veterans Bubba Watson, Zach Johnson, Matt Kuchar, Phil Mickelson, Stricker, Furyk and Dustin Johnson. The American rookies were Jason Dufner, Keegan Bradley, Webb Simpson and Snedeker. Besides McIlroy, the European squad consisted of Justin Rose, Paul Lawrie, Graeme McDowell, Francesco Molinari, Luke Donald, Lee Westwood, Sergio Garcia, Peter Hanson, Martin Kaymer and Ian Poulter. Their lone rookie was Nicolas Colsaerts.

Love had his prospective partners play practice rounds together. His team combinations did not vary in any of the four sessions involving team play. It would be Stricker and Woods, Mickelson and Bradley, Watson and Simpson, Dustin Johnson and Kuchar, Dufner and Zach Johnson, and Furyk and Snedeker.

The most prolific pairing wound up being Mickelson and Bradley. These two players would feed off each other throughout the week. Bradley seemed to gain confidence from the constant encouragement he received from Mickelson. In return, Phil was obviously energized by Bradley's passion and enthusiasm. They combined for a 3–0 record, culminating with a 7 and 6 dusting of Westwood and Donald on Saturday morning.

The Americans dominated play during the first three sessions and opened up an 8–4 lead. After Mickelson and Bradley walloped their opponents Saturday morning, they were back out on the course rooting on their teammates. Furyk and Snedeker won the final match Saturday morning, 1 up, over McIlroy and McDowell. Phil was standing in the 18th fairway when the match ended, and he asked me to drive him and his wife Amy back to the clubhouse.

In order to avoid autograph-seekers, we took the long way around through the corporate tents on the left side of the 18th hole. Phil said to Amy, "I told Davis to sit Keegan and me this afternoon. We need a break. I want to be fresh for the singles matches tomorrow. Those are worth two points (his match and Bradley's)."

It made sense to me, but many have criticized Love for allowing his hottest team to sit out when the Americans could have stepped on the jugular of the Euros. As it turned out the Saturday afternoon session was tied 2–2, and the Americans took a 10–6 lead into Sunday. Mickelson was 42 years old and suffers from psoriatic arthritis. I still support Love and Mickelson in the decision to not play in that fourth session Saturday afternoon. Phil had also spent a lot of mental energy in those three wins.

The most amazing thing on Friday and Saturday was the 0–3 record posted by Stricker and Woods. As partners, those two had dominated team competition virtually every time they had been paired. Woods was driving it all over the place, and Stricker lacked any kind of overall sharpness with his game, including his vaunted putting stroke.

A telling incident happened Friday afternoon during their four-ball match against Westwood and Colsaerts. I was crouched by the golf car on the No. 8 tee when Lee Trevino approached. The golf legend had been on foot following matches in every session. He knelt down beside me. "If you want to do something positive, grab that damned driver of Tiger's and break it," Trevino exclaimed.

Woods had been lethal with the galleries. He dropped a spectator on the 18th tee during a practice round when his ball hit a guy in the head. Twice during the matches he had beaned spectators with errant tee shots.

On Saturday morning a British betting parlor had hired a skywriter to fly the skies over Medinah on Saturday morning. The harmless messages were pro-Europe.

Paddypower.com had some clever messages. "Seen Tiger?" was one, referring to his winless performance. "#RyderCup #ForSeve" was another. "#GoEurope" was the theme. You could even send a tweet to the U.S. team and the theme was Help a Yank to Shank. The PGA of America had worked in conjunction with some local officials to block the airspace on Saturday from Paddypower.com, forcing them out of the skies by mid-morning.

Despite all of this, the Americans were still in a great spot heading into the Sunday singles matches. It would have been a complete blowout had it not been for the late Saturday afternoon heroics by the Europeans. Garcia and Donald had beaten Stricker and Woods, 1 up. Thanks to sterling play by Poulter and McIlroy, Europe had also rallied to a 1-up victory over Dufner and Zach Johnson just before sunset.

The U.S. could have easily been up 12–4. I saw Jon Miller, the president of programming for NBC Sports, on Saturday night. "Thank God Europe won those last two matches or nobody would be watching tomorrow," Miller exclaimed.

"What are you smoking?" I said to Jon. "We are trying to win a Ryder Cup. It would have been great to be ahead 12–4!"

It was a special time in the U.S. team room Saturday night. We were joined by George H.W. Bush, the 41st President of the United States, and his son, George W. Bush, No. 43. Rarely, if ever, have two former presidents joined a Ryder Cup team for its Saturday night dinner. The Bushes were highly engaged with the team. Both spoke to the team, but neither really offered much in the way of inspiration for the following day. The glaring absence was from Love, who was tied up with media activities and failed to dine with the presidents. I guess that instance would be the type of distraction Couples spoke of earlier in the week.

Speaking of Couples, he elected not to take a radio with him during the matches. In fact, he bounced all over Medinah and didn't really stick with his assigned group. He could be spotted much of the weekend watching the action with basketball legend Michael Jordan. On Sunday, when he was supposed to be with me for the final three singles matches, he was hanging out with Jordan. Those three matches, of course, ended up being huge.

Further encroaching on his time, Fred's girlfriend had gotten into town late in the week, and he had elected not to attend any of the nightly meetings Love held with his vice captains. This decision created some obvious friction among the vice captains.

I think this behavior on the part of the former Masters champion—one of Love's closest friends, mind you—went a good way toward Fred being passed over in favor of Love as the 2016 U.S. captain for the upcoming Ryder Cup at Hazeltine National. There were other factors, which I will get into later, but Fred did himself no favors that week.

Sometime later on Saturday night, Love called a meeting with his assistants. They were joined by Stricker, Woods, Furyk and Mickelson to discuss Sunday's order for the singles matches.

"Too many guys in the room. Information overload," Stricker told me later.

Sunday would go down as one of the wackiest and disheartening final days in the history of the Ryder Cup.

The day began when the British betting parlor won an injunction and was back in full force with more skywriting. Obviously inspired by the PGA of America's attempt to block the air space, Paddypower.com stepped it up a notch. This time they got personal and wrote some of the names of the women with whom Woods had his extramarital affairs. Followed by "#Tiger likes it rough."

The attention soon shifted from the skies to the drama building in what would be the third match of the day between Bradley and McIlroy. Their tee time was nearing, and Rory was nowhere to be found. Davis' brother, Mark and I were watching Golf Channel's coverage on the veranda leading into the U.S. locker room. Bradley had just come off the range, and I told him that his opponent still wasn't on property. He stopped, looked shocked and headed through the locker room to the putting green.

A few minutes later, McIlroy came rolling into Medinah in a police car. The report was that the young Irishman had overslept. Attempts by Olazabal to reach him by phone were unsuccessful. The huge American gallery on the No. 1 tee started singing a chant, "Oh where, oh where, has my Rory gone." He would claim that he was confused on the time. He jumped out of the police car with a protein bar in hand. Rory put his golf shoes on while standing next to the putting green, stroked a couple of putts, and headed to the first tee. The crowd started chanting, "Central Time Zone."

As we watched this incident unfold on TV, Mark Love looked at me and said, "How many times as a kid did he just go to the first tee and hit a tee shot with no warmups? This is not a big deal for him." It was great insight from someone who had spent his whole life in golf.

The Europeans stormed out of the gate Sunday morning and quickly erased the Americans' four-point lead. In fact, Europe won the first five matches of the day and seized control. It was the greatest Ryder Cup comeback in history since 1999, when the Americans pulled off the same feat at The Country Club in Brookline, Massachusetts—only in some ways it was even more amazing because Europe had accomplished the feat on foreign soil. The drama that unfolded at Medinah included some phenomenal shots by Justin Rose in his come-from-behind win against Mickelson, causing Phil to tip his hat to the Englishman.

In the end, it was Germany's Martin Kaymer who dropped a 6-foot putt on the 18th green to beat Stricker, 1 up, in the 11th match of the day. The pressure of the Ryder Cup was never more apparent than on that Sunday in Chicago.

I remember one scene very well. During the Kaymer-Stricker match, both players had dumped their second shots on the 16th hole into a greenside bunker. Bad shots affected by pressure. To their credit, both made great up-and-downs from the sand and saved pars.

When Kaymer holed his putt to halve the hole, Olazabal looked to the sky with eyes closed and hands raised as if gesturing to Ballesteros. Jose Maria then wiped the tears from his eyes. It was as if a special karma had fallen over Medinah that day and the Europeans were not going to be denied.

One match was still on the course after Kaymer locked up the Ryder Cup with his putt. Woods and Molinari were on the 18th tee, and Tiger led, 1 up. Kaymer had given the Euros the 14 points they needed to retain the cup because they were the defending champions. I could not help but think back to Wales and the half-point that was lost in the Furyk-Fowler match, which ultimately cost the U.S. a tie that would have retained Ryder Cup.

If the U.S. would have pulled that off, it would have again needed just a 14–14 tie to retain the Ryder Cup at Medinah. That would have allowed Woods to halve the 18th hole to preserve a 1-up victory and give the U.S. the Ryder Cup-retaining tie. The Americans would then have held the Cup for three straight matches. History would have been drastically changed, and the Americans would be dominating the Ryder Cup.

In the meaningless final match at Medinah, Woods conceded a putt on the 18th green to Molinari, which tied their match. Because of that, history will show Europe as a 14 ½ to 13 ½ winner.

All of America was pretty much shell-shocked over the developments of the day. The team seemed to have a different sense of defeat than it did at Wales. The loss at Medinah had left the U.S. players feeling empty and remorseful because they felt they had let down Davis Love. But the fact is, Europe got hot at the right time, made some key putts—especially Rose against Mickelson and Poulter starting on Saturday night—and rode the momentum as America's players got tight.

In my opinion, no Ryder Cup captain could have been better prepared and done more to put his team in a position to win. Love had masterfully put the pairings together in foursome and four-ball competition. The team's success then boiled down to players finishing it off in Sunday's singles matches. Based on the Official World Golf Ranking, the U.S. was favored in eight of the 12 singles matches. But that was on paper, and we all know from experience that means nothing in the Ryder Cup.

"We really may have dropped the ball on pin placements on the last few holes," Love told reporters in the aftermath. "We wanted pins on the left and in the middle of the green because a lot of our guys were drawing it (the ball) in there. The most two important holes in the singles came down to 17 and 18, and we had pins where if you hit it long and left, it was tough to get close to the pins because they were on the right. Should we have thought of that? Maybe."

After the press conference, the players and officials loaded up in vans and headed back to the clubhouse. I was in a van with Couples and some of the rookies. One of the players in the back of the van said, "Did you guys see what those skywriters were doing this morning? They were writing the names of the women Tiger was with. There must have been 10 or 12 names."

To which Couples jokingly replied, "Yeah, we all know it was more like 50 or 60." Make no mistake: Couples and Woods have a close relationship, and this comment by Freddie was just an attempt at humorous sarcasm.

Woods finished the Medinah Ryder Cup with a record of 0–3–1. At the time, nobody would have figured it to be his last Ryder Cup. But now it looks like that could be the case. His career Ryder Cup record stands at 13–14–2, and it wasn't going to change for 2016 given his back problems keeping him on the sidelines. Phil, on the other hand, was 3–1, and he was clearly no longer in Tiger's shadow in terms of the Ryder Cup.

As I drove home to Franklin the following day, I received a phone call from Love. He thanked me for all the PGA of America had done in the time leading up to and including the Ryder Cup. He also offered that Woods had sought him out and apologized for his performance at Medinah. He said Tiger was taking this Ryder Cup loss very hard. Love said Woods felt singlehandedly responsible for the defeat. This is a point worth stressing—Tiger cares about the Ryder Cup. Maybe he didn't always care as much as he did at Medinah, but to think the losses didn't bother him is wrong. In a way, it would be a shame if Medinah was his last appearance as a player because apparently the Ryder Cup had come to mean more to him over time.

Medinah certainly produced a demoralizing loss for everyone involved with the United States Ryder Cup efforts. It meant the U.S. had now lost seven of the past nine Ryder Cups. Changes were needed. All eyes were turning to Gleneagles in 2014. I felt I was ready for the challenge. But there was no way to prepare for the drama that would unfold in Scotland.

# Chapter Nine

# A Brilliant Choice

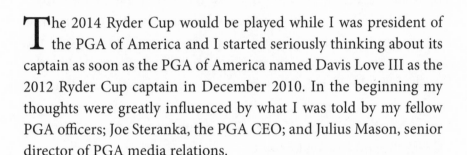

The 2014 Ryder Cup would be played while I was president of the PGA of America and I started seriously thinking about its captain as soon as the PGA of America named Davis Love III as the 2012 Ryder Cup captain in December 2010. In the beginning my thoughts were greatly influenced by what I was told by my fellow PGA officers; Joe Steranka, the PGA CEO; and Julius Mason, senior director of PGA media relations.

David Toms, the 2001 PGA champion and a member of three Ryder Cup teams, was the next man up on the napkin Julius always referred to when it came to this generation of Ryder Cup captains. David is a good guy who was the 2011 recipient of the Payne Stewart Award for his contributions to the game. I had two reservations about him, however. His career Ryder Cup record as a player was 4–6–2, and the three U.S. teams he played on from 2002–06 all lost to Europe—and twice by significant margins. But David fit the PGA mold. He would be 47 years old in 2014 at Gleneagles, and he was a former major champion who played on multiple Ryder Cup teams.

In October 2011, the PGA hosted its Grand Slam of Golf in Bermuda. Jim Huber, the renowned and award-winning essayist, was once again the host of the PGA's Fireside Chat with the Major Champions. Jim had just finished and released a book titled *Four Days In July,* which chronicled Tom Watson's attempt at winning the 2009 Open Championship at Turnberry. The book was given to everyone who attended that fireside chat.

I started reading Huber's book on the flight home from Bermuda. Honestly, I could not put the book down. It was an intriguing look inside Watson's valiant try at becoming the oldest major championship winner in golf history. Of course, everything went up in flames for the 59-year-old Watson when his brilliantly played 8-iron rolled over the back edge of the green on his 72nd hole, forcing him into a bogey and dropped him into a tie with Stewart Cink. In the four-hole playoff, Watson, emotionally and physically drained, played poorly, and Cink won the Claret Jug.

While Huber's story of Watson's near-miss at Turnberry was extremely insightful, I found his portrayal of Tom Watson, the man, to be even more interesting. In his unique style, Jim described the love affair between the Scottish people and Watson, a five-time winner of the British Open. Huber also dove deeply into the character of Watson. Jim poignantly exposed Watson's strengths and his weaknesses.

It was somewhere over the Atlantic Ocean on that October day in 2011 when I first asked myself the question, "Why not Tom Watson as the 2014 Ryder Cup captain?" After all, Tom was the last U.S. captain to win on foreign soil—in 1993, when he led the Americans to victory at The Belfry in England. It would be 21 years since a U.S. victory when our team would journey to Gleneagles in 2014. Tom Watson in Scotland as a U.S. Ryder Cup captain? It was sounding better all of the time, and I could hardly contain my enthusiasm.

A couple of days after getting home, I placed a phone call to Huber, who lived in Atlanta. We chatted for a few minutes about Bermuda and his book. I then asked the following question: "Jim, here is an off-the-wall idea. What do you think about Tom Watson as the Ryder Cup captain in 2014 at Gleneagles?"

There was a pause. Dead silence.

"Brilliant. That is a brilliant idea," Jim finally responded.

We continued to talk, and you could sense the excitement in Huber's voice. I asked him about Watson in 1993 versus today. "The big difference is that Tom is more at peace with himself now than he was then," said Jim. "He's licked the drinking thing, and I think that is the biggest difference."

This conversation with Huber was at least a validation that my idea to explore Watson as the 2014 captain had merit. The next thing that needed to happen for me was a conversation with Watson. When I asked Huber for Watson's cell phone number, his response was comical.

"I'll give it to you, but don't tell Tom where you got it," Jim firmly said.

I continued to do a lot of research on Watson on my own. At this point, no one else besides Huber had any idea Watson was on my radar. In early November, I finally called Watson to talk. When he answered the phone, it was clear he was outside because I could hear the wind blowing over the phone. It turned out he was in South Dakota hunting pheasants with David Feherty, the talented golf television personality from Northern Ireland. They were joined by a group of Wounded Warriors. Tom asked me to call him back later that night.

When I reached out to Watson that evening, he said, "What was your name again, and who were you with?" Tom would later say he really has no idea why he even answered the phone while he was hunting.

I told him I was the vice president of the PGA of America. I explained the PGA had a meeting earlier in the year with a group of former Ryder Cup captains in Savannah that he obviously had not been able to attend. I asked Tom if he had a few minutes to answer some questions and give me his insight into the Ryder Cup. Watson is a guy who can take a while to warm up in a conversation, and this was my first significant interaction of any kind with the man. While I found him to be somewhat intimidating in the first few minutes, we soon became more relaxed with each other, and the conversation flowed freely.

"Tom, why do you think the Americans have had so much trouble winning the Ryder Cup lately?" I asked.

"Right now, the Europeans have better players. I watch their swings, and they are fundamentally more solid," Watson replied.

"Why do you think it's been almost 20 years since we won in Europe?" I asked.

"It's several things," Watson answered. "Like I said, right now they have better players. But, they also have a familiarity with the courses over there that our players don't have. And when the weather gets bad, I think their swings hold up better."

As we talked, Tom conceded that the Ryder Cup had changed a lot since 1993. "I had one assistant captain—my teaching pro, Stan Thursk. Now they have four. That's overkill in my opinion. It seems there's a lot of pomp and circumstance today. Players are asked to do more things than when I was the captain," Watson said.

Finally, I popped the question. "Look, Tom. I called because I wanted your opinions. But I would also be curious to know if you would have any interest in being a Ryder Cup captain again?"

"Ted, I have been waiting a long time for this phone call. I had reached out to the PGA before and told them I would have interest in doing it again," Watson said. "I need to think about it, but I would be interested in talking again."

We ended our conversation with me telling Tom we obviously still had a Ryder Cup yet to play at Medinah. The PGA needed to give Davis Love III its full attention and support. Nothing could happen that would cause a distraction. Watson totally agreed. We exchanged email addresses and agreed to stay in touch.

I got to work early the next day, and there was already an email from Watson. He asked me to call him.

When I did, Tom told me there was something we probably needed to talk about that might preclude him from being a Ryder Cup captain. It was pertaining to some comments that he had publicly made about Tiger Woods and his behavior on and off the golf course. I had read a lot about Watson before I ever called him. I knew exactly what he was talking about.

In an interview from the United Arab Emirates while playing in the Dubai Desert Classic in 2009, Tom had said, "I'll let the cat out of the bag. Tiger has to take ownership of what he has done. He must get his personal life in order. I think that's what he's trying to do. And when he comes back, he has to show some humility to the public.

"I feel that he has not carried the same stature that other great players have like Jack (Nicklaus), Arnold (Palmer), Byron Nelson, and Hogan, in the sense that there was language and club-throwing (by Woods) on the golf course," Watson said.

"You can grant that to a young person who has not been out here for a while. But I think he needs to clean up his act and show respect for the game that other people before him have shown," Tom added.

In my conversation with Watson that morning, he referred to Woods as "the elephant in the room." I assured Watson I had seen and read all of his remarks on Woods. In my opinion, he hadn't said anything that wasn't true. Others had said far worse things about Tiger. His statements were all a non-issue for me.

Tom and I then spent over an hour discussing the details of the modern-day Ryder Cups. He asked the questions, and I answered them to the best of my ability. On that day, I knew Tom Watson was absolutely the right guy to lead us at Gleneagles.

A few nights later, I called Steve Stricker. I started my conversation with him the same as I had Watson. Steve had been on the last couple of U.S. Ryder Cup teams, and I wanted his perspective as a player. When we spoke about captains, Stricker had an interesting perspective.

"Some of the guys, like Tiger and Phil, have joked to me and said that I will never be a Ryder Cup captain until I win a major," Stricker said. "It's funny, but I never looked at Paul (Azinger) or Corey (Pavin) as major champions when they were my Ryder Cup captains. I looked at them as former Ryder Cup players.

"I know the PGA always picks guys in their late 40s as captains, but I don't know why they don't bring back some older guys like Tom Watson," Stricker remarked.

I about fell out of my chair.

"Well, Steve, that is actually why I am calling. Confidentially. Totally confidential. How would you feel about Watson as the 2014 Ryder Cup captain in Scotland?" I asked.

"That would be really cool. Tom Watson in Scotland. Those people over there would go crazy. I want to play on that team!" Stricker exclaimed.

In the next few weeks, I reached out to others with whom I felt I could have candid conversations regarding Watson.

"He might be the toughest competitor in the history of the game," said Tom Lehman, the 2006 Ryder Cup captain. "Tom will be the type of guy who inspires and motivates young players. It's one thing to play for guys like Paul (Azinger), Corey (Pavin), Davis (Love) and me. But, it's another to play for Tom Watson. He is a true legend of the game, and I love the idea."

Pavin, who was the U.S. Ryder Cup captain in 2010 in Wales, was also a player on the '93 Ryder Cup team that Watson captained at the Belfry. He said Watson had masterfully put together the Saturday afternoon pairings. Pavin gave Watson lots of credit for getting the U.S. in a position to win with his strategic decisions.

While addressing his team at Celtic Manor, Pavin had said. "Tom Watson is the greatest bad-weather player of all time. He told me the key is keeping your hands warm."

Pavin clearly had great respect for Watson—in his own way. Corey is a lot like Tom and not shy to voice an opinion. However,

Corey also had strong feelings about somebody else being the 2014 Ryder Cup captain. "The PGA needs to make things right with Larry Nelson. In my opinion, he needs to be the next captain you name."

Another former Ryder Cup player I reached out to was Jim Gallagher Jr. He is from Indiana, and he was also part of the '93 team at The Belfry.

"I remember flying to England, and before we landed Tom got up and addressed everybody. He said 'Gentlemen, we are going to the part of the world where they invented the game. But we are going to show them who perfected it.' There was no way that we were going to lose for Tom Watson," Gallagher said.

"We had a situation during the Ryder Cup when somebody put an extra club in Payne (Stewart's) bag one night while it was in the U.S. locker room. Fortunately, it was discovered before he started playing the match, or it would have violated the 14-club rule, causing a penalty. A lot of the guys were really fired up because we thought somebody was trying to sabotage us," Jim said. "Tom just took control of the situation. He told us to go play golf and let him worry about that. The story never got out. Tom had our backs the whole week."

The more people I talked to, the more it just strengthened my opinion that Watson was definitely the right choice. That still did not mean it would be easy to persuade my fellow PGA officers and key staff that Watson, not Toms, needed to be the captain. So, I went to work compiling an extensive document.

It consisted of 85 pages and told everything there was to tell about Watson: all of his playing accomplishments; details of his 10–4–1 record as a Ryder Cup player; the 1993 matches at The Belfry. I also included information about Tom's failed marriage to his first wife, Linda. In addition, I highlighted his ability to recover from alcoholism and his firm political stance in 1990 against the Kansas City Country Club's prejudice against Jews, which was later reversed. And, of course, I included his comments about Tiger Woods.

I tested the waters informally with Jim Remy, the honorary PGA president. He immediately liked the idea. As Remy thought more about it, he became my biggest supporter of Watson. Steranka was not crazy about bringing back Watson. Mason clearly was a little distressed about breaking up the order on his napkin. Allen Wronowski, the PGA president, was totally against the idea of Watson. Allen was firmly in the David Toms camp. Kerry Haigh, our championships director, and Susan Martin, from Haigh's department, both worked with Watson in 1993, and they spoke highly of Tom.

Unfortunately, Huber passed away on January 3, 2012, from an aggressive form of leukemia. Jim would never see the day when Watson was announced as captain, but he had played a crucial role.

During a meeting of the PGA officers later in winter 2012, I officially proposed the idea of Watson as the 2014 captain to Remy, Wronowski, Steranka and Derek Sprague, the newly elected PGA secretary. The presentation was not about making the decision at that moment. It was simply to put the concept officially on the table for discussion. Mine was just one of the four votes. Steranka didn't have a vote, although he was going to have input as the CEO.

It was clear that Sprague supported Watson as the next captain. I decided to wait until November 2012 to pursue the matter further until we had our next PGA Officer and a new CEO.

Watson and I traded a few emails over the next few months. It was actually at the Masters during a practice round when we finally met face to face. I caught him as he was walking from the 14th green to the 15th tee. I introduced Sprague to him, and we exchanged brief pleasantries.

Some people have reported I had a longstanding relationship with Watson and that is what influenced my interest in him as a Ryder Cup captain. That could not be further from the truth. Obviously, I had watched him play over the years and met him briefly after he won the 2011 Senior PGA. I always admired Tom's competitiveness and his grace on the course. More than anything, I admired his ability to deal with adversity.

My first Open Championship was in 2009 at Turnberry. There was a moment on Sunday morning when Watson walked from the player dining room to the locker room. He was by himself and totally immersed in his thoughts. For those few seconds, it was just he and I. We passed in silence separated by inches. I wanted to wish him luck, but I respected the moment.

After Tom played nine holes in that final round, I left the golf course and headed back to Ayre to watch the tournament unfold on the BBC. Not only could I better see the action, but the great Peter Alliss would be making the historical call of Watson's quest for something no golfer had ever done before. In my opinion, Alliss delivered one of the greatest telecasts of all time. He eloquently conveyed the hope and despair of Watson's round, shot by shot. Truly, the outcome wasn't what Alliss or anybody else wanted. Poor Stewart Cink.

As fate would have it, the following morning on my flight from Glasgow to London, I was seated one row directly behind Watson; his wife Hilary; and Andy North. During the flight, people started asking Tom to sign a British tabloid containing a picture of him watching Cink raise the Claret Jug. The headline read "Cruel in the Sun."

After eight people had approached the weary Watson, a flight attendant asked Tom if he wanted the parade of autograph seekers stopped.

"No, they are fine," Watson said with a gentle smile. That was the same Tom Watson I had observed 25 years earlier at Augusta. It was a defining reason why I had so much respect for Tom and his ability to lead our Ryder Cup team.

All eyes were focused on Medinah as summer 2012 unfolded. NBC announced it would do wall-to-wall coverage of the matches, which were scheduled for the week of September 24–30. Golf Channel would devote hours of coverage to the Ryder Cup. John Cook, a member of Watson's 1993 team, would join Larry Nelson for much of the analysis during the week of the matches. I felt Nelson used his week on Golf Channel in part as an opportunity to campaign on the air for consideration as the 2014 Ryder Cup captain.

Nelson is a three-time major champion who had a 9–3–1 career Ryder Cup record. He actually won his first nine matches and showed tremendous guile with his domination of Seve Ballesteros, the great Spaniard. Nelson is also a veteran of the Vietnam War. He is a soft-spoken guy who has an impeccable reputation.

There is no question Larry should have been a Ryder Cup captain, but in the mid-1990s. The PGA could have waited in 1993 to choose Watson, who was only 44 years old at the time, but didn't. Nelson was passed over for other players in that era including Lanny Wadkins (1995) and Tom Kite (1997). Larry's omission as a Ryder Cup captain is still a great mystery.

Dick Smith served as president of the PGA in 1991–92, and he recalled: "I think I remember that each cycle that Nelson might have been a consideration, there happened to be a "bigger" name also available, and that his non-selection was more a matter of poor timing than anything else. Watson in 1993 and Wadkins in 1995. Also, I think he was still an active player on the TOUR, and we seemed to always shy away from that."

Gary Schaal, who served as PGA president in 1992–93, said, "I would have to agree with (Dick) Smith, but would add that the matrix we were using was a bit congested with choices, and Kite (1997) seemed to make sense at the time."

On Sunday morning before the start of the final round of the Medinah Ryder Cup, I was summoned to the putting green by

NBC's Jimmy Roberts. He made an impassioned plea for Nelson as the 2014 captain. Roberts emphasized Larry's military service, and I later found out Jimmy was going to Vietnam with Nelson for a segment on Golf Channel's "In Play."

There was no doubt Larry rekindled the fire for his captainship during that week at Medinah. And I say this in a curious way because before that, there had been no discussion about naming him as the 2014 Ryder Cup captain. While I was sympathetic to Nelson's plight, I did not feel it was the responsibility of today's PGA of America to correct a 20-year-old mistake. For me, this was all about Tom Watson being the best choice in Scotland. I have never felt anyone should be picked as a ceremonious Ryder Cup captain to recognize his playing accomplishments. The PGA has a responsibility to pick the most qualified man for the job. In my mind, that was clearly Watson in 2014 at Gleneagles.

When Martin Kaymer sank the winning putt at Medinah late Sunday afternoon to give Europe yet another win, I was more convinced than ever that Watson was the right guy. Davis Love would get criticized for being soft and too much of a player's captain—particularly given his decision to let Mickelson and Bradley sit on Saturday afternoon at Mickelson's behest. Love would take the criticism for that, not Mickelson.

Less than two weeks later, on Tuesday, October 9, 2012, I headed to Kansas City to do a lengthy Medinah debrief with Watson. Tom and I spent nearly six hours discussing all aspects of the Ryder Cup. At times we were joined by his wife, Hilary; Kelly Fray, Tom's administrative assistant; and Steve Glassman, who represents Watson. The primary purpose of the meeting was to make sure there were no impending issues between Watson and the PGA of America. As soon as I became president, we would be conducting the "formal interview" with him. I wanted no surprises down the road, and there were none.

David Toms had sent me a short three-sentence letter in October. It was his formal request to be considered as the 2014

Ryder Cup captain. It was the only written request the PGA received. We got nothing from Nelson. Soon after Medinah ended, I did start to receive phone calls from people who had opinions on who the next captain should be.

Love called me late in the month and opined that it should be David Toms. He told me he had advised Toms to notify the PGA of his interest, and he told David to not be overly persistent. I informed Love we had received David's letter, but we were headed in a different direction. Love asked if it was Nelson. I told Love that Watson was probably going to be the choice. Love was shocked but unequivocally supported the choice. "I would give anything to be an assistant captain under Tom," Love said.

"Watson has a tremendous amount of respect from the players. People say you need to go out of the box with the next captain, and this is just that. I got criticized for being too soft, and Tom is the opposite of that. And I think he is more relatable than Larry (Nelson) because Tom is still out there at the majors playing. Let's face it, Watson can still beat a lot of the guys."

Curtis Strange had captained the 2002 Ryder Cup team at The Belfry in England. He called me to offer strong support for Nelson. "The PGA needs to correct the mistake it made years ago and name Larry Nelson as the next Ryder Cup captain," Strange said. "We need a guy who can command respect from the players. A guy like a Nicklaus or a Palmer or a Watson. Larry is that kind of guy." I listened intently to him, but I got great satisfaction on his remark about Watson. I didn't tell Curtis where we were headed—not just yet.

Lanny Wadkins was another former Ryder Cup captain who was profoundly in Watson's corner. He felt Tom was just what the U.S. needed at that moment. Wadkins viewed Watson as a guy who had the fortitude to make tough decisions. "He won't hesitate to sit anybody down or tell them to get out there and play. Tom will always do what's in the best interest of the team. It won't make any difference who the player is, he's not afraid of anybody," Lanny remarked.

On November 10, 2012, I became the 38th president of the PGA of America. Sprague moved up to vice president, and Paul Levy was elected secretary. Derek and I brought Levy up to speed on what had transpired with Watson over the past two years. Levy supported Watson's captainship. It was typical for the newly elected PGA secretary to be in this position. Lehman was picked before Remy was elected PGA secretary. The same was true for Wronowski with Azinger, me with Pavin, and Sprague with Love.

The PGA officers were scheduled to be in Kansas City on November 14 for the formal Tom Watson interview. Joining us would be Pete Bevacqua, newly appointed CEO. He thought the Watson pick was "brilliant." Also in the PGA party would be Mason, Haigh and Martin. As we sat in the West Palm Beach airport, awaiting our flight, Tim Rosaforte of Golf Channel strolled by. We sank down in our seats so he wouldn't see us. Tim was the one guy in the media who took pride in scooping the PGA on its Ryder Cup captain choices. At this point, not even Rosaforte suspected Watson.

Our interview that afternoon lasted for about an hour and a half. It was a great chance for my fellow officers and Bevacqua to get to know Watson better. There were no surprises, and Watson was "officially" approved as the 2014 Ryder Cup captain in a unanimous vote.

That evening we had dinner in a private room at the Capital Grill at The Plaza in downtown Kansas City. For me, it was a combination of relief and great satisfaction. When I proposed a toast to our new captain, everyone but Tom raised a glass of wine. He lifted his water glass. I had asked Watson earlier how he felt about people drinking in his presence. He had no problem with it. For the next two years nobody in the PGA ever would have more than one drink in Tom's presence. We all respected what he had overcome.

Over the next few weeks, the PGA somehow managed to keep the Watson choice a secret to the media. In early December, I shared the Watson pick with the PGA Board of Directors and asked to ratify the decision. The board did unanimously and with much enthusiasm.

The PGA announcement was slated for Thursday, December 13, 2012, in New York City. Bevacqua and I attended meetings with many of our broadcast partners early in the week. CBS, NBC and Turner were all excited with the choice of Watson. His stature in the game had taken this Ryder Cup announcement to another level. In an unprecedented move, NBC insisted we do the announcement live on The Today Show with Matt Lauer.

The PGA had scheduled media training with Watson and me on the day before the announcement. It was held in my suite at the Waldorf-Astoria. Inga Hammond, formerly of CNN and Golf Channel, conducted the intense session. The PGA anticipated that Watson would be questioned about his role with Woods, so the bulk of his work was centered there.

My media training wound up more complicated than I had expected because the Larry Nelson situation had taken a turn for the worse. Early that Wednesday morning, I had called David Toms to thank him for his interest in being a Ryder Cup captain, and told him we were announcing Tom Watson as the choice. David, who answered his phone from a duck blind in Arkansas, took the news very graciously.

A few minutes later I did a national radio interview with Matt Adams. He asked me if I had talked to Toms or Nelson. I simply said, "Yes," because I just had spoken with Toms. The PGA was still not confirming Watson as the captain. After the Adams interview, Golf Channel reported that I said I had talked to both Toms and Nelson. Larry was playing in the annual Father-Son tournament in Florida. He was informed by a member of the media that "Ted Bishop has said he spoke with you about the Ryder Cup captainship."

As you can expect, Nelson wasn't happy. And neither was I because I never said I talked with Larry. By mid-afternoon, I did have a chance to speak with Nelson. I told him I had not called him previously because the PGA did not make it a practice to notify everyone we did not choose. I explained I decided to call Toms earlier that morning because he had been the only one to actually write the PGA a letter requesting consideration as a captain.

"This is the second time I have been passed over because of Tom Watson," said an irritated Nelson. "It's not fair to me, and I think I deserve to be a Ryder Cup captain."

I told Larry I could sympathize with how he felt, and I agreed he should have been a captain back in the 1990s. That being said, Watson was clearly our choice because of his success in Scotland as a player, plus Tom had been the last winning U.S. captain on foreign soil. I went on to tell Larry that the choice of Watson did not mean future PGA officers might not still choose him. In my opinion, Tom had broken down the age barrier for captains, and that was in Larry's favor. Nelson is two years older than Watson.

But it was still a stressful conversation. I wish Nelson would have been more direct with his desires to be considered as the '14 Ryder Cup captain early on, rather than lobbying publicly for the job on television and through the media. Maybe Larry figures he deserves some consideration as a captain for each Ryder Cup. He probably feels that his time is running out. In retrospect, I wish I would have called Larry after Medinah and told him where we were going with the captain's choice.

Wednesday night, I called Curtis Strange and informed him we did listen to what he had said about the next captain. He said, "You mean Larry is the guy?"

"Not exactly," I said. "We picked someone you said would command respect from the players. We selected Tom Watson."

"Well, you can't argue with Tom as a captain. But I still think Larry deserves it at some point," Curtis said.

After the Today Show announcement at 8:30 a.m. on Thursday, December 12, we attended the official press conference at 10 a.m. in the Empire State Building. It was an incredibly exciting day. Accolades were rolling in from around the world on the Watson selection. Even Tiger Woods had sent Tom a congratulatory text.

I told the crowded group of reporters, "We haven't won a Ryder Cup on foreign soil since 1993 at The Belfry, and Tom was the captain when that happened. We are tired of losing Ryder Cups. That is why we picked Tom. He is a proven winner as a player and captain. Tom is the greatest modern player in the history of Scotland, and we are honored to have him as our captain at Gleneagles in 2014."

Tom Watson was a popular choice.

"I think he's a really good choice," Tiger Woods said in a statement. "Tom knows what it takes to win, and that's our ultimate goal. I hope I have the privilege of joining him on the 2014 United States team."

"My relationship with Tiger is fine," Watson said. "Whatever has been said before is water under the bridge. No issues. He's the best player maybe in the history of the game."

"Tom Watson will be an excellent captain, as he was in 1993 when I played for him," Paul Azinger said. "The PGA of America did the right thing at the right time."

"I remember the Saturday at Royal St. George's in 2011 when the rain was coming down sideways, and Tom had a smile on his face when he went out to play the third round," Rickie Fowler said. "He enjoyed every minute of making the best of the weather. I saw that, and I wanted to do the same, and I played my best round. I love his attitude, and it will carry over to the team."

"Tom Watson makes perfect sense to me," Steve Stricker said. "He's one of the all-time best players and winners, and he's beloved over the pond. It's a great choice."

"I'm a huge Tom Watson fan. I'm thrilled the PGA of America was thinking outside the box, and Tom is a great choice," Brandt Snedeker said. "He's a decorated winner over the world, and his success in Europe and Scotland gives us a lot of credibility over there."

Even players from Europe thought Watson was a great choice.

"It's very hard to quantify how much difference a captain makes to the end result, but Tom Watson will very much be welcomed in Scotland," Luke Donald said. "He has a no-nonsense approach to golf—he's all about winning, and I'm sure his players will feed off that mentally."

"Watson is one of the legends of the game. I am sure he would be a fantastic captain, not just for the team but that whole aspect of the Ryder Cup," Darren Clarke said. "The man is a huge name in the world of golf and rightly so. I think he will make a fantastic captain for the Americans."

The Europeans had not yet announced their next Ryder Cup captain. The Watson selection prompted people like Colin Montgomerie and Clarke to say their side would have to take a step back. Both felt the Europeans now needed to select someone who had a strong stature in the game because that would be needed to match wits with Watson. The countdown to Gleneagles officially began.

In October 2013, NBC announced it would televise every shot hit during the Scotland event. This was a first for a foreign Ryder Cup. With the five-hour time change on the East Coast of the U.S., it meant that Golf Channel would come on the air at 3 a.m. Eastern time when the matches started Friday morning. I'm confident this happened in large part because of the excitement the Watson selection generated. Ryder Cup fever was reaching an all-time high. Never in the history of the matches had the hype reached this level so far in advance of the start of the matches.

"The difference between Europe and the United States when it comes to the Ryder Cup is this," Watson once told me. "In Europe they talk about the Ryder Cup every day of the year. Here, they don't start writing about it until the majors are over in the summer of the Ryder Cup."

Tom Watson had changed all of that. And I felt confident that he was going to change our recent fortunes in the matches the United States had once dominated.

Minutes before throwing out the first pitch before the Nationals-Brewers game. Listening to Davey Johnson talk about almost becoming a PGA member, but lamenting the fact that the PGA made it harder than he wanted it to be.

The PGA did its part in recognizing Derek Jeter's great career as a Yankee by presenting him with a set of golf clubs to enjoy in his retirement. As a lifelong long Yankee fan it was a thrill to be at home plate in The Stadium.

With Tom Watson prior to the start of the pro-am at the 2014 Senior PGA Championship at Harbor Shores Golf Club in Benton Harbor, Michigan. I spent many happy times with Tom.

The last official photo? On the first tee at Gleneagles. Little did I know that this would probably be it for me with Pete Bevacqua, Derek Sprague and Paul Levy. Guys that I once talked to on a daily basis, but basically never again after 10/24/14. Particularly in Bevacqua's case. A guy I hired, promoted and formed a tremendously productive working relationship with. I can't help but feel betrayed and unfriended by Pete more than anyone else.

Ian Poulter has truly been the heart and soul of the European Ryder Cup team in the past decade. I have always respected his competitive spirit and meant no disrespect to him when I labeled his comments about Tom Watson and Nick Faldo as "lil' girlish." Bad choice of words on my part. However, Watson and Faldo combined 14 majors and 75 PGA Tour titles compared to Poulter's zero majors and two PGA Tour wins-laughable.

Sharing a few laughs with Sergio Garcia and Justin Rose at a 15-inch cup outing sponsored by TaylorMade's Mark King. I had friends on the European Ryder Cup team, too!

Jason Day finished runner-up to Louis Oosthuizen in the PGA's Long Drive Contest at the 2014 PGA Championship. Jack Nicklaus had won this long drive contest years ago. We brought it back to Valhalla after we found out he was still carrying a money clip commemorating his win.

These were the inaugural Drive, Chip and Putt winners at Augusta National in 2014. I know that Tom O'Toole, USGA President and Billy Payne, Masters Chairman, loved the day as much as I did.

Rickie Fowler is one of my favorites on the PGA TOUR. A great player who understands his role when it comes to inspiring today's youth. Hopefully, Rickie continues to attract new players to the game.

Enjoying a light-hearted moment with the media at the 2013 PGA Championship at Oak Hill Country Club in Rochester, New York. Most of the media were my friends and I enjoyed that part of my presidency very much.

On stage at NBC's Saturday Night Live Studio during the Captain's pick announcements. G-Fore owes me lifetime royalties for promoting those stars and stripes socks!

With my wife, Cindy, at a school in Auchturarder, Scotland one year before the Ryder Cup. The Scots implemented a class on the history of the Ryder Cup into their educational curriculum in 2013. The Europeans take the Ryder Cup to another level.

I have been asked many times about my greatest accomplishment as PGA president. Without question it was working with Tim Finchem to elevate the relationship between the TOUR and the PGA. The Commissioner was a great friend and ally- and still is.

Rory McIlroy saved the day when he snatched the top of the Wanamaker Trophy before it fell on the ground during the presentation in the darkness at Valhalla. The trophy weighs 35 pounds and I lost control when I tried to shake his hand. "I knew that top came off," said Rory afterwards. "I have taken a drink from the Wanamaker on several occasions!"

Captain's Announcement: Tom Watson explains his captain's pick during a live televised show on Golf Channel. No Ryder Cup captain has ever been asked to do more by the PGA than Watson was. He handled the good and as well as the bad with grace and class.

# Chapter Ten

# Victory Has a Thousand Fathers But Defeat is an Orphan

Tuesday, September 23, 2014, brought a crisp Scottish morning. The Ryder Cup was finally here. For me, it was like being a kid again and waiting for Christmas. Two long years had passed since that bitter loss at Medinah in Chicago, but it felt so much longer.

There had not been a day since I became the 38th President of the PGA of America in which I had not devoted some task or thought to this Ryder Cup at Gleneagles. I had one priority, and that was a United States victory. I am sure the same could be said for Tom Watson, our captain.

"If we win this thing, why would we not ask Tom to come back and do it again? He has done an amazing job," PGA CEO Pete Bevacqua said to me that Tuesday morning as the Scottish sunshine started to break the chill.

"Obviously that's not my call," I replied to Pete. "That decision will be Derek (Sprague) and others'. I don't even know if Tom would agree to do it again. But I do know that no one could have done a better job as captain than Tom has."

"I agree with that," Pete replied.

The PGA asked Watson to have more media interaction in the two years leading up to Gleneagles than any captain in Ryder Cup history. Tom never balked. But there were a multitude of other reasons Pete and I both thought Tom Watson was a great captain.

In that first conversation I had with Tom in November 2011, he talked about the PGA TOUR schedule leading into the Ryder Cup. With the advent of the FedExCup playoffs, the players no longer had a week off before the Ryder Cup. Most of the players on the U.S. team had to play five of six weeks before heading into the pressure cooker of the Ryder Cup matches.

"I think our players are tired when the Ryder Cup begins," Watson had told me. "If I am the captain, I will talk to (Tim) Finchem about moving the TOUR Championship up a week so the players can have some time off before the Ryder Cup starts."

When Tom relayed his thoughts to me, I immediately reached out to Finchem. This change would cause the PGA TOUR to make a major adjustment in its 2014 schedule, one piece in the puzzle of collaborations between the TOUR and the PGA of America. From the beginning of our relationship, Tim and I continually had discussions about what our organizations could do for each other and how decisions could would benefit TOUR players and PGA members.

In summer 2013, the PGA TOUR Policy Board approved the elimination of the week off between the BMW Championship and The TOUR Championship. This was huge legislation because it meant the FedExCup would be played four straight weeks in 2014, giving Watson's team a week off before the start of the Ryder Cup.

The TOUR was making a major sacrifice for the sake of the Ryder Cup. That was unparalleled. At the PGA TOUR Policy Board meeting, Jim Furyk and Steve Stricker adamantly supported Watson's request. "If this is what Tom wants, then this is what we need to do," Furyk said. The measure passed unanimously.

Ryder Cup details were Watson's obsession. He was committed to working with Polo Ralph Lauren on developing U.S. rainsuits that would perform in Scotland. With Tom's influence

Polo created several different thicknesses of Gore-Tex, the waterproof garment. This would ensure the players had the appropriate weight of outerwear no matter the temperature. The team would have three different rainsuits when we got to Gleneagles.

Watson took great care in choosing the proper outerwear. He had Polo send samples to his house near Kansas City, Missouri. His wife, Hilary, laughs when she tells the rest of the story.

"Can you believe that Tom put those rainsuits on and stood in the shower for long periods of time making sure they didn't leak?" Hilary once confided to me.

Yes, I could believe that. Tom also had Polo embroider "United We Stand" inside the team uniforms. He was hoping to create an atmosphere of solidarity within our team. I was actually able to persuade Tom we should allow PGA members to sell the official Sunday Ryder Cup shirt in their golf shops. What better way for Americans to show their support to our team? It would be like fans wearing jerseys to football or baseball games. After some convincing on my part, Tom begrudgingly agreed with my "All in for the Win" idea.

Watson had obtained the topographical maps on the Centenary course at Gleneagles. This would be the venue where the 2014 Ryder Cup was played. It was a Jack Nicklaus design deemed to be "a modern classic." Tom knew the course well in advance of the Ryder Cup.

Watson also made a concerted effort to get to know his players. Every time he played in a major championship or in a PGA TOUR event, he would make a point of playing practice rounds with guys who might be on his team. He was evaluating their games but, more importantly, their minds. Tom was looking for a combination of talent and toughness.

One of Watson's strengths was that his golf game could still compete with today's players. Even though he was the oldest Ryder Cup captain ever, he was beating many of the potential European and U.S. team members at the majors in 2013–14. Watson's sharp playing skills built up credibility with the players.

It was very satisfying to hear many of the young American stars on the PGA TOUR talk about how much they wanted to make this Ryder Cup team and play for Watson. My first experience with Jordan Spieth was in an elevator at The Presidents Cup in 2013. Spieth was just a rookie and he had made the U.S. team as one of Fred Couples' captain's picks at Muirfield Village Golf Club in Columbus, Ohio. Tom was pleased to see Spieth get the chance at some international team experience.

"I can't tell you how happy Tom was to see you make this Presidents Cup team," I told Spieth. "We are all rooting for you to have a good year so you make the Ryder Cup team."

"That is my main goal for 2014," Spieth said. "I want to play for Tom Watson."

In the two years that led up to Gleneagles, I thought Watson firmly established himself as a player's captain. At the "Year-to-Go Celebration" in September 2013, Tom spent considerable time doing a walkthrough of the elaborate Gleneagles Hotel, the official Ryder Cup hotel for both teams. He was into every detail. With the cooperation of the PGA, Tom and Hilary designed a massive team room plus other amenities, including a private meeting room where team strategy could be discussed.

It was during these few days in Scotland when Tom came to me with a request. He asked that the team room at the Gleneagles Hotel be devoted solely to the players, captains and their wives. Watson wanted no presence from the official PGA party, which included our officers along with Tim and Holly Finchem.

"I want an environment where I don't have to worry about asking people to leave the room because I have something to say to just the players. I hope you understand, Ted. This is important to me," Watson said.

The request caught me off guard because the official party always had access to the team room. I asked Watson if there had been problems or complaints from the past. The PGA official party had always gone to great lengths to stay out of the way. Watson assured me there were no problems in the past, but this is how he wanted it done this time. I agreed and eventually told the rest of the official party that Tom had requested this. It was our job to support him.

For my own piece of mind, I did reach out to Davis Love III, Steve Stricker and Jim Furyk when I returned. All three had been involved with the past two Ryder Cups, and I wanted to confirm that there were no previous issues with the official party in the team room. They all said there were no problems. Furyk even took it further.

"I hate to hear that you guys won't be in the team room," Jim said. "It was always a good way for the younger guys to put a name with a face and better understand what the PGA of America is to the Ryder Cup."

The PGA officers would still work with the team during the Gleneagles matches. We would help the assistant captains drive golf cars and assist with player and caddie needs. We would also have full access in the locker room and team dining area during the matches. Watson did let me address the team upon our arrival Monday night at Gleneagles. It would give me a chance to inform the players better on what the role of the PGA of America is at the Ryder Cup.

Watson scheduled practice rounds at Gleneagles in July 2014 on the weekend before the Open Championship, which was being held at Royal Liverpool. This also came during the weekend of the Scottish Open. Several potential members of the U.S. team were playing at Royal Aberdeen and only two players took up Tom on the chance to get a look at Gleneagles.

Keegan Bradley flew in early on Saturday morning. Bradley had established himself at Medinah as a fiery character racking up a 3–1 record in his debut. If Bradley was going to make the team, it would probably need to be as a captain's pick unless he won a PGA TOUR event in the next few weeks. Keegan, Tom and I were set to play around 10 a.m. when Watson noticed Golf-week's Alex Miceli hanging around the first tee of the Centenary course. Tom told Alex to get his clubs and join us as our fourth player.

There were several hundred Scots who had gotten word Watson was playing the course. They followed us during the round. It was a fun day, and the course appeared perfect for Brad-ley's style of play. He was long, and the greens were relatively flat.

"I can't let this influence my decision," Tom confided later to me. "It was a great effort by Keegan to get here and play. As much as I want him on the team, he has got to earn his spot based on his performance the rest of the year."

After we played golf, the four of us were joined by Kerry Haigh, chief championship officer from the PGA of America. We had a private lunch in the Gleneagles clubhouse. Bradley soon left and headed to Liverpool. For the next three hours, Watson grilled Miceli about American players. At that point, there were probably still 30 guys who could make the U.S. team.

When Alex departed that Saturday afternoon, I asked Tom what his plans were with the assistant captains. Watson had named Andy North early on as his first assistant captain. Ray-mond Floyd had been chosen in February to be another assistant. Tom always said he wasn't a big fan of four assistant captains, but I thought he needed them. It was pretty apparent that the best hope was for one more assistant captain, and I felt it needed to be a younger guy who could relate to today's players.

"You need at least one more assistant captain," I told Tom. "You would be doing the PGA a big favor if you would consider Steve Stricker because there is a good chance that he might some-day be a Ryder Cup captain."

"Duly noted," Watson said firmly with a nod of his head. Less than a month later, Tom introduced Stricker at the PGA Championship as his third assistant captain.

On Sunday, Furyk joined Tom and me for his practice round on the Centenary course. Like Bradley, Jim had flown all night to get to Gleneagles. He was operating on little or no sleep, and he was also headed to Royal Liverpool. I had breakfast with Jim and asked him why he made the effort to be there, given that he was a lock to make the 2014 team.

"I'm tired of getting my ass kicked in the Ryder Cup," Furyk said. "I'm like everybody else. I'm tired of losing, and I'm willing to do whatever it takes to win this thing."

It was another enjoyable day on the course. Watson loved sharing the intricacies of the Centenary course with these players. Bradley and Furyk had contrasting styles, and that was beneficial for Watson to see how players with different lengths would attack Gleneagles. Tom told me he was disappointed more players didn't show up that weekend; it was an extremely valuable experience for him as the captain.

Talk about a dream week for me. It started Wednesday, when I played with Phil Mickelson and Alex Salmond, the first minister of Scotland, in the pro-am at the Scottish Open. In the previous five days, I had played with Tom Watson twice, Phil Mickelson, Keegan Bradley and Jim Furyk.

After we finished our round, we all boarded a plane headed to Liverpool. Furyk and Watson talked about the Centenary course, and both thought it was very much "an American-style" course, which would be good for our team.

"There will be times when the wind is not a factor, and this course will be a birdie fest," Watson said. "Other times, if the wind is blowing, holes like No. 3 and No. 5 are going to be tough."

Tom knew what he was talking about. He had arranged for the services of a Scottish weather expert who had given him a bevy of weather history and what to expect during the last week of September at Gleneagles.

Soon after I returned home from the U.K., I was playing in my Saturday morning men's club when I received a call from

Tom. I apologized to my playing partners and took Tom's call in the middle of the No. 2 fairway at The Legends.

"I've been thinking," Tom began. "One piece that we are missing is a team doctor. I think we need our own doctor. Somebody that speaks our language and who will make our players and wives feel at ease if they need any kind of treatment.

"I have a doctor who has treated me at the Mayo Clinic," he continued, "and he would do this for the PGA. What do you think?"

This was another case of Watson covering the details. To my knowledge the PGA had never done this. When I checked with Haigh, he confirmed that the U.S. had always used the European medical staff on-site. I told Kerry this was important to Tom, and I consented. So, Dr. Ian D. Hay, who actually has Scottish roots, joined the U.S. team.

Watson also insisted the team eat in Atlanta before heading to Scotland on Sunday night. This would allow us to forego meal service on the plane, which would give everyone a chance to get more sleep, reducing the ill effects of jet lag. He always told me it took five days for the body to adjust to Scotland's time difference.

The only real drama that existed with the Watson captaincy in the months leading up to the Ryder Cup stemmed from questions about Tiger Woods and his health. Would Tiger be physically ready to play at Gleneagles? He had a stellar 2013 season, winning five times on the PGA TOUR, but a back injury in '14 had limited Woods to only seven starts by midsummer.

From the beginning of his captaincy, Watson had told me Woods and Mickelson would be on this team. Tom had been more public in his comments about Tiger than Phil. But there was never any doubt in my mind that both would be on Watson's team unless injury prevented it.

Watson's relationship with Mickelson intrigued me. Both were strong personalities. Both liked being in control. Tom had won eight major championships and 39 PGA TOUR events, compared to Phil's five majors and 42 PGA TOUR victories. But there was a rub between the two that was evident in the lead-up to Gleneagles.

Watson had miffed some players, including Mickelson, when he made a comment that he would not be afraid to "tell one of these prima donnas they were going to sit, or play" if the circumstances dictated so. This comment quickly circulated around the caddie yard.

Jim "Bones" Mackay, Mickelson's caddie, had remarked to another caddie, "What's Watson thinking about with that 'prima donna' comment?" It was evident Phil's camp took Tom's comments personally.

During the Scottish Open pro-am I asked Phil why the U.S. wins Presidents Cups and loses Ryder Cups. He credited Fred Couples and his ability to utilize lunar and solar effects when it comes to pairing players. Phil was serious.

"Certain players are just going to have good or bad weeks based on the position of the sun," Phil told me. "There are charts that depict this, and Fred studies them."

I asked Mickelson if he had ever discussed this with Watson.

"No, Tom would never listen to that," Phil said. "He has his own way of doing things."

A week later at a dinner hosted by the Royal and Ancient during the Open Championship, I ran into Mark Steinberg, Woods' agent. He pointed his finger at me and offered the following: "You tell your man that my man wants to be on that Ryder Cup team."

After I texted the message to Watson, he responded, "Tell Steinberg to have his man call me."

When I passed this on to Steinberg, he fired back by saying Tiger had already spent time with Andy North, reminding me they shared a long lunch, and Tiger had expressed his desire to be on the U.S. team.

I told Steinberg that Andy was not the Ryder Cup captain. "Your man should call the captain," I said.

Woods did call Watson before the PGA Championship. Tiger was on vacation with his kids and, according to Tom, they had a very good conversation. Tom trusted Tiger would be honest with him. Watson expressed this very point on August 7, 2014, at his press conference on the Wednesday before the start of the PGA Championship at Valhalla Golf Club in Louisville, Kentucky.

"I've said it before that he's an automatic pick," Watson told the media. You can't have a player of that caliber not on the team. But that has to be weighed next to what his health is. I hope he can get back in the swing, because he wasn't playing his best even before the surgery. But if he's not physically right, Tiger will be the first one to tell me."

At the same time, there had been no public validation by Watson for Mickelson's position on the team. Phil headed into the PGA Championship in a precarious spot, outside of the automatic nine to make the team on points and needing Watson's nod as a captain's pick. That all changed Sunday, when Phil finished in second place to Rory McIlroy as darkness fell over Valhalla. The runner-up finish had given Mickelson enough points to move into fifth place on the points list and secure his position on the 2014 Ryder Cup team.

I will always feel Mickelson's ego had been bruised because Phil had not received the same public assurance from Watson that Woods had received about a guaranteed spot on the team. But there was never any doubt in my mind that Mickelson was always going to be on Tom's team. In fairness to Watson, he had to be hoping he didn't have to burn a captain's pick on Phil.

The mystery surrounding Woods' injury came to an end in the week after the PGA Championship. Woods had flown in Wednesday of the PGA, played a nine-hole practice round and left Valhalla with no chance of playing in the PGA, due to his back. Watson called Woods, and Tiger informed Tom he would not be able to play in the Ryder Cup. Tiger's status was officially revealed August 13.

A couple weeks earlier, Dustin Johnson announced he was taking a leave of absence from the PGA TOUR for "personal reasons." Johnson had already locked up one of the nine automatic Ryder Cup spots, but he would forego the competition at Gleneagles. Jason Dufner, the defending PGA champion, withdrew from Valhalla with a neck injury, and that eliminated any chance he'd be on the U.S. team.

The U.S. had now lost three players who earlier figured to be pivotal on Watson's 2014 team. Johnson and Dufner had both played brilliantly at Medinah. Johnson was 4–0 and Dufner was 3–1 for the U.S. in 2012. Many had felt the Centenary course was tailor-made for Johnson's length. Dufner had ice water in his veins at Medinah and would be missed. Tiger Woods was still one of the most intimidating players in the game.

Even with the loss of three players, Watson stayed extremely positive, and so did I. Getting back to what Jim Gallagher Jr. had said about his experience at The Belfry, in my mind there was no way we were going to lose for Tom Watson. It was false optimism because when the matches began at Gleneagles, the European team was be much stronger on paper, boasting four of the top five players in the Official World Golf Ranking.

The nine automatic U.S. berths went to Bubba Watson, Rickie Fowler, Jim Furyk, Jimmy Walker, Phil Mickelson, Matt Kuchar, Jordan Spieth, Patrick Reed and Zach Johnson. At No. 4 in the world, Furyk was the highest-ranked American. Walker, Spieth and Reed were all Ryder Cup rookies.

Tom's last duty before we headed to Scotland was to announce his three captain's picks on Tuesday evening, September 2, in a made-for-TV event on Golf Channel. The PGA staged this at 7 p.m. from the studio of "Saturday Night Live." In attendance were real estate magnate Donald Trump and former New York

City Mayor Rudy Giuliani. It was the most widely publicized captain's pick announcement in the history of the Ryder Cup.

Two of Watson's picks were seemingly obvious. Hunter Mahan was the hottest player outside of the automatic nine. He had won The Barclays, which was the first leg of the FedExCup Playoffs in late August. Hunter owned a 3–2–3 career record in two Ryder Cup appearances. Bradley was the other choice, and I felt it was mainly because of his success with Mickelson at Medinah, where they compiled a 3–0 record as partners.

The final captain's pick was coming from muddy waters. Chris Kirk won the Deutsche Bank Championship on the day before Tom announced his picks. But Kirk had faltered down the stretch and did nothing to endear himself to Watson with the way he played the final hole as he limped to victory. It boiled down to Webb Simpson or Bill Haas. Flip a coin. Ultimately, Watson chose Simpson because he had partnered successfully with Bubba Watson at Medinah.

The European team, led by captain Paul McGinley, would consist of Rory McIlroy, Henrik Stenson, Victor Dubuisson, Jamie Donaldson, Sergio Garcia, Justin Rose, Martin Kaymer, Thomas Bjorn, Graeme McDowell, Stephen Gallacher, Ian Poulter and Lee Westwood. Dubuisson, Donaldson and Gallacher were all Ryder Cup rookies.

In retrospect, there was no way the Americans matched up well with the Europeans. McGinley's players had participated in a combined total of 32 matches and compiled an overall Ryder Cup record of 69–42–18 for a .622 winning percentage. Watson's team, on the other hand, played in 29 Ryder Cups—17 of those by Furyk and Mickelson. The Americans had a record of 43–52–18 for a winning percentage of .453.

The only player who opted not to fly with the team to Gleneagles was Mickelson. Tom approved Phil's request to arrive a few days earlier with his family and justified it publicly as "Phil needing to take care of some business and get his body acclimated to the different time zone." Watson's only request was that Phil and his wife, Amy, meet the U.S. team at the airport when it arrived in Scotland in order to be part of the U.S. team picture upon arrival.

The Europeans won the 2014 Ryder Cup at Gleneagles by a lopsided margin of 16 ½ to 11 ½. Over the three days of competition, they outperformed the Americans by 35 shots. That being said, Watson's squad was snakebitten in a couple key match losses when McIlroy and Poulter pulled off heroics with long putts and chip-ins.

Even on Sunday, when the U.S. was down 10–6 heading into the singles matches, a fast start by the Americans gave some slim hope that an unlikely comeback might be in the making. But eventually the U.S. team faltered.

I spent the entire week driving Watson around the Centenary course. No PGA president ever spent as much time with the Ryder Cup captain during the practice rounds or matches than I did with Tom. When it was apparent Sunday that our efforts over the past two years were going up in flames, it was hard to describe the emotions.

The only time Watson ever expressed any regrets to me came Sunday morning as we watched Zach Johnson play the opening hole in the final singles match of the day. Tom wasn't giving up by any means, but I think the reality of what might happen was setting in.

"Ted, I will tell you my biggest mistake this week. I did not make these guys prepare the way you have to for a Ryder Cup," Tom said softly. "I let them do their own thing in the practice rounds, and I just don't feel like I did all I could to help them get ready."

I knew exactly what Tom was referring to. Those damned money games they play. It was a telling comment, and it demonstrated the generational differences between Watson's era and that of today's players in terms of Ryder Cup preparation. I look back at that now and think how this was another example of Tom truly being a "player's captain" and letting his guys prepare in their own way. Can you imagine how Phil would have reacted to Tom trying to coach him on how to play a practice round at the Ryder Cup? His comment also immediately brought me back to a couple incidents earlier in the week.

Wednesday, there had been a terse exchange between Mickelson and Watson when Phil's foursome was stuck behind Furyk, Kuchar, Johnson and Mahan in the practice round. It was Phil, Fowler, Walker and Bradley waiting, and they were involved in their own money game. Mickelson was frustrated because it was the day of the Ryder Cup Gala, and he was afraid his group might not get the match completed. Tom told Phil he was welcome to skip a hole and go around the group ahead. Mickelson wasn't pleased with Watson's response, and you could sense the tension.

On another occasion early in the week, Tom and I were sitting in the golf car watching a group hit shots into the 14th green. There was a front pin placement that day, and Watson was lamenting the fact that the players were actually aiming at the pin.

"The pin will never be there during the matches," Tom said. "When I was playing, we would be firing at that shelf over on the left because we knew that's where the pin might be on Sunday."

No sooner than those words left Tom's lips, Webb Simpson threw his iron shot into the back left corner of the green. The captain nudged me and said, "See, that's what I'm talking about."

He jumped out of the golf car and approached Simpson with a fist pump. "Great shot, Webb. Wasn't that where you were trying to hit it?" Watson asked.

"No, captain, I just came over the top of it and tugged it left," Simpson said.

Watson dejectedly sat back down in the cart. He looked at me with a grin and just rolled his eyes.

The post-Ryder Cup critics, many who had lauded his choice in 2012, would say Watson was too old and that he wound up not being relatable to the modern-day players. Tom's choice of two older assistant captains in North and Floyd also became a source for criticism.

In a practice round on Tuesday, I was with Floyd on the 11th green while Tom tended to some media duties. Raymond was accompanying Webb, Bubba, Spieth and Reed. There was a Jumbotron screen right next to the green, and they were showing highlights from previous Ryder Cups. At the moment our group was on the green, Floyd showed up on the big screen, and he sank a putt to win a Ryder Cup match. The players were all entranced watching highlights of Raymond's Ryder Cup performance.

"Raymond, when you were playing in the Ryder Cup, who was the one guy you really wanted to have as a partner?" Simpson asked the eight-time Ryder Cup stalwart.

Floyd never hesitated and pierced him with his competitive eyes. "Webb, it's the Ryder Cup. You play with whoever they put you with." End of story.

It was a tough week for Simpson. While he looked pretty impressive in the practice rounds from a ball-striking standpoint, that soon changed when the matches began. He and Bubba were first out on Friday in the four-ball matches. Webb popped up his opening tee shot, and that first swing told the story of the rest of his week. He struggled mightily in that first match, causing Tom to bench him until Sunday. I'm sure Tom was disappointed because he had put his own neck on the line with the pick of Simpson over Haas. Supposedly, Webb was so distraught by the benching that he had been reduced to tears and sought counseling from Mickelson.

If anything was happening behind the scenes in terms of friction between players and the captain, it was not evident to me throughout the entirety of the matches. There were decisions on pairings that would naturally ruffle a player's feathers, particularly when he was told to sit out.

Early in the week, Patrick Reed had looked like a duck out of water in Scotland. He was playing miserably Tuesday and Wednesday. At one point, Tom told me he just didn't see how he could ask anyone to pair up with Patrick as badly as he was playing. Thursday, Tom and I went to rehearse our roles in the opening ceremonies.

"I am going to put Jordan and Patrick out there on Friday morning," Watson said in a change of attitude. "It'll be like throwing two guys into the Atlantic without life preservers. They will either sink or swim. But I have to get Patrick out there. I can't wait until Sunday to play him and create that kind of pressure for him."

The decision worked out well for the two young Americans. They delivered a 5 and 4 whooping to Gallacher and Poulter. Tom was set to send them out again on Friday afternoon when he was made aware of the fact that Spieth really didn't want to be paired with Reed in the alternate-shot format because of Patrick's erratic driving. That caused Watson to send Fowler and Walker back out on Friday after they had halved their morning match.

Watson had decided to keep the Mickelson/Bradley combination intact from Medinah. Tom sent them out in the fourth match Friday morning, and the Americans delivered an emotional 1-up victory over McIlroy and Garcia. Phil began lobbying Tom on the sixth tee for an afternoon appearance with Bradley in the foursome session.

"Captain, you know I have only missed five fairways in alternate shot play in The Presidents Cup and Ryder Cup since 2007," were the words Phil had conveyed to Tom.

When I heard that I just laughed to myself. "Who but Phil would keep track of that?" I thought. I'm not sure whether Phil's driving statistics impressed Tom.

But Mickelson and Bradley did get the call from Watson on Friday afternoon. They were 3 down after eight holes, and both were driving the ball erratically. Phil was on his way to missing more fairways that afternoon than he supposedly had since 2007. With arms folded, Tom approached Bradley and Mickelson on the ninth tee.

"When are one of you two guys actually going to hit a fairway?" asked a bewildered Watson, who then turned around and walked away. Keegan proceeded to rope-hook his tee shot off of the par-5 hole, and they would eventually succumb to Dubuisson and McDowell by a 3 and 2 margin.

It turns out that neither Bradley nor Mickelson would play again until Sunday. They probably expected to take a break Saturday morning, but when they were told late morning of Watson's decision to sit them out in the afternoon alternate-shot session there were some fireworks. Bradley became highly emotional. Mickelson began texting Watson, pleading to get another chance with Bradley, but Watson stuck to his guns.

Tom decided to send out Kuchar, Johnson, Furyk, Mahan, Spieth and Reed along with Fowler and Walker. Watson felt they were his best chance to improve upon the prior day's 3 ½ to ½ shellacking that the U.S. had received in the alternate-shot format. In hindsight, Watson would admit he should have rested Fowler and Walker because they were coming off three tough matches that all wound up being halved. The two Americans were visually drained, physically and mentally, in their Saturday afternoon 5 and 4 defeat to Dubuisson and McDowell. The U.S. again got smoked 3 ½ to ½. The foursome sessions would be the difference in this Ryder Cup.

Saturday night, after the Americans had lost 7–1 combined in foursomes, Watson addressed the team and made an attempt at levity: "You guys suck at foursomes."

That comment, along with his benching Saturday, was evidently the tipping point for Mickelson. When he was asked to present Watson with a Ryder Cup replica from the U.S. players, Phil refused, saying, "You don't want me up there talking tonight."

Furyk would accept the task of presenting the trophy to Watson. When Jim handed it to Tom, the words from Watson's mouth were not what some of the team had hoped for. Watson told the players he didn't care about the replica. He wanted the "real thing."

The week after the Ryder Cup was over, Tom told me that when he got to his room that night, Hilary advised him his comments probably didn't come across the way he meant them. Watson expressed regret that he didn't thank the players for their gesture when they presented him with the replica. Tom admitted he could have done a better job of explaining what he actually meant.

All of this set the stage for what happened in the media center Sunday evening following the closing ceremonies. With a question posed to Mickelson about the recent U.S. Ryder Cup losses, Phil reflected back to 2008 at Valhalla, saying captain Paul Azinger had developed a system in which players were divided into small groups that ate, slept and practiced together.

"So we were invested in the process," Mickelson said. "Unfortunately, we have strayed from a winning formula for the last three Ryder Cups, and we need to consider maybe getting back to that formula that helped us play our best."

As Mickelson spoke, Tom Watson stared ahead. Hunter Mahan was seated next to Phil, and he fidgeted in his seat. Other players were noticeably uncomfortable at Mickelson's public words. The fidgeting became even more obvious when a reporter told Mickelson his comments sounded like a brutal destruction of Watson's leadership during the entire week.

"Oh, I'm sorry you're taking it that way. I'm just talking about what Paul Azinger did to help us play our best," Mickelson said. "You asked me what I thought we should do going forward to bring our best golf out, and I go back to when we played our best golf and try to replicate that formula."

When asked if that had happened at Gleneagles, Mickelson replied. "Uh, no. Nobody here was in any decision."

Tom was asked what he thought of Mickelson's remarks, and you could hear a pin drop.

"I had a different philosophy as far as being a captain of this team. You know, it takes 12 players to win. It's not pods. It's 12 players," Watson said. "Phil's style of leadership is different than mine."

Furyk was drawn into the fray when he was asked a question about the back and forth between Mickelson and Watson.

"Gee thanks. Just sitting over here minding my own business," Furyk remarked. "I think that I have a lot of respect for both gentlemen. I've known Phil my entire life. Since I was 16, I've competed against him. He's one of my dearest friends on the PGA TOUR. And I have a lot of respect for the captain. I know he put his heart and soul in it for two years."

Sitting in the back of the interview room, I was shocked by what I was seeing. Here was the leader of the U.S. team absolutely doing a public dismembering of our captain. It was an embarrassing moment for everyone associated with the United States Ryder Cup team, and I would later tell Phil that.

Several reporters, including Martin Dempster from *The Scotsman* and Alan Shipnuck from *Sports Illustrated,* tried to get me to comment on the fiasco at the press conference. I declined. When we got outside the media center, I drove Tom and Julius Mason over to the locker room. It was a silent ride until I finally broke the ice.

I looked at Tom and said, "I can't believe what I just saw."

Tom looked over at me with a broken smile and said, "Phil and I are at odds with each other right now. This, too, shall pass."

I felt rage as I walked to my locker and gathered my things. I slammed my locker door and walked back to the Gleneagles Hotel by myself. I was still shocked at the way this all ended. It was bad enough to lose, but now everybody in the world would mock the Americans for how the latest defeat was handled. If Phil had issues with Tom, he should have expressed them privately.

Mostly, I felt horrible for Tom. The U.S. had been beaten soundly on the golf course by the better team in the Europeans. None of Watson's decisions had truly decided the outcome at Gleneagles. Ironically, the two Americans who wound up performing the best for Watson were Reed and Spieth. Patrick had a 3-0-1 record, while Jordan was 2-1. For all of the criticism Tom would receive about being too old and not relatable, his two youngest players prospered in the environment Watson created.

The three assistant captains—North, Floyd and Stricker—made a pact that none would ever comment about the ugly aftermath of Gleneagles. But not long ago North did offer the following in a long phone conversation:

"I can say that no captain in the history of the Ryder Cup worked as hard as Tom did to put our team in a position to succeed," he said.

Indeed, and that is how I will always remember my friend Tom Watson.

As for what I will remember about Gleneagles, well, for several years I had dreamed about the jubilation of lifting that victorious Ryder Cup and sharing the moment with Tom Watson as a fruitful reward for how hard we had worked together to bring that trophy back to American soil. Winning was what Tom and I were both about. I've written it repeatedly throughout this chapter: There was no way we were going to lose with Tom Watson as our captain. But we did.

Gleneagles turned out to be far more than a nightmare for me. It also was the beginning of the end.

# Chapter Eleven

# Lefty Leads a Task Force

Monday morning after the Ryder Cup, our official party gathered in the team room for our departure back to the U.S. My wife, Cindy, and I joined the Watsons for breakfast. Tom was fairly upbeat. In some ways it seemed eerily similar to his heartbreaking defeat at Turnberry in 2009, but the aftermath was really much different. This time, Tom never hit a shot. His leadership had been challenged, and he was gutted in public by one of his team members.

As we departed the Gleneagles Hotel and boarded our buses, we were greeted by Ryder Cup Europe's official party. Paul McGinley, Europe's captain, was there, and he shared a private moment with Watson. The two captains shook hands after their brief conversation and headed in opposite directions. McGinley was a hero, and Watson was tarnished.

Paul told Tom that in all of his Ryder Cup experiences he had never seen a European player publicly criticize a captain like Phil Mickelson had Watson. According to McGinley, there were plenty of occasions in the past when Europe's players had an occasion to attack their captain. One example was in 2008 when players were dissatisfied with Nick Faldo's performance at Valhalla in Louisville, Kentucky. But Paul said it was an unwritten rule that dirty laundry is not aired in public.

At least the flight home would be less stressful. Phil was once again on his own and not with the team. When we got airborne, the details of what he had witnessed in the team room over the course of the week began to emerge.

Apparently, some of the players were upset by some of Tom's remarks when he addressed the team. Phil took it upon himself to speak to the team, praising them one by one, and pointing out the positive things each player brought to Gleneagles. Phil sat on top of a couch with his back to Watson. It could all be interpreted as a defiant and disrespectful display by Phil. I passed it off to his ire over being benched Saturday. Others might take it as Phil taking a conciliatory leadership role to smooth what some players might have perceived as Tom's directness.

Let me make this clear: I like Phil Mickelson. I certainly don't agree with what he did at Gleneagles, but his actions were in the emotions of the moment, and it demonstrated how much the players do care about the Ryder Cup, perhaps none more than Phil. At the same time, Phil is a dominant personality, and he is a master manipulator. In my opinion, his motives were self-serving.

While his actions tore our team apart to some extent, they did not influence the outcome of the matches. Phil had a 2–1 record at Gleneagles. He had now won six of his last eight Ryder Cup matches. In a lot of ways, Mickelson used Scotland to elbow his way to the forefront of the next decade of Ryder Cups.

I sat in my seat and reflected on the week. Eventually, I leaned over the aisle and spoke to PGA CEO Pete Bevacqua, who was seated across from me. "You know going forward the PGA is going to have to do something different with the Ryder Cup. There are going to be many critics who will demand changes in how the PGA does things now that we have lost eight of the last 10 Ryder Cups."

Pete nodded in agreement, and I continued.

"For lack of better words, I think we need to name a task force or a committee made up of former Ryder Cup players and captains. The PGA of America should listen to what those guys have to say and then set the course."

We discussed who should be involved. Obviously, it started with Mickelson and Tiger Woods. Paul Azinger also had to be included. From there, we would need to discuss it with Derek Sprague, who would be the next PGA president, and Paul Levy, who would move up to vice president. A conference call was set for midweek to start the process of naming the Ryder Cup Task Force.

A couple days after I got back to Indiana, Tom Watson called me.

"Ted, how are you doing? I just wanted to call and make sure you are OK. I know this has been a tough few days for you, too," he said.

I was totally moved that Tom would do this given the abuse he was taking by the media in the immediate fallout over what happened at Gleneagles.

"I'm doing fine, Tom. I'm only getting criticized for doing one thing, and that is picking you as captain. I know you are getting ripped for many things," I jokingly said.

Watson was in a good place that day. He was seemingly his old self, self-assured and confident. He told me he had called all the players on the team, including Phil. I thanked Tom for calling me and once again let him know how proud I was to be associated with his captainship. I made sure Tom knew I thought he had done all he could to put the U.S. team in a position to win.

Watson had already sorted through the statistics from Gleneagles, and he informed me his team had lost to the Euros by 35 shots over the three days of competition. That summed it up for me. You could clone a captain from Vince Lombardi, Red Auerbach or Joe Torre, and they couldn't overcome that. It's always been amazing to me that the golf media didn't focus more on the 35-shot deficit than they did.

I felt it was important Tom hear about the impending Ryder Cup Task Force from me. I assured him it was not an indictment of his captaincy. The PGA simply needed to get more player input moving forward and make a very public move that we were going to everything possible to do a better job preparing for the Ryder Cup from our end.

"I think that's a smart thing do," Watson said. "The players will appreciate that."

As you might imagine, many so-called experts were weighing in publicly on what the PGA should do with the Ryder Cup. There were those who felt the PGA needed to bring in someone like Jerry Colangelo from USA Basketball. They said that the PGA needed an opinion from someone outside golf who had been successful in team sports. It was even proposed that we include Dottie Pepper, a successful Solheim Cup player- the women's version of the Ryder Cup. The Ryder Cup has always been a male only event. The PGA officers listened respectfully to lots of different people and ideas.

People were coming out of the wood work and wanting to be part of the Ryder Cup task force. The officers assembled a short list which was comprised of former players and former captains. We tried to get a wide range of ages involved, but in the case of the players we were relying heavily on experience- albeit losing Ryder Cup experiences in most cases.

Mickelson was the first player to get my call about the task force. I figured it was "put up or shut up time" for Phil after Gleneagles. As I suspected, he was all in for the task force. Phil has repeatedly said since the task force was formed that he was highly in favor of giving the players more input. Although he had lobbied for Paul Azinger's system on Sunday night at Gleneagles, Phil was indifferent about Paul's role in the Ryder Cup going forward.

I am still shocked by Phil's perspective on this. Just a few days before in Scotland, he had sliced and diced Watson at the loser's press conference with his ringing endorsement of Azinger's captaincy in 2008 at Valhalla. Now Phil was being more specific by saying it was the system and not the captain that produced the victory.

After Phil, we assembled a group of players that included Tiger Woods, Steve Stricker, Jim Furyk and Rickie Fowler. All of the guys were highly engaged and excited to be part of the group. Several high profile agents even contacted me and asked that the PGA consider their player as a task force member. Interestingly, one of the primary concerns that the players had was getting too many people involved and creating such a large number of people in the room that it would be impossible to get any consensus.

I had several occasions in the summer of 2015 to ask Steve Stricker what he had learned from his experience as an assistant captain at Gleneagles. "I went into Gleneagles looking at everything as a player, but as the week went on my thinking totally changed. It's so much different when you are the one making decisions instead of the one playing," Stricker said.

"In the future I would like to see us assign an assistant captain to the guys who are not playing on Friday and Saturday. That person needs to take the players out on the course behind the last match and play certain holes. (Padraig) Harrington did that at Gleneagles."

The Ryder Cup rules allow the players who are not involved in the matches to be on the course practicing after the final match of each session has teed off.

It was apparent to me after speaking to Stricker that the PGA needed guys to be assistant captains before they ever became a Ryder Cup captain. Strangely enough, only Love had done that in recent years.

As you can imagine, many former Ryder Cup captains were reaching out when they heard about the task force. It was going to be impossible to engage all of them. For example, Julie Crenshaw posted criticism on social media that her husband, Ben, had not been asked to be on the task force. I'm sure every living captain rightfully thought they could contribute, but it would be the responsibility of the former captains who were on the task force to assimilate that information.

Love was the first who agreed to be on the task force. "You went out of the box when you picked Tom. People said I was too soft, and now they say Tom was too tough. It is a thankless job," Davis told me a few days after I got back from Gleneagles. Love jumped at the chance to continue his Ryder Cup involvement.

Tom Lehman was excited to be asked to serve on the task force. He enthusiastically called me several times after being appointed to the task force. We spoke about Tom's thoughts on Hazeltine and the golf course setup during the Ryder Cup. Lehman is from Minnesota, and he is very familiar with Hazeltine. He was an easy choice to be part of this task force.

Azinger continued to ignore my requests to talk and I don't think he ever had any real desire to be on a task force. He would later tell the media that he had no interest in being part of the PGA's process.  In my opinion, Paul wanted to be the next captain, and the task force was a road block. I think Azinger felt he was entitled because was he was the only winning U.S. captain since Crenshaw in 1999.

When the task force was announced, Raymond Floyd wound up with a spot that might have gone to Azinger. But Floyd clearly had his own credentials.  He never had been part of a losing Ryder Cup team before Gleneagles. Eight times as a player, once as a captain and then again as an assistant to Azinger at Valhalla, Floyd had been part of teams that never lost Ryder Cup competition.

Sprague, Levy and Bevacqua would all appoint themselves to the task force. That brought the total to 11 people who would construct the road map that will hopefully lead to future U.S. Ryder Cup victories. Will the task force be effective and will it accomplish what I had hoped for? Only time will tell.

Candidly, I was surprised at the long term commitment given Davis Love III. Not because Davis isn't a great guy and a worthy captain. But, he will be the '16 captain and remain on as an assistant in the years to come. If Love loses at Hazeltine he will be the only 0-2 captain in the history of the Ryder Cup for whatever that's worth.

In my opinion, Phil called the shots inside the task force meetings, although I was already gone by then. I say that in part because the changes that were made to the Ryder Cup points system mirrored his playing schedule. Don't get me wrong, I am not saying that Phil's passion and influence on the next decade of Ryder Cups is a bad thing. Just understand that his finger prints will be all over the Ryder Cup planning for quite awhile and hopefully that leads to his prints being on the actual Ryder Cup! You can bet on Mickelson being the 2024 captain at Bethpage.

I would have almost guaranteed that Fred Couples would have been the 2016 captain based on conversations with players over the last couple of years. Obviously, I was not in the task force meetings and I don't know the reason for the pick of Love. Word from a veteran golf writer was that Couples had sent a text Furyk and told him that he was choosing Spieth as his final pick for the 2013 President's Cup team. Supposedly, Furyk was not happy about the impersonal manner that Couples used to break the news. This situation, on top of his more than casual attitude at Medinah as Love's assistant, might have doomed Couples forever as a Ryder Cup captain.

Many media critics poked fun and mocked the PGA for constructing the task force. Some European players openly called it "an overreaction by the PGA." We were in a no-win situation no matter what we did. Then again, we had no wins since 2008, and only two going back to Watson in 1993.

I announced the Ryder Cup Task Force at the PGA Grand Slam of Golf in mid-October. Sprague and Bevacqua would serve as the co-chairmen. The three of us recorded a video for the PGA membership while we were in Bermuda. While there, I was officially passing the baton to Sprague and stepping aside from the Ryder Cup. There was only a month left in my term and it was pretty evident I was officially a lame-duck president.

A few days before the Grand Slam, I received a call from PGA Past President Pat Rielly. He had cautioned me to watch my back. The sentiment that he expressed to me was, "The sooner Bishop goes, the better. He got us into this whole Ryder Cup mess."

I was starting to feel like the PGA of America had become a cloak-and-dagger society. Little did I know how true that would turn out to be.

There is one poignant memory from the 2014 Grand Slam. After we announced the formation of the task force, Bubba Watson, who was there as the Masters champion, approached me.

"I just want to tell you that I'm OK with everything the PGA has done in the past with the Ryder Cup. I have no problem with naming a captain as a reward because of what they accomplished as a player. Tom Watson was a good captain. I didn't do my part. I just needed to make more putts," Bubba said.

I appreciated those words from Bubba. He wasn't the only player who spoke out after Gleneagles. Rickie Fowler was playing in China at the World Golf Championship-HSBC Champions when he told Dave Shedloski of GolfDigest.com the following:

"The unfortunate part, I believe, is that stuff that happens in the team room should stay there. I thought Tom did a great job of talking to the guys. He had been there plenty of times, and I enjoyed the time I got to spend with him. He is a legend. Some things may have got blown a little bit out of proportion. But obviously we didn't play well enough to win, and that has got to change."

I was very frustrated with the PGA of America, my fellow officers and senior staff. In my opinion a line was drawn in the sand, and everyone was either in Watson's camp or Mickelson's. The PGA should have been far more public in its appreciation and support of Tom for his steadfast dedication over the two years of his volunteer captainship. The PGA had discarded Tom. On the other hand, Phil would be involved with future Ryder Cups. The PGA leadership sought his approval because he was a former PGA champion. His attendance at future PGA champions' dinners could not be jeopardized by siding with Watson.

The Ryder Cup Task Force would eventually meet a couple times over the winter and release its findings at a press conference held during the Honda Classic in March 2015. There were several major surprises.

First of all, Love wound up being named as the 2016 Ryder Cup captain. Based on the endorsement of Couples by Mickelson, Woods and Stricker, this was a shocking development. Personally, I had come full circle on the thought of Fred being a Ryder Cup captain. It made sense to me to have Couples be the "transition captain" while the PGA put a long-term plan in place as long as we surrounded him with experienced assistants captains such as Love, Floyd and Lehman, who could handle the details. Fred's fourth assistant could have been the guy who was in the pipeline to be the captain at Paris in 2018.

Obviously, I was not in the task force meetings and I don't know the reason for the pick. A story later circulated that Furyk had been upset when Couples chose Spieth as a captain's pick in the 2013 Presidents Cup at Muirfield Village. Evidently, Fred had sent Jim a text notifying him of the decision instead of making a personal phone call. Furyk was more upset about the method of communication than he was the pick of Jordan. As the story goes, this incident may have influenced the task force to scrap Couples and pick Love as the next Ryder Cup captain. Obviously, there had to be other reasons too.

From his pub-stool perch in the second row at the press conference, Phil presided over the proceedings like a hawk surveying its prey. When a reporter asked Love how he evolved as a task force member to captain, Phil practically knocked down Davis to grab the microphone. Mickelson was quick to point out Love had not lobbied for the job. He said Davis sees the big picture and is a perfect fit.

Phil also acknowledged Love had made mistakes at Medinah and that he had learned from those mistakes. Phil capped his remarks by saying, "Davis will put us in a position to succeed rather than create obstacles to overcome."

I took that remark as another backhanded slap at Watson.

The task force retooled the Ryder Cup points system by no longer awarding points for the Fall Series events. At the press conference, Mickelson said the players who competed in the fall were "in the bottom half" of the group vying for spots at Gleneagles. Phil said these players gained a distinct advantage by accumulating early Ryder Cup points. Jimmy Walker was one player who enjoyed success in those fall events and used it as a springboard to make the '14 U.S. team. Walker lost only one match out of the four he played in at Gleneagles.

The Fall Series, which Mickelson and many other top players skip, was replaced for Ryder Cup point purposes by the limited-field World Golf Championships events and The Players Championship in the year prior to the Ryder Cup. Coincidentally, those changes mirrored Phil's playing schedule.

The move to eliminate the Fall Series from the Ryder Cup points list totally took PGA TOUR Commissioner Tim Finchem by surprise. Adding the Fall Series to the 2014 Ryder Cup points was a critical part of the collaboration between the TOUR and the PGA of America. Then, it was eliminated, unbeknownst to Finchem.

"I kind of whiffed it on that one, to be honest with you. I didn't really think through that particular change. It's particularly annoying to me that I missed it because we had just been wrestling with this on FedExCup points for the last number of years," Finchem said. "We would like to see (Ryder Cup points) included."

The PGA of America also announced at the press conference that future Ryder Cup captains would have at least two former captains among their assistants. Love immediately appointed Lehman to his staff in '16 because of Tom's knowledge of Hazeltine. A few months later Love announced Woods, Stricker and Furyk as three additional assistant captains. He specified that a fifth would be named later.

This raises several interesting questions given the commitment to have two former Ryder Cup captains as assistants. If Phil Mickelson does not make the 2016 team, what will his role be? Is Fred Couples, who may have cooked his own goose in Medinah with what some saw as a disinterested attitude, no longer under consideration as a future Ryder Cup captain?

Or will a sixth assistant captain eventually be added? To paraphrase what Stricker said about Love at Medinah, it could be information overload at Hazeltine with so many voices in his ear. My only criticism of Davis Love is that I sometimes think he lets consensus-building impair his ability to make the spontaneous decisions.

To promote continuity, Love agreed to stay on as an assistant captain in 2018 and '20. The PGA also announced Davis, Phil and Tiger would remain on a permanent Ryder Cup committee.

The glaring absence at that press conference was Woods. The man who simply had to drive across town to attend the proceedings at Palm Beach Gardens was nowhere to be found. Conversely, Phil had made his presence felt. I can't help but think Phil's taking charge of the U.S. Ryder Cup process might represent the first time in years that he isn't living in Tiger's shadow, although I suppose you could say that the 2008 Ryder Cup at

Valhalla was perhaps one other such occasion, with Tiger on the sidelines and Phil the veteran presence under Azinger.

I await with great anticipation the 2024 Ryder Cup at Bethpage Black in New York. Phil Mickelson will most likely be the U.S. captain, and he will then become the one making the decisions—not just a guy swinging a club.

I'm certain he will be a good captain. He does like to be in control. But then he will find out, like all captains before him, how much control over the outcome he truly has. Or doesn't have. Win or lose, perhaps only then will he truly have an understanding of what he did to Tom Watson at Gleneagles.

# Chapter Twelve

# A Less than Stellar Past

In my 23 months as president of the PGA of America, our mission statement revolved around two things—serving our PGA membership and growing the game of golf. Everything we did was geared toward getting more people to play golf and searching for ways to help our PGA members be more successful at their jobs.

Diversity and inclusion were certainly important components that influenced many of the decisions we made. It's safe to say that today's PGA professionals go to work every single day searching for ways to make their businesses prosper. A key fundamental to that success is making golf open and inclusive to everyone, which, incidentally has been a priority of mine for more than 40 years.

Since its formation 100 years ago, the PGA of America has battled a stigma that it is a predominantly white male organization. Because it is. The PGA's past is sordid, with prejudice and bigotry toward minorities and women, but over the past 50 years the PGA has worked hard to change that perception. Still, it can't seem to get out of its own way when it wants to beat its chest on accomplishments.

Since October 24, 2014, when I was impeached, many PGA members have been kind enough to reach out to me and offer their condolences as well as thanks for my service to the association. I sense there is a tremendous amount of discontent within today's rank-and-file PGA members who feel their association has become too corporate and less member-centric since my removal.

PGA CEO Pete Bevacqua has a canned message he continually feeds our membership: "Our mission is to serve our 28,000 members and grow the game." The message is not resonating with the rank-and-file. Many PGA members feel Bevacqua's top priority today is more about a commitment to diversity and inclusion than truly serving our members and growing the game.

Let me make this clear: I fully support diversity and inclusion. But in Franklin, Indiana, I am extremely limited in how I can increase minority participation at my golf course based on the local population demographics. Many PGA professionals around the country are in the same position as I. I feel my impeachment served as a stepping stone for what today's PGA of America is trying to look like. It caught me like a left hook out of nowhere, particularly given my commitment over the years to women and minorities. That said, I am extremely pleased the PGA is doing more for this cause. It has only taken us a century.

On January 17, 1916, a New York City department store magnate named Rodman Wanamaker invited a group of golf professionals to lunch at the Taplow Club in the Martinique Hotel on Broadway and 32nd Street. Wanamaker believed golf professionals could enhance equipment sales if they formed an association. On April 10, the PGA of America was founded with 35 charter members.

Less than half of the original members of the PGA were American-born. Most were of Scottish descent, and they migrated to the U.S. to help promote the game of golf as caddies, clubmakers or club professionals. The United States Golf Association is credited with founding the sport in America in 1894.

The early PGA of America clearly reflected what was seen on golf courses across America in the first part of the 20th century. It was a white, all-male association, and it would remain that

way for decades. Even in 2016, nearly 93 percent of its membership is white males.

The modern-day PGA of America is admittedly ashamed
of its first 45 years of racial inequity. In 2009, the PGA bestowed
posthumous membership upon three African-American pioneers—Ted Rhodes, John Shippen and Bill Spiller. These men had
been denied the opportunity to become PGA members during
their professional careers. The PGA also granted posthumous
honorary membership to Joe Louis, the legendary world heavy-
weight boxing champion who became an advocate for diversity
in golf. Also in 2009, the PGA presented its Distinguished Service Award to William Powell, who overcame many racial barri-
ers. According to the PGA, Powell is the only African-American
to design, build, own and operate a golf course.

It was a great gesture by the PGA, but there was a glaring
omission. Dewey Brown actually became the first African-American PGA member in 1928 after he worked as a caddie in New
Jersey. He was also a renowned golf clubmaker and golf teacher
during the 1920s and '30s. Brown actually built a set of golf clubs
for President Warren G. Harding. In 1934 he worked as an assistant at Shawnee in Pennsylvania.

A 1934 "Caucasian Race" clause prohibited minority golfers
from joining the PGA and playing in its events. Until the removal of the clause in 1961, African-American golfers were left to
organize their own association and tours. The PGA of America
ultimately terminated Brown's membership when it discovered
he was African-American. The PGA previously believed he was
white because of his light skin color. Brown purchased the Cedar
River Golf Club in Indiana Lake, New York, in 1947. His son took
it over after Brown retired in 1972.

Unfortunately, Dewey Brown, the first black man to be a
PGA member, was not recognized in the 2009 celebration of
black pioneers. It's safe to assume he never had the opportunity
to be a head pro because of the color of his skin. That is proba-

bly what prompted Brown to buy his own course a year before Powell opened Clearview Golf Club in East Canton, Ohio. An argument could be made that Dewey Brown might be the first African-American to own a golf course in the U.S.

Ann Gregory, a 2016 Indiana Golf Hall of Fame inductee, became the first African-American woman to play in a national championship conducted by the USGA in 1956—five years before the PGA rescinded the "Caucasian Race" clause. In 1963, Althea Gibson was selected as the first African-American member of the Ladies Professional Golf Association. But the PGA of America again lagged behind, and it wasn't until 1964 that Charlie Sifford became the first African-American to hold a full PGA membership.

Women's golf started gaining momentum in the 1920s. By the 1930s and 1940s, a new breed of professional women's golfers were on the scene. These women were seldom from exclusive country clubs. They learned to play on public courses or less-exclusive clubs. Few could support themselves from the purses of prize money for which they were playing. Several women's tournaments of national prominence started evolving and the Women's Professional Golf Association was formed in 1944. The WPGA disbanded in 1949, and the newly formed LPGA was founded the next year by 12 golfers, including Louise Suggs of Georgia.

Suggs was not only a founder and charter member; she was the LPGA's best player. She won more than 50 LPGA events and seven women's major championships. Suggs became the first woman to beat male professionals playing from the same tees, besting Sam Snead and Gardner Dickinson in the Royal Poinciana Invitational in 1949 at the Palm Beach Par 3 Golf Club in Florida in 1949. In 1951, Suggs was elected to the World Golf Hall of Fame, and in 1956, she was the first woman inducted into the Georgia Athletic Hall of Fame.

With the advent of the Civil Rights Act of 1964 and Title IX legislation in 1972, women began demanding greater access to a sport that has been historically laced with discrimination. While African-American golfers had limited playing opportunities before the mid-1950s, white women also faced discrimination.

Women were denied access by many private clubs. Even if admitted as wives or daughters, they were restricted on when they could be at the club. Most women's locker rooms paled in size and scope to the men's. Women were not allowed to serve on the club's administrative boards and were restricted to outdated roles.

The most significant challenge to the game's exclusionary practices involved Barrie Naismith, then an assistant golf professional at Brookfield West Golf and Country Club in Atlanta. According to the Atlanta Historical Society, she applied for membership as a teaching professional to the PGA of America on March 15, 1978, and as an apprentice on March 21, 1978. On both occasions, she was denied.

After appealing to the Georgia Section of the PGA, she was told by a GPGA official that she could "call Jimmy Carter, but it won't do you any good." Judge Joel Fryer, one of Naismith's friends and students at the Standard Club where she had taught golf, urged her to hire Lawrence Ashe, a noted Atlanta employment discrimination attorney.

On May 5, 1978, Naismith brought a class-action employment discrimination suit against the PGA of America in U.S. District Court in Atlanta. In her suit Naismith charged the "PGA certification requirements had prevented her and other females from being employed as head pros at courses operating under the sanction of the PGA which had no females among its 4,000-plus members."

Ashe presented numerous affidavits to make their case. One involved Louise Suggs, who could not accept a position as head professional at Sapphire Valley Resort in North Carolina because she did not have PGA status. Ashe also submitted letters from the LPGA that complained to the PGA about its guidelines and rules.

"The Suggs situation was damning to the PGA of America. That put us in a strong position going forward," Ashe recalled. "Barrie was a classy person. The PGA of America thought it could throw money at us and we would go away. But this was not about money for Barrie. It was all about what was right for women."

According to Ashe, his client was willing to take the PGA courses required for membership and do the playing standards. The PGA of America has a playing ability test that must be passed before gaining membership. Ashe even offered to waive his attorney fees if the PGA would give Naismith the opportunity to become a member. "They (PGA) said, 'Go to hell,'" Ashe recalled.

Mark Kizziar served as president of the PGA of America in 1983–84. His recollection of the Naismith Decree went as follows: "I remember Don Padgett, the PGA president at the time, calling me in 1978 and asking me to present a resolution on the floor of the Annual Meeting that would change the PGA Constitution to allow women to try and gain membership. There was a great deal of opposition to this."

At that point, the PGA of America had spent close to $375,000 on legal fees fighting Naismith and Ashe's quest to have women become PGA members. Frank Cardi from the Metropolitan PGA Section was slated to succeed Padgett and become the next PGA president. According to Kizziar, Cardi was adamantly opposed to allowing women to become members of the PGA.

Kizziar formulated a lengthy presentation at the bequest of Padgett for the delegates at the PGA's Annual Meeting at Atlanta's Omni Hotel. Kizziar estimates he spent 18 hours on the floor of that Annual Meeting devoted to the resolution allowing women to pursue PGA membership. On December 11, 1978, the PGA of America passed a resolution amending its constitution to allow women to try and become members.

"The PGA of America was a boys club at that time. That's the way we had always done it. We had no choice but to give women the opportunity to join the PGA. The LPGA probably wasn't really thrilled about women being admitted to the PGA either because it was viewed as a potential threat to their ability to attract members," Kizziar said.

The PGA resolution passed, but it was only a small victory for women. Even though they could become PGA of America members, it also demanded women gain entry through the playing ability test by shooting the same target score (a prescribed number over the course rating) from the same set of tees as the men.

In her book *From Birdies to Bunkers,* Alice Dye offered this insight.

"The toughest obstacle was the Playing Ability Test. It required her (Naismith) to shoot an average of 75 from the men's tees on a course with a distance of approximately 6,500 yards. This was impossible for her and almost any woman at the time. My lawyer friend (Ashe) asked for my assistance in determining the distances that would allow a woman to play well enough to qualify.

"I researched the yardage of the Women's Western Open, the USGA Women's Open, and the tournaments on the LPGA Tour and gave a deposition detailing the yardages that the best tournament professionals and amateurs were playing in tournaments. I knew the PGA of America was being unfair."

Alice's husband is Pete Dye, the legendary golf course architect. Pete ran into Mark Cox, the PGA's executive director, in the Atlanta airport in 1979. Cox confronted Dye and said that he was angry with Alice for being involved in the lawsuit that helped women gain entry into the PGA of America. He felt it was a man's organization and it should stay that way. He accosted Pete by saying, "What is your wife doing suing the PGA?"

Pete was caught off-guard because Alice had not informed him of her conversations with Ashe. Pete informed Cox that Alice would never do that because they were just starting out in the golf course architecture business and certainly would not want to offend the PGA of America. When Pete arrived home that evening, he informed Alice of "Cox's mistake."

Alice informed Pete it was not a mistake and that she was in fact helping Naismith and Ashe with their lawsuit against the PGA of America. Pete, knowing the negative ramifications her involvement could have for their fledgling golf course architecture business, asked Alice, "How could you do that?

"Because they were wrong," Alice told Pete.

The case of Naismith vs. Professional Golfers Association would linger in the courts for three years. In 1979, the PGA agreed to accept Naismith as a Class A member and extend similar status to a small group of professional women golfers and grant conditional status to others. The PGA also agreed to give full credit for membership purposes to women in all 50 states who had worked as an assistant to a PGA Class A professional and grant them retroactive credits as they sought PGA membership.

In addition, the PGA waived the playing ability test for players who had turned professional and could have joined before April 1, 1974, but were denied because of their gender. The PGA's membership department estimates as many as 19 women were "grandmothered" into to the PGA under these conditions.

Naismith was truly a champion for women. She forever changed the modern-day professional career opportunities for women in golf. An intriguing sidelight to the Naismith saga occurred in 1981 when she was terminated from the PGA's membership role for nonpayment of dues. It seems she was engaged to be married in 1980 and elected to not pursue any future career opportunities in golf even though she had reportedly been offered a position as head professional at a golf course in Birmingham, Alabama.

There has been a steady increase in the number of female PGA of America members and apprentices since 1985. Had it not been for the efforts of people like Naismith, Ashe and Dye, who knows what the PGA of America would look like it does today?

Growth of Women in the PGA of America
1985—240 Female PGA members and apprentices
1995—704 Female PGA members and apprentices
2005—903 Female PGA members and apprentices
2015—1,128 Female PGA members and apprentices

By comparison, in 2015 the Ladies Professional Golfers Association had about 1,500 members and applicants in its Teaching and Coaching Division within the United States. In 1990, the LPGA had nearly 500 members, meaning that it tripled and increased its membership in the last 25 years by 300 percent. Meanwhile, the PGA of America saw an increase from 508 female members and apprentices in 1990 to 1,128 in 2015 for an uptick of 122 percent. There are approximately 200 female golf professionals who belong to both the LPGA and the PGA.

Almost 40 years after Naismith carried the torch for women, the playing ability test still remains the biggest barrier for women trying to become members of the PGA of America. There is a substantial difference in the playing ability requirements between the LPGA and PGA. The LPGA clearly has a more relaxed standard with an 18-hole playing ability test allowing a higher target score. The PGA invokes a 36-hole playing ability test with a much lower target score.

The LPGA's 18-hole playing ability test requires the player to shoot a score within 13 strokes of the course rating. In other words, if a woman took her LPGA playing ability test on a course of 5,200 yards with a rating of 70.0, her target score could be no higher than 83. The yardage required for an LPGA playing ability test is between 5,100 and 5,700 yards.

The PGA of America changed its playing standards in 2015. The PGA's playing ability test consists of 36 holes in one day. Women use a yardage that is 78 to 85 percent of the men's. The minimum course yardage for men is 6,000 yards, meaning women could play a course as short as 4,680 yards. One problem facing the PGA is that when the course gets shorter during a playing ability test, the course rating is lowered, meaning the target score is also lowered and requires the golfer to shoot a better score to pass. PGA women are required to shoot a score that is 15 strokes over twice the course rating. If a woman is playing a 5,200 yard course with a rating of 70, the target score for 36 holes would be (70 x 2 plus 15 = 155) or an average of 77.5 per round.

Most women in the LPGA are golf teachers or coaches. Many females pursue a PGA membership because they desire to be an assistant or head professional. Others might elect to be a general manager or director of golf. Currently, out of the 928 female PGA members, only 181 serve in managerial positions at golf courses. Since the Naismith Decree in 1978, that amounts to an average of 24 women per year who have joined the PGA of America. Factor in the LPGA roster, and there are fewer than 3,000 women nationwide who are employed in golf as members of either the LPGA or PGA.

While all of golf is recognizing that women represent the largest group of untapped resources, to a large extent the sport still remains a "boys club."

The PGA of America listed its "Milestones in Diversity" as part of the 2016 Centennial Celebration. "While tremendous opportunity exists for continued growth, and there is work to be done, let's take a moment to celebrate and reflect upon some of our achievements in recent history." Some of their highlights are:

- Implemented an open membership practice requirement for our championship host sites.
- Appointed the first multicultural members to the national PGA Board of Directors.
- The first woman PGA member was elected to the national PGA Board of Directors. Suzy Whaley elected as the 39th secretary of the PGA and the first woman to hold national office in the history of the association.
- Women comprise 51 percent of the PGA of America national staff.
- Implemented a national Diversity and Inclusion Committee.

Other things are noted, such as: supplier diversity at the PGA's major championships; community relations programs at major championships that support diversity and inclusion initiatives; ownership and operation of the Minority Collegiate Championship; implementation of the golf industry's "Connecting with Her;" and a reciprocal membership program with the LPGA to increase the number of female professionals in both Associations.

During my term as the 38th president of the PGA in 2013–14, we expanded our commitment to diversity and inclusion in many different ways. The PGA hired Wendell Haskins to serve as senior director of diversity and implemented a dedicated Diversity and Inclusion Department at PGA headquarters. We joined the Diversity and Inclusion Sports Consortium alongside Major League Baseball, Major League Soccer, NASCAR, the NBA/WNBA, NCAA, NFL, NHL, the United States Olympic Committee and the United States Tennis Association.

The PGA of America joined forces with the LPGA to launch the KPMG Women's Championship and the KPMG Women's Leadership Summit. We were instrumental in the formation and participation of the Annual Sports Diversity and Inclusion Symposium. With the help of key sport influencers and allied golf associations, the PGA of America spearheaded a successful campaign that resulted in Charlie Sifford being awarded the Presidential Medal of Freedom.

I was proud to present Lee Trevino, the greatest Hispanic golfer of all time, with the PGA's Distinguished Service Award. Annika Sorenstam from Sweden was our First Lady of Golf during my term. In 2013, I publicly questioned the Royal & Ancient's intent to grow golf in the United Kingdom when in fact it excluded women as R&A members and several of its Open Championship sites did not allow women to join. Soon after, women were named as members of the R&A, and several more Open Championship clubs allowed women as members.

My passion for women's rights in golf began early in my career. A group of women approached me when I started at the Phil Harris Golf Course in Linton in 1976. They were frustrated because even though the course was public, they felt their access was limited. As a 22-year-old pro, I got that changed. Rosie Griffith became the first female to serve on the city of Linton's golf committee when I recommended her to the mayor. As I raised my two girls and they began to play golf, my commitment to promoting women in golf naturally increased. Both of my girls wound up playing in college and chose careers in golf. My youngest daughter is a PGA member.

Our facility, The Legends Golf Club, has hosted every significant statewide women's golf championship in Indiana. That list includes the formation of the Indiana Women's Open and a 10-year run as host. I became heavily involved with girls junior golf and served as volunteer assistant coach at Franklin High School for seven years. At The Legends, we created countless playing opportunities for women and girls in Indiana. Additionally, in 2005, I cofounded the Central Indiana Executive Women's Golf Association with my oldest daughter. Throughout my teaching career, I have taught more women than men.

In August 2015 the Horizon Planning Group organized a dinner and golf tournament in my honor to commemorate my time as the 38th president of the PGA. I agreed to do this if we could raise money for some people who needed it. Greg Fisher, a high school buddy of mine, did a tremendous job with the guys at Horizon in putting on a tremendous two days. It was called "The Mulligan Open: A Charity Event Creating Second Chances." That was certainly appropriate in my case.

Tom Watson, Tim Finchem and Steve Stricker joined Alex Miceli of Golfweek in Franklin for a Tuesday night dinner and fireside chat. There was a golf outing on the following day, and we raised nearly $50,000 for The Little Red Door Cancer Agency, PGA Tour Wives' Association, Indiana Golf Foundation and the Steve Stricker Foundation.

One of the groups that generously donated to the event was the Indiana Women's Golf Association. I was totally humbled when I was informed that the IWGA had written a $1,000 check to the event. The IWGA is a nonprofit with limited funds. But I was informed by Mike David, the executive director of the Indiana Golf Association, that IWGA insisted on doing this to express appreciation and show support for what I had done for women's golf in Indiana.

As Geoff Shackelford said in his 2014 profile in *Golf World's* Newsmakers of the Year, the PGA of America has "had a less than stellar record on progressive matters." While that is true, the staff at the PGA of America is trying to change that image. Still, there are many PGA members, including women and minorities, who are not seeing significant changes take place.

The timing of my "lil girl" remarks came on the eve of the conclusion of the Sports Diversity and Inclusion Symposium hosted at PGA headquarters in Palm Beach Gardens, Florida. Undoubtedly, the powers that be at the PGA of America saw fit to make a profound statement by using me as an example. What better way to show a commitment to diversity and inclusion than to impeach the PGA president after he made a very stupid comment?

In my research for information contained in this chapter, I discovered that in conjunction with the PGA of America's Centennial Celebration, there is a Web page devoted to 100 years of the association's history. Contained on that page at pga.com is a clock that proudly counted down to April 10, 2016—the official date commemorating the formation of the PGA of America. Also contained on the first page of the web site is a decade-by-decade historical profile highlighting the significant milestones in the PGA of America's history.

Curiously, there was no mention of the "Caucasian Race" clause in 1934 or its elimination in 1961. Nor was there any mention of the Naismith Decree in the late 1970s which forced the PGA of America to allow women to become members. There was also no mention of Dewey Brown and Barrie Naismith, whose courageous careers have forever influenced the PGA's history.

The PGA of America should not try to hide from its past. And worse than that, the leaders at the PGA used me as a way, it seems, to try to partially make up for that past—even though my own personal history shows strong support for women in the game. That got lost in the ensuing brouhaha over my remarks to Ian Poulter. I'm not trying to justify the remarks. I just want to put them in the full context of my journey in golf so that I can be judged fairly and honestly, nothing more.

# Chapter Thirteen

# I'm Offended that You're Offended

My impeachment as the 38th president of the PGA of America was as close as I could come to dying without actually dying. I was embarrassed. I was humiliated. I was enraged at times. I felt betrayed. I felt like a victim. I felt lonely. I felt like a complete idiot for letting my emotions drive my irresponsible use of social media. My emotions were all over the board, and they would fluctuate many times throughout a day. I had nightmares. Sometimes I would awaken thinking that it was all a bad dream—only to realize that it wasn't. I was edgy and irritable. Conversely, I sometimes felt extremely upbeat and glad that I could now finally focus on the rest of my life with my family and business.

My life changed in the blink of an eye. What I had always envisioned it would be in my post-PGA presidency, it would never be. All of a sudden, my dedication and devotion to the PGA of America all seemed for naught.

It could have been a hopeless time for me and my family, if not for the tremendous outpouring of support I received in the form of phone calls, letters and emails from hundreds across the country. Many were total strangers. They offered encouragement and expressed appreciation for what I had done for the sport of golf during my career with the PGA. It was exactly the therapy that I needed in order to move on with my life. Looking back at those weeks following my impeachment, it all seems so surreal now.

Some crazy things would happen.

A few days after the PGA debacle, I received a call from Rudy Giuliani, the former mayor of New York City. He was calling to "see how I was holding up."

Rudy and I had played golf together at Liberty National Golf Club in summer 2013, and our friendship developed over the next year. I thoroughly enjoyed the mayor's company. The PGA arranged a lunch between Rudy and me at the Havana Cigar Bar in Manhattan on the day Tom Watson announced his Ryder Cup captain's picks in September '14. Rudy presented me with a picture taken of us during our round of golf. The Statue of Liberty was in the background. Included inside the framed photo was a handwritten note from him, extolling my leadership virtues as president of the PGA of America.

I considered Rudy to be a true American hero for the courageous leadership he displayed during the aftermath of 9/11. We dined together on multiple occasions when he was our guest at PGA Championships. Pete Bevacqua, our CEO, had even retained Giuliani as a paid consultant for the PGA of America. Rudy helped us raise money for the PGA Foundation, including accompanying a group of potential PGA Foundation donors on a trip to Scotland during the Ryder Cup.

During my phone call with Giuliani, he told me the PGA Board of Directors had no choice but to take the action it had to me. He said corporate boards simply had no options but to terminate a leader under circumstances such as these. Giuliani said, despite my troubles, he still had great respect for me. Rudy said it pained him to see the split that had taken place between the PGA and me. He thought he could serve as a mediator and patch the damaged relationship. Rudy recommended I come to New York and spend a day with him so he could share his plan to reunite me with the PGA.

I told him I appreciated the gesture, but I was sure he had heard only one side of the story and that I was extremely frustrated by the way the PGA had dealt with things from a public relations standpoint. I informed the mayor that I had compiled a lengthy chronological timeline of events I would like to share with him. (I shared this time frame at the outset of this book.) It might help him better understand my viewpoint. He agreed to read the information. The next day I emailed 70 pages of information about my impeachment.

A few days later, I received a follow-up call from Giuliani. He said he appreciated the information and that he had read it. Rudy again said he thought it would be good if I could come to New York and spend a day with him. He still insisted he might be able to help resurrect the relationship between me and the PGA. Then he asked me a very random question.

"Are you planning on attending the PGA Annual Meeting?" The meeting was scheduled for Indianapolis in just a few days. Many PGA friends had reached out and encouraged me to attend the meeting, which was scheduled 30 minutes from my house, so that I might receive the appreciation I deserved from the Section leaders I had served.

I immediately started asking myself if the PGA had put Giuliani up to this in hopes of finding out if I had plans to attend and potentially disrupt things.

"Presently, I have no intention of attending the meeting. Many have encouraged me to do so, but I see no worthwhile purpose in going," I told Giuliani.

"That's good," he said. "It wouldn't be beneficial for you or the PGA."

The tone of Giuliani's question and response bothered me. I thanked Rudy for his gesture to mediate my situation with the PGA and told him there was no merit in me coming to New York.

My gut told me he was operating as the paid PGA consultant and that he was to do what was best for it, not for me.

Giuliani wound up recording a video message for that PGA Annual Meeting in Indianapolis. He said the PGA delegates should support the board on its decision to remove me as president, and he spoke to the importance of the PGA being a leader for diversity and inclusion. That was all of the evidence I needed when it came to where Rudy's allegiance resided.

Shortly after my impeachment, TaylorMade notified me that my professional staff agreement was being terminated. I had joined that team in January 2014 because I felt aligned with Mark King, the company's CEO at the time. King had some innovative ideas on how to grow golf, and he came up with a concept called "Hack Golf." It was "hack" as you would break into a computer, not "hack" a shot in golf. King's idea was to introduce things such as 15-inch cups and FootGolf to open golf to new people. I also helped broker a deal with King that would make TaylorMade the major sponsor of the PGA Junior League.

Mark and I became good friends. He was an outside-the-box guy who, like me, embraced new ideas. King hosted a 15-inch cup event at Reynolds Plantation on the day after the Masters. I joined Mark, Sergio Garcia and Justin Rose in a fun nine-hole day of golf. Garcia and Rose were the top TaylorMade staffers from the PGA TOUR in 2014. Later in the year, King left Taylor-Made and became president of Adidas Group North. Ben Sharpe replaced him as CEO at TaylorMade.

My fateful phone call from TaylorMade came in early November at around 9 p.m. on a Saturday night. I was at home with Cindy when I received the call from Dwight Segall. He informed me TaylorMade could not have me as part of its club professional staff given my "gender-insensitive" remarks as PGA president. I was surprised but not totally shocked. The order came from Sharpe, who had never taken the time to speak with me when tough issues such as the massive PGA member layoffs at Dick's Sporting Goods had taken place.

"I only have one question for you, Dwight," I began. "When Sergio made those racially insensitive remarks about Tiger Woods at Wentworth in 2013, did TaylorMade terminate his staff contract?"

"Well, you know we didn't, but Sergio is in our Tour division, and that is different than the club pro division here at TaylorMade," Segall responded.

I considered it a lame but predictable response. Garcia had been on stage with the rest of the victorious 2012 European Ryder Cup team when he was asked by Golf Channel's Steve Sands, who was emceeing the event, whether he would invite Woods over for dinner at the U.S. Open next month.

"We will have him 'round every night. We will serve him fried chicken," Garcia said. The Spaniard soon apologized for the insensitive comment, saying in a statement he was clearly making a joke with a silly remark, but in no way was the comment meant in a racist manner. The Garcia comment was reminiscent of the remark made by Fuzzy Zoeller at the 1997 Masters, when he urged Woods to not serve fried chicken or collard greens at the following year's Champions Dinner. Fuzzy was excoriated for it, and he lost some sponsors for what was intended as a flippant remark to get a laugh but only made folks cringe.

I was glad to see Sergio was spared from any major fallout from his remarks. Like me, Garcia had done a stupid thing. But I couldn't help scratching my head at the difference in how TaylorMade dealt with Sergio and me.

About 30 minutes after my phone call with Segall, Mark King called me to see how I was doing. He had no idea about being me being fired by TaylorMade. "I am so sorry, Ted. You know this never would have happened if I was still at TaylorMade," King said.

The happy ending to the story is that Chip Brewer, CEO at Callaway Golf, reached out and welcomed me his staff.

"We are on a mission to make Callaway Golf the best golf equipment brand in the world. To do that we need to strengthen our position with PGA professionals and key influencers. You have an impressive background and have done a lot for the game of golf. We welcome you to the brand team and believe you can continue to be a force for good in the game and helpful for the positive development of Callaway. And, for the record … Welcome to team Callaway!" – Chip.

It is a gesture I will never forget, and I hope to die a Callaway staffer.

In early November 2014, the PGA of America would meet with Paul Azinger in Palm Beach Gardens. Even though Paul had elected not to be a part of the Ryder Cup Task Force, the PGA felt compelled to listen to Azinger's thoughts. The PGA's ongoing dialogue prompted my youngest daughter, Ambry, herself a PGA member, to write a letter to the PGA officers and staff.

*PGA Officers and Senior Staff:*

*I have had a few weeks to reflect on the "Ted Bishop Dismissal" and have many thoughts and perspectives that I am sure you can imagine would differ from your decision. One thing I do know for sure is that as a female and PGA member, the PGA of America has continued to tell me I should be offended by Ted Bishop's remarks. You have done this personally through member emails, but also through the media and our section leaders. It has been communicated widely from the PGA of America over the last few weeks that you felt the comments Ted made were "insensitive gender-based."*

*As a female and PGA member, I was not personally offended by those comments. In fact the way I found out was through my women's college golf team. My players sent a group text saying "we think he is a legend for calling out Ian Poulter" with a screenshot of Ted's Twitter post. Even though that is the way I felt as well as other females around me, that is not how the leaders of the PGA of America perceived it.*

*Sticking to your theme that Ted's comments were "insensitive gender-based," and you telling me I should be offended, I am highly disappointed with an article I read this weekend stating PGA of America officials and Paul Azinger met last week about Ryder Cup topics and plan to meet again in December. You have spent weeks criticizing and ridiculing one of your own in Ted Bishop, but yet within the same time frame you would entertain opinions from someone that has made "insensitive gender-based" comments in a public interview that is still aired and replayed today. The story that Azinger told on a XM/Sirius Radio interview states that in a gambling match with Payne Stewart and Phil Mickelson, Azinger turned to Mickelson and said "putt it bitch!"*

*This is a story that has been widely publicized in a positive light and I can't help but think of the Ted Bishop injustice when I turn the PGA Tour Radio Network on every morning and hear Azinger repeating this line. I try and wrap my head around how this statement is less offensive than what Ted Bishop said. If that is the case, the PGA of America was treating Paul Azinger different than Ted Bishop. You have told Ted he could not serve the Association in a Past President capacity and he could no longer have a vote or voice his opinion in a leadership role. With that being communicated about Ted, how can Paul Azinger serve as a Past Ryder Cup Captain and still voice his opinion, have influence, and maybe even down the road serve in another Ryder Cup Captain role?*

*I know how I view the definition of "bitch", but I decided to clarify by looking at the dictionary. In the Merriam-Webster English dictionary when "bitch" is used as a noun it means the following:*

1: *the female of the dog or some other carnivorous mammals*
2a: *a lewd or immoral woman*
  b: *a malicious, spiteful, or overbearing woman—sometimes used as a generalized term of abuse*
3: *something that is extremely difficult, objectionable, or unpleasant*

*If we are going to oust one of our own who actually served the PGA of America for a number of years and tell him he can no longer be a part of the leadership process based on his comments, then why is our Association speaking to someone about their opinions and potential leadership role in the future that has made worse comments on a public forum? The PGA of America has told me numerous times I need to be offended by "insensitive gender-based" comments, so after reading this article about the PGA of America and Azinger…I am offended!*

*Sincerely,*
*Ambry Bishop, PGA*
*Assistant Golf Professional*

The point of the letter is self-explanatory. Where does the PGA draw a line with insensitive gender-based comments? Are former Ryder Cup captains held to a different standard than PGA presidents? It was a fair question from a PGA member. Ambry received what appeared to be the standard form letter the PGA composed to deal with complaints from members who supported me. It came from Derek Sprague, the interim PGA president. To me, it was an impersonal reply. In addition to being the daughter of a former PGA president, Ambry had served as a volunteer the previous four years as a PGA national committee member. A better way to answer her questions might have been to make a phone call, but the PGA was sticking to communication forms that were clearly being driven by its legal counsel.

*Ambry,*

*Thanks for your email yesterday. The Board stands behind its decision regarding Ted. We do not condone any insensitive gender-based comments and hopefully the PGA can use its resources and influence to truly champion progress in diversity and inclusion as it is such a critical part of its strategic mission. We wish you well and thank you for your continued service to the PGA.*

*Derek*

When Sprague referred to diversity and inclusion as such a critical part of the PGA's strategic mission, it was bitter irony for me. I believed that Derek wanted no part of Suzy Whaley as the next PGA secretary. When it came to opening the door to a woman as the next PGA officer and embracing that strategic mission, I don't think that Sprague was walking the walk.

In fact, Derek was working hard behind the scenes to defeat Whaley. Furthermore, on November 14, 2014, Dottie Pepper announced her support for Russ Libby, another candidate for PGA secretary. Pepper and Sprague both reside in the Northeastern New York PGA Section, which was in Whaley's PGA district, and it appeared to me this was a backroom strategy to block Whaley. Well, it didn't work, and Whaley was elected. Given the sensitivity the PGA was exhibiting outwardly toward gender, it was a curious move.

During the summer of 2015 Brad Faxon, a PGA TOUR player and analyst for Fox Sports, took issue with criticism that Ian Poulter had given the USGA on the condition of the greens at the U.S. Open at Chambers Bay. Faxon used a term that some would interpret as an offensive reference for a woman's genitalia to insult the European Ryder Cup star while doing an interview on Boston's WEEI sports talk radio.

Brad conceded the greens were not exactly great, but the average guy sitting at home watching the Open didn't want to hear golfers complain about course conditions. "The greens weren't perfect. Everyone was saying things about that, even the USGA," Faxon remarked.

A day later, a Fox Sports spokesman explained that his unflattering description of Ian Poulter was not meant as a derogatory term or one intended to have a sexual connotation. Faxon's intent was to pay homage to his friend from Britain, where the word has come to mean "a person regarded as stupid or obnoxious."

Fox Sports said that Brad's use of the word was "a misunderstanding in that…in the English and British context of it, it's pronounced differently and it means like an obnoxious or ignorant person," the Fox spokesperson said. "I guess it's a word that Poulter uses on his Twitter feed from time to time, so it's kind of an homage to that."

"Those two know each other," he said, "and Brad had made the point that, 'I totally didn't mean it in the way that people thought, I didn't say it in the way people thought.'"

Out of curiosity, I made a thorough but certainly not exhaustive search for Poulter tweeting that same word, but came up empty. Interestingly, Rory McIlroy used the term to describe English footballer Robbie Savage. Rory took heat for it and offered an apology.

I've always liked Brad Faxon a lot. We appointed him to serve on Pete Bevacqua's special advisory committee at the PGA of America while I was president. I sent Faxon a message on Twitter after his controversial remarks about Poulter. Faxon responded by offering his support to me saying that none of his four daughters had taken offense to my remarks about Poulter.

It was unbelievable to see the difference in how Fox Sports handled Faxon's comment compared to how the PGA of America dealt with me calling Poulter a "lil girl." Brad remains on Pete's special advisory committee at the PGA of America.

Speaking of Poulter, I did call him and offer an apology on the Friday after Thanksgiving about a month after my impeachment. Predictably, it was an awkward conversation. I told Ian I wanted to say how sorry I was for what I had said about him. I told Poulter I always respected him as a player and I viewed him as one of the greatest competitors in the history of the Ryder Cup.

Poulter didn't have much to say other than, "It was a tragic situation for you." When I hung up I told Cindy it was a call I needed to make, but I didn't get much satisfaction from it. I wasn't sure it was worth the effort on my part. If anything, as I have read Poulter's vain and vulgar social media posts over the past couple years, it just makes me sicker that I let somebody like him get under my skin.

Since my impeachment, the landscape of political correctness has changed continually and with implicit censorship the result is much different. What is viewed as an "acceptable" comment has changed dramatically over the past two years and the most frustrating thing of all—not just for me, but for any reasonable person—is that it's constantly shifting ground. What's acceptable one day is unacceptable the next. It's a ridiculous set of circumstances. And it seems that some people can get away with things others can't. Standards are applied unevenly, as my previous examples exhibit.

"Freedom of speech only exists in America if you are politically correct," said Gary Player in an interview at the 2016 Masters. "Your career can be ruined if you are not politically correct."

Yet another example would be when President Barack Obama hosted the U.S. women's national soccer team at the White House in October 2015. He praised the World Cup champions and remarked: "This team taught all of America's children that 'playing like a girl' means you're a badass." After the crowd in the East room cheered and clapped, Obama said he probably shouldn't have said that. All was forgotten.

We can probably thank my friend Donald Trump for doing a lot to expose the increasing frustration and rage the American public has with the current state of political correctness.

"I think the big problem this country has is being politically correct. I've been challenged by so many people, and I don't, frankly, have time for total political correctness. And to be honest with you, this country doesn't have time either," Trump said.

As I said earlier in the book, Donald Trump was the first to reach out to me and offer his support on the day I was impeached. For that reason, I feel a tremendous amount of personal loyalty to the man. The Trump Foundation also financially supported The

Mulligan Open, which honored my accomplishments as PGA president. Personally, I am not offended by Trump's outspokenness in his role as a presidential candidate even though of course I don't agree with everything he says. I understand the context in which they are delivered, and it seems many other Americans do as well.

I reflect back to my 23 months as president of the PGA, and I could never have imagined the exciting journey I encountered. It was predictable that I would get to know the biggest names in golf, given my position. When I made the decision that could lead to becoming the president of the PGA of America, it was because I wanted to enhance the lives of PGA members. I believe that did happen.

My critics said I thrived on being the center of attention. They said I relished the media exposure and was a "news hound," that I was continually looking for a microphone or TV camera. The fact of the matter is, the PGA of America controlled all my media appearances. They put me out there because they knew I could handle it. My presidency coincided with the first couple years of Bevacqua's tenure as PGA CEO. Pete had no institutional knowledge of the PGA of America. That meant I was the most experienced spokesperson the PGA had.

Golf Channel, Sirius/XM Radio, Facebook and Twitter all hit their strides in 2013. As a result, I was exposed to the golf world like no other president in PGA history. With that came consequences for me. Some of the same people who encouraged me to use those platforms in order to elevate the profile of the PGA member later criticized me for over using it and were, in fact, accomplices in my demise.

My impeachment will always be part of my legacy. But I would like to think history will judge my accomplishments more on how I tried to help PGA members and make golf a more inviting game. There is not a week that goes by that I still don't hear from a PGA member thanking me for my service and apologizing for the way the PGA treated me. The same can be said for feedback I get from the everyday golfers I run into at my course, the grocery store or a restaurant.

One such call from a PGA member came well over a year after my impeachment. Eddie Merrins, the 82-year-old legendary golf pro from Bel-Air Country Club in Los Angeles, called me on a winter's afternoon. Merrins, who also was the head professional at Merion Golf Club and Westchester Country Club has been inducted into 10 different halls of fame. He served as longtime golf coach at UCLA. Known as "The Little Pro," thanks to his diminutive stature, Merrins had a teaching clientele that included a host of tour pros and several entertainment giants, past and present, including Jack Nicholson, Dean Martin, Sean Connery, Glenn Frey, Ringo Starr and Fred Astaire.

"You did an outstanding job as president," Merrins began. "You made members proud to be part of the PGA. I was embarrassed by the way the PGA handled your situation. It was the worst thing I had seen in my time as a PGA member. I just want you to know that there are a lot of PGA members who feel the same as me," Merrins said. I was humbled that Eddie took the time to call, particularly so long after my service was over.

In a 2015 Golf.com poll of LPGA Tour players, the question was asked: "Should Ted Bishop, the former PGA of America president, have been removed from office for calling Ian Poulter a "lil girl" on social media? The results: Yes, 36 percent. No, 64 percent.

The outcome of the poll by LPGA players was in total contrast to the LPGA's immediate endorsement of my impeachment with its public statement that said, "The PGA's quick and decisive action sent a strong message. There is simply no room nor willingness to take a step backwards."

From *"Undercover Tour Pro"* in *Golf Digest*: "Whenever someone makes a mistake and the whole world righteously piles on, as they did to Ted Bishop, that mob mentality really bothers me."

Many leaders in the golf industry also took the time to offer kind words to me in the months that followed my removal by the PGA, none more profound than these from Jerry Tarde, the editor-in-chief from *Golf Digest*.

"Ted, you've opened the doors to golf's hierarchy and let the breezes flow through the game's inner sanctums. You uniquely looked at all sides before coming to a conclusion. You championed the underdog and the underprivileged. You saw a future in the industry when so many only saw a past. And you represented your constituency with honesty and integrity and honor."

On September 28, 2015, one year to the day after the United States lost the Ryder Cup at Gleneagles, Jaime Diaz of *Golf World* reported the following.

"The ire over the dismissal last October of Ted Bishop as PGA of America president still lingers. Tom Watson, who was Bishop's first choice to captain the 2014 U.S. Ryder Cup team, has refused induction into the organization's Hall of Fame. In a texted statement, Watson, a member of the World Golf Hall of Fame, wrote: 'While I was very flattered by PGA President (Derek) Sprague's honoring me to be inducted into the PGA Hall of Fame, I couldn't accept in good conscience because of how the PGA mishandled the firing of my friend and immediate past president of the PGA, Ted Bishop.'"

In my lifetime, I am not sure anyone outside of my immediate family has ever shown me a greater display of friendship and loyalty than Tom did when he turned down the opportunity to be inducted into the PGA of America Hall of Fame.

As I close this chapter and finally bring closure to what has been a very difficult period in my life, I won't try and say I wouldn't change anything. Of course I would. I would change two silly minutes out of two successful years. But, that's life.

Put in that context, I'll leave it to you to be the judge of my tenure as the 38th president of the PGA of America.

# Acknowledgements

The most important people to me during my 23 months as President of the PGA of America were my constituents. Those were the 28,000 men and women of the PGA plus all of the amateur golfers who frequent our facilities. To you, I say thanks for your support and encouragement during the past couple of years of my life. The thousands of notes, phone calls or emails that I received after my impeachment lifted me to the next phase of my life.

Alex Miceli, group publisher of *Golfweek,* came to Indianapolis in late November 2014 to cover the PGA Annual Meeting that had been scheduled to honor my accomplishments as the 38th president of the PGA of America. He visited me at The Legends Golf Club and we spent the good portion of an afternoon reflecting back on the previous two years. Trading stories and sharing secrets. When Alex got ready to leave he said, "You know, you really need to write a book."

Enter Dave Shedloski, veteran golf writer, who was recommended by Miceli and who agreed to read my manuscript. I didn't know Dave very well, but I had read some of his material, including *Golden Twilight,* his book on Jack Nicklaus' final year of playing the major championships in 2000. The best recommendation I got on Dave was from another golf writer—the great Jaime Diaz. "Shed is a pro's pro. He is perfect for this project." And Shed was, as an advisor.

Dave challenged me, but he shut me down when I got carried away. I owe him a tremendous debt of gratitude. His insight on the sport of golf was instrumental in making sure the end product of *Unfriended* delivered the story I wanted to tell.

Throughout this project I also leaned on the advice and counsel of veteran writers such as Diaz, Michael Bamberger, Matt Adams and ESPN broadcaster Mike Greenberg. The respect I have for those who report on our great sport of golf is immeasurable. The guys I just mentioned are the best storytellers on the planet and they all inspired me throughout this process.

When Tom Watson, Tim Finchem and Steve Stricker came to my facility in August 2015 for a dinner in my honor, associated with The Mulligan Open, it was an incredible display of friendship and support. We raised approximately $50,000 that night for charity and I was able to share the evening with over 200 of my friends. The Mulligan Open offered closure for me in many ways because it once again demonstrated the tremendous amount of goodwill that existed around my PGA presidency.

Mike Beckerich, of Classics of Golf publishing, discovered *Unfriended* after I tweeted that my manuscript was finished. Something good actually came from my social media interaction! Mike asked to see what I had written and made the decision to publish my book. Mike felt the story behind my impeachment driven by the PGA's corporate governance structure was one that history should record. I owe the completion of this project to Mike Beckerich and Brian Lewis at Classics of Golf publishing.

When I decided to write my book, I never dreamed that I would need a First Amendment lawyer. *Unfriended* would never have come to fruition without Tom Curley and the firm of Levine Sullivan Koch and Schulz, LLP in Washington D.C. Tom guided me through some perilous times with the PGA of America. In the United States we take Freedom of Speech for granted. This project awakened me to the fact that the legal system in this country, at times, can be a barrier to those basic freedoms. Thank you Tom Curley for getting me to the finish line.

My family has been on a lifelong roller coaster ride with me. It all started 40 years ago with my wife, Cindy. She has been my biggest critic as well as my most loyal advocate. While Cindy accompanied me to a few of my PGA officer events, most of time she stayed at home by herself. She has always allowed me to pursue my professional dreams and never complained about the personal sacrifices she had to make. Cindy insisted I write this book, if for no other reason than to preserve my journey for future generations of our family.

Ashely and Ambry, our two daughters, followed in my footsteps when they chose golf as a career. Is there a greater honor a dad can have? I have said many times that my girls are my finest accomplishment. I love them both very much. They are very good golfers, but more importantly, they are great people.

In the end, I do hope that someday my two grandchildren—Reid and Remy—(and maybe their kids) will find the time to read *Unfriended*. And like you, they will have the opportunity to make their own judgments on the 38th president of the PGA of America.

I wrote this book for one reason—to set the record straight and tell my story honestly without filter of media interpretation or spinning from those who had my fate in their hands when my "wrongdoing" led to my impeachment. I didn't look to burn anybody. But I figured if I was going to pay such a high price for my unintentional indiscretion, then people deserved the whole story. It was important to give you a more complete picture of the people around me who have their own imperfections and questionable viewpoints and yet who judged me so harshly.

Unfortunately, my impeachment by the PGA of America is part of history and I will always be connected with that. You might come away still thinking the punishment fit the crime, and that's OK. You are entitled to that opinion, but at least I've had the chance to tell my side of the story. Theodore Roosevelt once said, "If you could kick the person in the pants responsible for most of your trouble, you wouldn't sit for a month." That would certainly describe how I feel about this part of my life.

Roosevelt also said, "It is not the critic who counts; not the man who points out how the strong man stumbles, or where the doer of deeds could have done better. The credit belongs to the man who was in the arena." I was definitely in the arena, but I'm not looking to take any credit for that. I simply tried to make golf better for my PGA constituents and all of the people who play the game.

# APPENDIX A

Several weeks before the 2014 PGA Annual Meeting in Indianapolis, I asked the PGA of America to provide me with a summary of the things that we had accomplished during my term as president. I asked for the information to help me frame my final speech as president on November 22, the day I was scheduled to leave office.

The PGA provided me with over five pages of single-spaced information detailing the many things that had taken place during 2013-14. This list was a culmination of the work of many people- PGA Officers, PGA Board Members, Section Executive Directors and PGA Staff. I do take great pride in the culture we created during my presidency. For the most part, there was great team work and an unselfish commitment by many people.

### Notable Achievements
### November 2012 through October 2014
(Key achievements are underlined)

## PGA Leadership
- Creation of Chief Operating Officer Position *(November, 2012)*
- Creation of Chief Championships Officer Position *(December, 2012)*
- Monthly Section ED Conference Calls *(December, 2012)*

- Monthly Board of Directors Conference Calls *(December, 2012)*
- Board minutes and update highlight documents *(December, 2012)*
- Naming Tom Watson 2014 Ryder Cup Captain *(December, 2012)*
- Asking for and receiving overwhelming PGA member feed-back during the USGA's 14-1b implementation *(November —December, 2012)*
- Introductory "State of the Game" Roundtable at the PGA Show *(January, 2013)*
- Creation of Chief Marketing Officer Position *(January, 2013)*
- Created Merchandising Department and hired Mike Quirk *(January, 2013)*
- Alternatives to "Handicapping" Committee and discussions *(January, 2013)*
- Creation of Chief Business Officer and Chief Administrative Officer & General Counsel Positions *(February, 2013)*
- Creation of Chief Financial Officer position *(July, 2013)*
- PGA of America Headquarters opens its first non-championship specific satellite office in New York *(September, 2013)*
- President Bishop's presence on *Golf World's* "Newsmakers of the Year" *(December, 2013)*
- Placing a new emphasis on Diversity and Inclusion with the hiring of Wendell Haskins *(January, 2014)*
- Budding relationship with Jack Nicklaus *(January, 2014)*
- Formation of a PGA of America Advisory Committee *(February, 2014)*
- Completion of Short and Long Term Strategic Plans *(March, 2014)*
- Growth of the Game Task Force *(March, 2014)*
- Work Force Task Force *(March, 2014)*
- President Bishop authors his "State of the Game" letter *(May, 2014)*
- Hired Jeff Price as Chief Commercial Officer *(June, 2014)*
- Roll out of Long Term Strategic Plan by Senior Staff to all of PGA HQ *(August, 2014)*
- Developed and instituted a Youth Safety Screening

Program for all HQ staff affiliated with PGA junior programs *(August, 2014)*

## Business Development & Merchandise

- Improved communication with CBS regarding 2014 PGA Championship broadcast; removal of Glory's Last Shot tagline *(December, 2012)*
- Standard Life Global Ryder Cup Partner deal *(February, 2013)*
- Mercedes-Benz renewal *(April, 2013)*
- NBC Ryder Cup Media Rights deal *(October, 2013)*
- Golf Channel covering Bethpage site announcements and PGA's Annual Meeting in San Diego *(November, 2013)*
- The Golf Channel broadcasting Morning Drive live from the PGA Show *(January, 2014)*
- Samsung Deal *(January, 2014)*
- Ryder Cup uniform retail plan with Ralph Lauren *(January, 2014)*
- NBC's Ryder Cup Live Coverage announcement *(March, 2014)*
- Overhaul of PGA Member merchandise system and inventory *(April, 2014)*
- Renewed Omega partnership agreement *(June, 2014)*
- Ralph Lauren named Official Partner and Outfitter of the PGA of America through 2020 *(September, 2014)*
- Partnered with Golf Channel in creation of Ryder Cup program "Alternate Shot" *(September, 2014)*

## Championships

- KitchenAid renewal *(June, 2013)*
- Near flawless PGA at Oak Hill *(August, 2013)*
- Bethpage 2019 PGA Championship and 2024 Ryder Cup *(September, 2013)*
- International PGA Championship analysis is initiated *(October, 2013)*
- PGA Championship purse increase *(November, 2013)*
- National Car Rental ProAm Series and Section Funding *(January, 2014)*
- PNC to Philly Cricket *(February, 2014)*

- West Coast PGA analysis and potential to go to Harding Park in 2020 *(March, 2014)*
- Initiating changes to the Grand Slam *(April, 2014)*
- <u>Creation of KPMG Women's PGA Championship</u> *(April, 2014)*
- Partnership with The Trump Organization *(May, 2014)*
- Ryder Cup rings to former Captains and Team Members *(May, 2014)*
- <u>Announced the 2020 PGA Championship at TPC Harding Park (first West Coast PGA Championship since 1998)</u> *(July, 2014)*
- Implementation of ShotLink scoring at 2014 PGA Championship *(August, 2014)*
- PGA of America Long Drive Competition at the PGA Championship *(August, 2014)*
- Successful 2014 PGA Championship with Rory McIlroy emerging victorious at Valhalla Golf Club *(August, 2014)*
- <u>Announcement of the Captain's Picks for the 2014 United States Ryder Cup team live on Golf Channel during an hour long television special held at the Saturday Night Live Studios</u> *(September, 2014)*
- 2015 Senior PNC Championship will take place on the West Coast at Bayonet and Black Horse Run *(September, 2014)*

**Education**
- Created PGA Speakers Bureau *(September, 2013)*
- Completed four year transition from PGM 1.0 to PGM 2.0 *(November, 2013)*
- Grew member education participation at PGA Merchandise Show by 550% *(January, 2014)*

**Employment**
- Filled 700 + PGA professional jobs and made 17,000 + contacts with PGA professionals *(November, 2012)*
- Reorganized department, new territory alignment and employment consultant management *(May, 2013)*
- Created new employer guide and communication plan on

PGALinks for supervising PGA professionals *(October, 2013)*
- Updated CareerLinks hiring solution, employment center and job hunter tool kit on PGALinks *(November, 2013)*
- *Boardroom Magazine* Association Program of the Year Award *(February, 2014)*

## Finance/IT
- Long overdue technology transition from Groupwise to Outlook at HQ *(February, 2013)*
- Inurement study *(February, 2014)*
- Reversing trends in budget re revenue versus spend *(January, 2014)*
- Revamped and opened budget process *(January, 2014)*
- Stabilization of Oracle Fusion *(January, 2014)*
- New Investment Committee management team *(March, 2014)*

## Human Resources & PGA HQ Culture
- Establishing "Town Halls" to brief HQ on new developments and ensure organizational transparency *(November, 2012)*
- PGA HQ dress code update—a tangible representation of our new culture *(December, 2012)*
- Weekly HQ Yoga classes offered to all staff members free of charge *(March, 2013)*
- Lunchtime Conversations with senior staff *(March, 2013)*
- Emphasis on promoting the PGA of America is an attractive environment for female employees by establishing the Women of the PGA Lunch Series *(March, 2013)*
- Authored a new and enhanced PGA Employee Handbook *(March, 2013)*
- New and more fiscally responsible approach to staff travel *(March, 2013)*
- Publishing executive organization charts *(April, 2013)*
- More collaborative, positive and productive staff culture with the Breakfast with a Department Series and Guest Speaker opportunities *(May, 2013)*
- Staff photo directory for Board of Directors *(May, 2013)*

- Flex hours policy for employees *(July, 2013)*
- Integration of PGA Golf Properties into HR at HQ including PSL and Valhalla *(July, 2013)*
- Posting new job opportunities on PGA Links and alerting HQ staff to the opportunities *(August, 2013)*
- Establishing new holiday hours (closing HQ between Christmas and the New Years) *(August, 2013)*
- Staff lead committees—Wellness, Activities and Professional Development *(September, 2013)*
- Towers Watson analysis is initiated *(December, 2013)*
- Revamping the HR hiring and recruiting process (utilizing LinkedIn as a recruiting tool thus expanding our applicant pool) *(January, 2014)*
- Revamping the HQ employee onboarding process *(January, 2014)*
- PGA HQ Internship Program enhancements – 12 Interns starting in May (largest group ever) *(January, 2014)*
- Staff Speaker Series *(January, 2014)*
- Enhanced on-boarding process with cultural integration *(January, 2014)*
- Compensation Assessment with Towers Watson: Part 1 Completed, Part 2 pending approval *(February, 2014)*
- Payroll Cycle Change for HQ providing higher level accuracy and efficiency *(May, 2014)*

## Marketing
- Built ProMotion tool *(March, 2013)*
- Adjusting the PGA of America's agreement with Rick Summers and PGA Magazine *(June, 2013)*
- Re-Branding of PGA Championship and Senior PGA Championship *(July, 2013)*
- Pick the Hole Location Challenge Presented by Jack Nicklaus *(July, 2013)*
- *Golf World* to our members free of charge via *Golf Digest* *(August, 2013)*
- New roles and titles for Arjun Chowdri and Julius Mason resulting in improved management structure of the MarCom team *(January, 2014)*

- Plan in action for PGALinks.com complete overhaul *(April, 2014)*
- New PSA campaign *(April, 2014)*

## Membership
- <u>Doubling ADP Section Funding</u> *(November, 2013)*
- Execution of the most productive and positive Annual Meeting in recent PGA memory *(November, 2013)*
- PGA TOUR tournament broadcasts highlighting PGA Professionals at host venue of TOUR stops *(November, 2013)*
- Updated Super Regionals Format *(February, 2014)*
- Creation of the Deacon Palmer Award *(November, 2014)*
- Naming Donald Trump as Keynote Speaker for the 2014 Annual Meeting *(November, 2014)*

## PGA REACH
- New energy behind PGA REACH with Scott Kmiec *(February, 2013)*
- Giuliani relationship *(November, 2013)*
- Re-branding of PGA Foundation to PGA REACH *(March, 2014)*
- A true, tangible plan to raise revenue with 2014 Ryder Cup trip hosted by Mayor Giuliani *(September, 2014)*

## Player Development
- Launched Drive, Chip & Putt *(April, 2013)*
- Launched Beyond the Green professional development events, featuring Connecting with Her education *(May, 2013)*
- Tremendous growth in PGA Junior League; 500% *(June, 2013)*
- Launched GGR employee talent development program; KPMG an early adopter *(July, 2013)*
- Game Golf Investment *(January, 2014)*
- Forty new Player Development jobs for PGA Members created by PDRMs *(February, 2014)*
- Developed initial Olympic teaching and coaching plan *(March, 2014)*

- Rory McIlroy's involvement in PGA Junior League *(April, 2014)*
- Built revenue scorecard to quantify PGA member value in Player Development *(April, 2014)*
- Wildly successful Drive, Chip and Putt expanded to 50 states and all 41 Sections; 121 sites to 314 and 17k kids to 50k participants *(April, 2014)*
- Drive, Chip and Putt Championships held at Augusta National Golf Club and shown live on Golf Channel prompting Augusta National Chairman to state "This is one of the most powerful days of my life." *(April, 2014)*
- Building from scratch a youth program background check and safety management plan *(April, 2014)*
- Testing a "Pay Per Minute" pilot program at five golf courses in the Midwestern portion of the United States in conjunction with the PGA Growth of the Game Task Force *(Summer, 2014)*
- Developed and launched Section revenue scorecard workshops *(August, 2014)*

## Properties
- Hiring Keith Reese at Valhalla *(January, 2013)*
- Hiring Jimmy Terry at PGA Golf Club Port St. Lucie *(May, 2013)*
- Critical staff hire with Dick Gray *(December, 2013)*
- Properties Advisory Committee *(January, 2014)*
- Improving the perception of Port St. Lucie and performance of the facility
- PGA Country Club transformation to a moderately priced public access golf course to better address the needs of the Port St. Lucie marketplace *(July, 2014)*
- Demolition and renovation of PGA Golf Club Port St. Lucie clubhouse are underway and set to be completed in November *(August, 2014)*

## Miscellaneous
- New perception in the golf industry; the PGA is no longer thought of as a "sleeping giant"

- More presence on Golf Channel programming than ever before
- A relationship with the PGA TOUR that is as friendly and productive as it has ever been
- <u>Viewed as progressive and perhaps the most progressive major entity in the game Named President Bill Clinton as the 2014 Distinguished Service Award Recipient</u>

# APPENDIX B

The following are the 17 members of the Board of Directors who voted to impeach me on October 24, 2014 as the 38th President of the PGA of America.

- Derek Sprague, Vice President
- Paul Levy, Secretary
- Allen Wronowski, Honorary President
- Donnie Lyons–District 1
- Dan Pasternak–District 2
- Bud Rousey–District 3
- Jim Antkiewicz–District 4
- Chad Seymour–District 5
- Jim Richerson–District 6
- Bob Philbrick–District 7
- Chris Thomson–District 8
- Scott Brandt–District 9
- Rick Murphy–District 10
- Bill Hulbert–District 11
- Dan Koesters–District 12
- Jack Binswanger–District 13
- Dan Hill–District 14
- Lynn Swann–Independent Director

There was one abstention by Dottie Pepper, an Independent Director.